Criminology and Criminal Justice

To my wife, Julie and my daughters, Emmeline and Eleanor

Criminology and Criminal Justice

A study guide

Peter Joyce

WILLAN
PUBLISHING

Published by

Willan Publishing
Culmcott House
Mill Street, Uffculme
Cullompton, Devon
EX15 3AT, UK
Tel: +44(0)1884 840337
Fax: +44(0)1884 840251
e-mail: info@willanpublishing.co.uk
website: www.willanpublishing.co.uk

Published simultaneously in the USA and Canada by
Willan Publishing

c\o ISBS, 920 NE 58th Ave, Suite 300
Portland, Oregon 97213-3786, USA
Tel: +001(0)503 287 3093
Fax: +001(0)503 280 8832
e-mail: info@isbs.com
website: www.isbs.com

First published 2009

ISBN 978-1-84392-336-7 paperback
       978-1-84392-517-0 hardback

British Library Cataloguing-in-Publication Data

A catalogue record for this book is available from the British Library

FSC
Mixed Sources
Product group from well-managed
forests and other controlled sources
Cert no. SGS-COC-2482
www.fsc.org
© 1996 Forest Stewardship Council

Project management by Deer Park Productions, Tavistock, Devon
Typeset by Pantek Arts Ltd, Maidstone, Kent
Printing and bound by TJ International, Padstow, Cornwall

Contents

Synopsis

This book is written for those commencing their studies in Criminology with Higher Education and assumes no prior knowledge of this subject. It will also be relevant for those who wish to develop their knowledge in Criminology with a view to embarking on a career in the criminal justice system or out of general interest.

The book presents a summary of the key ideas that seek to explain why persons engage in criminal behaviour and of the measures that have been developed to prevent crime. A broad overview of the criminal justice system is provided in order to explain the operations of the key criminal justice agencies and the processes that are involved in bringing offenders to justice. Readers are encouraged to develop the basic knowledge they have obtained in these areas by tackling a number of questions, making use of additional reading of key texts suggested in the book. Brief pointers regarding the approach that should be adopted in answering these questions are provided in Chapter 7.

Attention is devoted to key sources from which information regarding crime and the criminal justice system can be obtained, one key feature of which is a list of websites of key agencies concerned with criminal justice policy and a discussion of the online information that can be obtained from them. Good practice regarding the presentation and assessment of written work is also provided, in particular in connection with referencing. Readers are also introduced to the wide variety of methods that can be used to carry out criminological research and are invited to engage in exercises that include the marking of sample essays and the design of a questionnaire.

A glossary of key terms in criminology and criminal justice is also provided.

Key features

- The book offers a comprehensive yet basic account of crime and the criminal justice system;

- It is written in a style that is easy to understand for those with no prior knowledge of criminology;

- It is interactive, containing a number of 'taking it further exercises' that are designed to encourage readers to extend their knowledge derived from the book into more complex areas, using additional material suggested in the book;

- Guidance is given regarding how the 'taking it further' exercises should be answered, thus expanding the coverage devoted to crime and criminal justice in the main chapters of the book;

- It provides (with examples) a comprehensive guide as to how a wide range of sources should be referenced;

- Readers are given information regarding websites for key agencies and organisations concerned with crime and criminal justice affairs and an indication of what online information can be obtained from them.

Introduction

What is criminology?

A simplistic definition would assert that criminology is concerned with the study of crime – why people commit actions of this nature and how society responds to their behaviour. However, such a definition omits a number of important considerations which substantially widen the scope of the material criminologists need to study.

Below we briefly consider some of the key areas that those embarking on a course of study that includes criminology will encounter.

The scope of the criminological enterprise

Criminology is concerned with a number of key areas of study. Key components of the study of criminology embrace the following:

- What constitutes a criminal act.

- The extent to which the definition of crime is socially constructed.

- Various explanations that are offered to explain criminal behaviour.

- The various objectives that society may wish to secure through punishment.

- The operations of the criminal justice system.

- The formulation of criminal justice policy.

- Crime prevention and community safety.

- The manner in which the needs of victims are catered for by the criminal justice process.

These components cover wide academic areas, demonstrating the multi-dimensional character of criminology that draws upon fields of study that include sociology, psychology, biology, politics, history, philosophy, economics, statistics and geography. These issues are considered more fully overleaf.

What is a crime?

The assertion that criminology is concerned with the study of criminal behaviour requires consideration to be given to what constitutes the kind of behaviour that interests criminologists. Defining what a criminal act consists of is not a straightforward task, and provides a good example of the wide breadth of criminological concerns.

It might be argued that crime is an act that breaks the law. However, in order to assess why people commit crime, it is important to go beyond knowledge of the content of the of law (which is chiefly the concern of those who study the academic discipline of law) and obtain an understanding of the factors that shape its content. These exert an important bearing on why a person breaks the law.

Let us consider some ideas relating to what constitutes criminal behaviour.

Crime is an expression of popular views as to what is right and wrong behaviour.

This perception gives rise to a suggestion that most members of society share a common perception of what constitutes 'right' and 'wrong' behaviour. It implies that there is a consensus within society regarding what is 'wrong' or 'unacceptable' behaviour and this is reflected in the law which criminalises actions of this nature. Criminals, therefore, are a minority who fail to adhere to common standards of behaviour.

There are, however, problems with this definition as to what constitutes a crime. Does the definition of a crime truly reflect popular views of right and wrong behaviour?

Consider the proposition that most members of society believe that the taking of one person's life by another is wrong and the law reflects this by imposing strict penalties on those who commit murder or manslaughter.

However, some might argue that killing another in defence of one's person or property is justifiable under certain circumstances (for example in the case of a woman defending herself or her children from a violent male partner), and others might contend that the law relating to abortion constitutes the legalisation of the murder of an unborn child.

This suggests that the definition of what constitutes a crime might be based on factors other than widespread popular beliefs and opinions concerning what constitutes right and wrong forms of behaviour and that on some occasions the law is not an expression of popular beliefs and attitudes.

Accordingly, let us consider a different view as to what constitutes criminal behaviour, which focuses on the social construction of criminal behaviour.

Crime is an action that is contrary to the interests of those who wield power within society.

The definition of acceptable and unacceptable behaviour is subject to constant change over historical periods. Is this because society alters its views regarding right and wrong conduct (in which the definition of crime merely follows the new consensus) or because law-makers use their position in society to lead it in new directions by redefining what constitutes a criminal act?

This latter view suggests that the definition of criminal behaviour is not simply based upon popular perceptions of right and wrong behaviour, but rather reflects the concerns of those who wield power in society. They use their position to criminalise behaviour that poses a threat to their position in society.

There are various definitions as to who constitutes of the power-holders in society but this view may suggest that the criminal, far from exhibiting the behaviour of a minority, may be representing majority opinion – a Robin Hood figure waging a popular war against the tyranny of a latter-day Prince John in order to combat laws that many find oppressive.

The suggestion that crime is a socially constructed phenomenon means that certain issues are of valid concern to criminologists. These include:

- The power structure of society – who wields power within it?

- The processes through which those who wield power are able to translate their concerns into legal measures that restrain the actions of those who might undermine their position in society.

Criminology, therefore, goes beyond biological, psychological or sociological interest in human behaviour to embrace elements of historical and political analysis and the study of how institutions such as the media can shape and mould human behaviour.

Both of the above definitions relate to definitions of crime in a specific country. However, it might be argued that definitions of right and wrong behaviour should universally apply to all societies. This provides us with a third definition of crime.

Crime is a violation of basic human values that all societies should embrace.

This definition suggests that common standards of what constitutes right and wrong behaviour should be universally applied. Additionally, it embraces behaviour that is not consistently defined as criminal but which many people would view as immoral. Exploitation of labour in developing nations by companies in first world countries is an example of this.

This definition also suggests that the designation of what constitutes right and wrong behaviour should be subject to international rather than national definition. It thus further extends the scope of the criminological enterprise to embrace a trans-national dimension in which the political culture and traditions of nations, the impact of processes such as colonisation, trading relationships between first world and developing nations, and the operations and institutions of international capitalism (in particular the behaviour of multinational companies) all become valid aspects of criminological study.

A key problem here concerns who defines these values and how they are to be enforced. An important departure in this respect is the European Declaration of Human Rights, which established legally enforceable standards of behaviour within all countries that signed up to this measure.

Why do people commit crime?

As with attempts to define what constitutes criminal behaviour, there is considerable disagreement as to why people engage in behaviour of this nature. Criminologists require knowledge of the key theories, which highlights the multi-disciplinary nature of the subject.

Various theories exist as to why people commit criminal acts. Some of the key ideas (which are discussed more fully in the following chapter) focus on:

- *Biological explanations*. These suggest that there is a defect in a person's biological make-up that accounts for their criminal behaviour; it may also mean that they commit crime because they cannot override impulses that derive from these biological roots – they are the 'prisoners of their genes', perhaps.

- *Psychological explanations*. These suggest that some form of personality disorder can explain criminal behaviour.

- *Sociological explanations*. Unlike biological or psychological explanations, which suggest that the cause of crime is rooted in the individual, sociological explanations focus on the operations of society and suggest that social factors (such as poverty, unemployment, poor education or inadequate housing) may underpin criminal behaviour.

It follows from this brief account, therefore, that the scope of criminological concerns extend across several academic disciplines, knowledge of which is important for a well-rounded student of criminology.

Additionally, criminologists need to develop a critical awareness of the methods used on which theories as to why people commit crime are based. These range from the philosophic speculation of the early classicist criminologists to the scientific forms of investigation especially associated with positivist criminologists.

Criminology embraces both knowledge of the wide range of methods that have been applied to study criminal behaviour and a critical awareness of the strengths and weaknesses of these methods. It also embraces an appreciation of the ethical considerations relating to the compiling of information of this nature, being able to appreciate what is, and what is not, acceptable practice. Research methods are more fully considered in Chapter 4.

How does society respond to crime?

In addition to considerations as to what constitutes criminal behaviour and why those who engage in it act as they do, criminology is also concerned with society's response to crime. This consideration embraces a number of areas of study.

The aims of punishment

Laws contain sanctions that are designed to ensure that they are obeyed. Those who break the law will thus suffer some form of penalty. An important area of criminological study concerns understanding the purpose society wishes to achieve by inflicting punishment on a law-breaker. This aspect of criminology is referred to as *penology*.

The rationale of punishment and the specific sanctions that are applied to particular crimes are not consistent, but are affected by what has been termed the 'penal temper of society' (Hudson, 2003: 96). Sociological perspectives of punishment are particularly concerned to provide an understanding as to why the aims and methods of punishment are subject to wide variation both between different countries and within one country across historical time periods. This 'mood' of society influences both what punishment intends to achieve and also how it is carried out.

Sentencing

The aims of punishment and the form that it takes are translated into a sentence that is applied to a specific offender. The 2003 Criminal Justice Act states that the purpose of sentencing is to:

- Punish offenders

- Reduce crime

- Secure the reform and rehabilitation of offenders

- Protect the public

- Enable offenders to make reparations to those affected by their actions.

There are three main categories of sentencing:

- *Sentences without supervision.* Historically these took a number of forms, including 'binding over' (a procedure that originated in the 1361 Justices of the Peace Act) whereby an offender undertakes not to repeat his or her behaviour, cautioning, conditional discharges, fines and fixed penalty notices. These are used for the least serious forms of criminal actions such as minor public order offences.

- *Sentences served in the community.* A range of existing alternatives to custodial sentences (that included probation orders and community service orders) were provided under the generic term *community sentences* by the 1991 Criminal Justice Act. Offenders would not receive a custodial sentence but instead be required to undertake some form of supervised activity within the community and might additionally be subject to restrictions on their liberty imposed by sanctions such as curfews. The 2003

▶

Criminal Justice Act rationalised community penalties by introducing a new community order containing a list of requirements that included unpaid work, curfew, electronic monitoring, residence and drug rehabilitation. Sentencers could impose as many of these requirements on an offender as they felt appropriate.

- *Sentences served in prison.* These are theoretically reserved for the most serious offenders whose removal from society is justified by the threat that they pose.

There are various reasons why society punishes those who break the law. However, a key distinction is drawn between methods of punishment that are directed at influencing future behaviour (an approach that is termed *reductivism*) and approaches that focus on criminal actions that have been committed in the past, seeking to punish those for the actions that they have already committed (referred to as *retributivism*).

Reductivism is associated with a range of strategies that include:

- Seeking to alter the behaviour of a criminal so that he or she does not re-offend in the future. This suggests that punishment, whatever mechanism it assumes, is a method of making bad people better.

- Aiming to deter the commission of criminal acts. This approach may be directed at the public at large, whereby the nature or severity of punishment acts as a disincentive to commit crime, or it may be directed at an offender, seeking to ensure that he or she does not repeat their criminal behaviour. Responses to crime that include tough sentences are likely to form an important aspect of strategies designed to deter criminal actions.

- Intending to incapacitate those who have committed crime so that they cannot cause further harm to society. This entails the physical removal of the offender from society, nowadays achieved through imprisonment: while in prison the criminal cannot commit further acts that endanger the public.

Retributivism is frequently associated with harsh forms of punishment whereby pain is inflicted on the offender. Although retributivism may have a deterrent effect, the chief rationale is to enable society to get its own back on those who have committed criminal acts – punishment ensures that criminals get their 'just deserts' for their actions.

An additional aim that may be served when society intervenes against a person who has committed a criminal act is to secure their reintegration into society. This intervention (to which the designation 'punishment' may not be appropriate) is a particular concern of *restorative justice*. This is discussed in Chapter 2.

The criminal justice system

Society's response to crime is delivered through a number of official agencies whose development, role and operations are important aspects of criminological study. These agencies are more fully considered in Chapter 2 and include the police service, the legal system and the probation and prison services.

Criminal justice policy

The functions that are performed by the key agencies of the criminal justice system are subject to frequent change. Criminologists need to be aware not only of the nature of these changes but also what has caused them to occur. This aspect of study emphasises the political dimension within which the criminal justice system functions and also highlights the importance of an understanding of public policy-making to assess the extent to which the concerns of those who make policy are translated into action.

How can society prevent crime?

The consideration of methods that might be used to prevent crime, as opposed to attempts to assess why people have committed criminal acts and how they should be punished, is an important aspect of criminological concern, and in relatively recent years has assumed considerable practical importance in connection with assessing methods best suited to achieve this objective. It has also exercised a key role in contemporary criminal justice policy in connection with the community safety agenda. We consider crime prevention policy in the following chapter.

Victims of crime

Criminology is also concerned with studying those who suffer as the result of crime. Victims (as opposed to offenders) take centre stage in this aspect of criminology – referred to as *victimology* – which also considers the nature and adequacy of agencies charged with delivering services to victims of crime.

Victims historically played a marginal role in the criminal justice system, which was primarily dominated by those prosecuting an offence on behalf of the state and the defendant(s). However, recent governments have sought to ensure that the victim is given a greater role in the criminal justice process. Support for victims is commonly coupled to measures that are designed to ensure support for witnesses to criminal actions, whether the direct victim or another party. We consider this aspect of criminology more fully in the following chapter.

Structure of the book

This book is designed as an introduction and is written for those with no prior knowledge of criminology. It aims to introduce you to the broad areas that are the subject of study of criminology courses in higher education and also seeks to provide information regarding how to study and how to present written work. The book also contains a list of key Internet sources and the kind of material you will find on these websites, and a glossary of key terms relevant to criminology and criminal justice studies.

Chapter 1 presents a brief survey of the main theories as to why individuals and groups engage in criminal behaviour and what activities might be undertaken to prevent it. This chapter contains a series of 'Taking it further' exercises. The aim is to encourage you to extend the basic knowledge you have derived from the chapter by constructing answers to more complex criminological issues. To do this you need to consult additional texts, some of which are referred to at the beginning of the chapter. The final chapter, Chapter 7, gives you some brief pointers as to the way in which answers to these questions might be constructed.

Chapter 2 adopts a similar format to Chapter 1. Here the focus is on the agencies that comprise the criminal justice process. The chapter provides some basic facts regarding the structure and development of these agencies and develops this material in two more focused sections. The first of these is written around the theme of 'bringing offenders to justice' and is designed to introduce you to the key stages of this process and the role played by the separate agencies within the criminal justice system.

The second of these sections highlights some general themes that have influenced the development of all criminal justice agencies. As in Chapter 1, a series of 'Taking it further' exercises aims to encourage you to conduct more detailed reading on the criminal justice system. Suggestions for additional reading required to undertake these tasks are mentioned at the beginning of the chapter, and suggestions as to how answers to these questions can be constructed are contained in Chapter 7.

The basic information provided in Chapter 1 and 2, complemented by additional reading related to the 'Taking it further' sections, will give you a good grounding in both criminology and the operations of the criminal justice system.

Chapter 3 seeks to develop the 'Taking it further' approach and is concerned with how to gather information and material related to the study of criminology and the criminal justice system. It distinguishes between primary and secondary source material and discusses the various formats within which this material is presented. The chapter especially refers to the Internet as a source from which you can gather material and provides details of a number of key organisations from which online information can be obtained.

Chapter 4 focuses on conducting research in connection with issues affecting criminology and the criminal justice system. It seeks to provide an elementary introduction to research methods by distinguishing between quantitative and qualitative research methods and discusses the key aspects of approaches associated with these two methodologies. Particular emphasis is placed on questionnaire design, which is a commonly used method for undertaking research at undergraduate level. The practical application of research methods is considered in connection with gathering information relating to the level of crime within society, and the strengths and weaknesses of various approaches that might be adopted to secure this information are considered. We also consider the ethical considerations underpinning the gathering of information that involves some form of field research.

As with earlier chapters, Chapter 4 contains a brief series of 'Taking it further' exercises that invite you (in conjunction with reading referred to at the beginning of the chapter) to consider more fully some of the applications and ideas that are discussed. Brief suggestions regarding these exercises are contained in Chapter 7.

Chapter 5 is concerned with the presentation of written work, providing guidance on how to write essays and other forms of written work that may be required in a university undergraduate course in criminology. It discusses the issue of plagiarism and provides detailed guidance as to how this might be avoided through the use of good referencing techniques. The chapter also considers how assessed work is marked. It provides you with an example of a scheme of assessment and has a 'Taking it further' exercise that invites you to mark two sample essays.

Chapter 6 contains material related to the study of criminology in higher education. It aims to advise you as to how to make the best use of lectures and classes and discusses the various mechanisms of assessment that you are likely to encounter. It also provides guidance concerning the writing of a piece of research, which typically takes the form of a project or dissertation, and includes advice as to good and bad practice and discussion of key aspects of such research including the sections relating to methodology and the literature review. A final section of this chapter provides some information on careers that are relevant when you have graduated with a degree in criminology.

Chapter 7 consists of guidance to the exercises contained in Chapters 1, 2, 4 and 5. These are not presented as model answers, but aim to provide you with an indication as to the kind of information that the 'Taking it further' exercises should contain.

References

Hudson, B. (2003) *Understanding Justice*, 2nd ed. Buckingham: Open University Press.

1 The causes and prevention of crime and deviancy

A major concern of criminology is why people commit crime. However, there is no one accepted explanation of why people carry out criminal acts; instead, there are many different theories as to why people commit behaviour of this nature. This chapter seeks to provide a brief introduction to some of the main explanations that have been offered by criminologists as to the cause of criminal and deviant behaviour. In particular it will:

- Discuss the key features of classicist criminology and identify the reforms associated with this approach.

- Distinguish between classicist and positivist approaches to the study of crime: a more detailed consideration of the theories and theorists associated with positivism will be found in the sections dealing with biological, psychological and sociological explanations of crime.

- Consider the wide range of biological explanations for crime, dating from the findings of Cesare Lombroso in the late nineteenth century to more recent attempts to identify the existence of a criminal gene.

- Examine psychological explanations for crime and deviance, particularly focusing on the contributions made by Sigmund Freud and Hans Eysenck.

- Evaluate a wide range of sociological theories related to the causes of crime and deviance that seek to explain the causes of crime and deviance in the social environment in which it occurs.

- Analyse the approaches associated with theories that place the operations of the state and the power structure underpinning it at the forefront of explanations for behaviour depicted as criminal: these approaches include new deviancy, Marxist, left idealist, left realist and critical criminologies.

- Discuss conservative and new right views concerning the occurrence of crime.

- Identify the key contributions made by feminist criminologies to the study of crime and deviance.

- Consider the implications posed for criminology arising from the emergence of late modern society.

Further reading

This chapter contains a number of questions that are designed to encourage you to take further the brief outline of a topic that has been provided. To do this you will need to undertake further reading from introductory books. These include the following:

Carrabine, E., Iganski, P., Lee, M., Plummer, K. and South, N. (2004) *Criminology: A Sociological Introduction*. London: Routledge.

Croall, H. (1998) *Crime and Society in Britain*. Harlow: Longman.

Hale, C., Hayward, K., Wahidin, A. and Wincup, E. (2005) *Criminology*. Oxford: Oxford University Press.

Jones, S. (2006) *Criminology*, 3rd ed. Oxford: Oxford University Press.

Lilly, J., Cullen, F. and Ball, R. (2007) *Criminological Theory: Context and Consequences*. London: Sage.

Muncie, J., McLaughlin, E. and Langan, M. (1996) *Criminological Perspectives: A Reader*. London: Sage.

Muncie, J. and McLaughlin, E. (2001) *The Problem of Crime*, 2nd ed. London: Sage.

Newburn, T. (2007) *Criminology*. Cullompton, Devon: Willan Publishing.

Vold, G., Bernard, T. and Snipes, J. (1998) *Theoretical Criminology*, 4th ed. Oxford: Oxford University Press.

Walklate, S. (2003) *Understanding Criminology: Current Theoretical Debates*, 2nd ed. Buckingham: Open University Press.

Walklate, S. (2005) *Criminology: The Basics*. London: Routledge.

Williams, K. (2001) *Textbook on Criminology*, 4th ed. Oxford: Oxford University Press.

Suggestions as to how to organise the new material you have consulted are contained in Chapter 7.

Classicism

Classicism developed in late eighteenth century Europe. A key classicist criminologist was Cesare Beccaria, who put forward a number of views concerning crime and how the state should respond to it. The key beliefs associated with classicist criminology were as follows:

- *Crime was an act carried out by a rational being.* Individuals possess free will and the decision to commit crime was viewed as the consequence of a logical thought process in which a person calculated the benefits to be derived from a criminal action compared to the personal costs it might involve. Classicists therefore sought to ensure that the costs associated with crime outweighed any advantage that an individual might secure from it.

- *Deterrence.* Classicists believed that the main aim of state intervention against crime was to deter persons from committing wrongdoings rather than to punish them after they had broken the law.

- *Crime should be responded to in a uniform and consistent way.* Classicists thought it essential that potential criminals were fully aware of the consequences of their actions. They thus argued that the most appropriate solution to crime was a clearly defined and consistently applied legal code and a criminal justice system that was predictable (and also swift) in its operations.

- *Discretion was to be avoided.* The emphasis on a uniform and consistent approach to crime inevitably rejected the exercise of discretion by professionals such as magistrates and judges. Classicists argued that the role of judges was to apply, but never to interpret, the law.

- *Punishments should fit the crime.* The harm that a particular criminal action did to society was the yardstick used by classicists to judge the appropriateness of punishments. Classicism focused on the act and not the person who carried it out. It was further argued that the degree of punishment to be inflicted on a wrongdoer should be no more than was needed to outweigh any advantage which the criminal action might bring.

Although we can identify some advantages associated with the views of classicist criminology, in particular their desire to move away from the harsh criminal code found in many European countries in the late eighteenth century, their approach can be challenged on a number of grounds.

- *There was no proof to support their ideas.* Their views concerning the commission of crime and the way society should respond to it were based on philosophic speculation. There was no 'hard' evidence to justify their views.

- *They placed too much emphasis on rationality.* Some people were mentally incapable of making rational choices, and, additionally, factors such as poverty might override logical considerations and cause people to commit crime. The classicists thus underplayed the role exerted by environment or social pressures on criminal behaviour.

- *The importance of discretion was underemphasised.* The classicist belief in the importance of a criminal justice system that operated in a consistent manner downplayed the importance of discretion. However, the ability of a practitioner such as a police officer or a magistrate to take the circumstances in which the law was broken into account might provide a more just outcome than would happen if the law was applied in a totally inflexible manner. The exercise of discretion is often seen as an important skill by those who work in the criminal justice system.

> **Taking it further 1**
>
> Jeremy Bentham was an influential English thinker (a moral philosopher) whose views on crime and its prevention were inspired by classicist thought. Identify the key reforms with which he was associated and indicate how these relate to classicist criminology.

Neoclassicism

This approach made some adjustments to classicist criminology without destroying its basic ideas. Concessions were made to acknowledge that the actions of some people were not based on free will and that rational choice might be undermined or overridden by factors that included social factors such as poverty and mental disorder.

Positivism

The classicist belief that crime was the result of rational calculation based on an individual's freedom of choice was challenged during the nineteenth century by a new approach to the study of crime. This was referred to as *positivism*.

This approach argued that criminals did not possess free will, but were instead motivated by factors over which they had no control. This meant that punishing people for their wrongdoings was inappropriate but it justified removing criminals from society and where possible offering treatment to overcome the urges that made them commit criminal acts.

Unlike classicism, positivism utilised scientific methods to justify opinions that were put forward. The evidence on which positivist assumptions were based was largely derived from quantitative research methodologies (see Chapter 4). Although there are several divisions within positivist criminology (the main ones being biological, psychological and sociological aspects of positivism) we can identify two key features shared by all branches of positivist criminology:

- *Focus on the offender*. All forms of positivist criminology concentrate attention on the behaviour of the individual. Positivists sought to gain an understanding of the person who committed the offence, unlike classicists who focused on the crime that had been committed.

- *Crime was viewed as an act that breached society's consensual values*. A common store of values was assumed to exist within all societies. The criminal, therefore, was an undersocialised individual who failed to obey these standards of behaviour. The reasons for such undersocialisation, however, were the subject of much debate within positivist criminology as to whether biological, psychological and sociological factors were the source of this problem. We consider these diverse views more fully below.

Although the approach adopted by positivist criminologists has exerted an important influence on the way we study crime, their views have been subject to a number of criticisms, including:

- *Determinism.* Positivism suggested that individuals were not responsible for their criminal actions. This implied that those who committed crime had no control over their actions and could not be held responsible for what they did.

- *Undersocialisation.* Positivism defined crime in relation to consensual values, but we may question the extent to which universally accepted standards of behaviour exist within any society. Marxism, for example (see below), believed that human behaviour was shaped according to values that mirrored the power relationship within society. This view may suggest that crime occurs not because of undersocialisation but as a form of protest against values (and the consequences of these values) that are imposed on society by those who wield power within it.

- *Crime as a working class phenomenon.* The identification of crime as an activity primarily associated with the undersocialised resulted in a tendency to suggest that crime was an activity carried out by those at the lower end of the social scale. This provided no explanation for the criminal actions of those in a higher social position. This issue is explored later in this chapter when we consider white-collar and corporate crime.

- *Over-concentration on the offender.* The focus on the individual who committed the crime rather than the nature of the crime itself could lead to injustices if the penalty imposed on the criminal reflected his or her personal circumstances and not the severity of the offence.

Taking it further 2

What do you regard as being the main differences between classicist and positivist explanations of criminal behaviour?

Biological explanations of crime

In the late eighteenth and early nineteenth centuries Joseph Gall explored the view that physical characteristics were an indication to a person's behaviour. He popularised phrenology, which suggested that the shape of a person's skull reflected the structure of their brain, which in turn influenced their behaviour. Cesare Lombroso developed these ideas by asserting that crime was related to a person's biological make-up. In the first edition of his book *L'Uomo Delinquente,* written in 1876, he came to two main conclusions:

- *Criminals were those individuals who had failed to evolve.* Reflecting the influence of Charles Darwin, he believed that criminals were primitive biological freaks who possessed characteristics that were displayed by earlier, primitive man. We refer to this view as *atavism.*

- *Criminals could be identified by their physical features.* Based upon his study of criminals who had been executed, Lombroso asserted that the 'criminal type' could be identified by distinguishing physical features (such as the shape of the skull or facial characteristics) which he referred to as 'stigmata'. Many of these were inherited, reflecting that person's biological inferiority and their predisposition to commit crime. Physical traits of this nature were often reinforced by non-hereditary features such as tattoos.

These views are compatible with the view that criminals were 'born bad' – that some persons were 'wired up' to commit crime. In his later writings Lombroso modified his 'born bad' stance by including factors external to the individual (such as climate or education) as causes of criminal behaviour.

Although Lombroso's methodology was criticised (for reasons that included the unrepresentative nature of the subjects on which he based his conclusions), we continue to view him as an important figure in the development of criminology.

His key contributions to criminology were to shift attention away from the criminal law and make individual offenders the focus of his studies, and to reject the classicist view that punishment should fit the crime by asserting that the purpose of state intervention should be that of protecting society. His belief that those who broke the law were physically different from law-abiding members of society was reflected in later approaches, in particular that of somatotyping (which suggested that the shape of a person's body was a guide to their behaviour).

Biological explanations for criminal behaviour have been subsequently developed in a number of different directions, which we consider below. Their common approach rejects free will and personal responsibility for this behaviour in favour of predetermination.

The search for the criminal gene

We often hear the assertion that crime 'runs in families'. This has been the basis of studies that assert this phenomenon is due to a genetic abnormality transmitted across the generations. It overrides free will and forces a person to commit crime.

Initial research in this field was based on the existence of chromosome deficiencies that may affect the chemistry of the brain. An early attempt to reveal the existence of a 'criminal chromosome' was the XYY syndrome – the belief that males with an extra Y chromosome were likely to commit violent or antisocial actions (Jacobs *et al.*, 1965). However, this failed to provide a universal explanation of crime since many persons with this abnormality did not exhibit criminal or violent actions.

Chromosome deficiencies are not inherited, but arise at the moment of conception. Subsequent research has centred on genes that reside on chromosomes. There are a large number of genes that are active in the brain and mutated genes may result in a person being unable to control his or her emotions. This condition *is* inherited.

The most important research that provided a possible genetic explanation for violent behaviour was provided by Hans Brunner. His study of a Dutch family, some of whose members exhibited extreme violent behaviour that stretched over several generations, revealed a deficiency in several of the males of monoamine oxidase A (MAOA) (Brunner *et al.*, 1993). However, we may query the extent to which a genetic abnormality may be viewed as the sole cause of violent or criminal behaviour. At best it might be concluded that genetic deficiencies may exert some influence on an individual's behaviour but are not the sole cause of his or her actions.

Biochemical explanations of crime

Biological explanations of crime are not confined to genetic explanations of criminal behaviour. It has been suggested that biochemical factors may explain criminal behaviour. Hormonal explanations (which include the impact of premenstrual tension on female behaviour and an excess of testosterone on actions performed by males) have been put forward to account for some forms of criminal activity. Biochemical explanations of crime have also asserted that abnormally low levels of serotonin (a chemical found in the brain which regulates mood) can result in violent behaviour. Other biochemical explanations focus on diet. These include arguments that behaviour may be adversely affected by factors that include a deficiency of glucose in the bloodstream, excessive amounts of lead or cobalt in the body or an insufficiency of vitamin B.

Other studies associated with biology have considered problems associated with the central nervous system as explanations for criminal activity. These include excessive amounts of slow brain activity and cerebral dysfunctions. The latter embraces learning disabilities and brain disorders that may arise from factors such as drug or alcohol abuse by a mother during pregnancy, difficulties in connection with the delivery of the child (such as being deprived of oxygen at birth), or by accidents that occur in later childhood.

A key difficulty with biochemical explanations is that these may be used to medicalise a social problem. They may justify a 'quick fix' approach based on drug treatment, which is far cheaper than social reform programmes.

Taking it further 3

'Criminals commit crime because they are "born bad" – it is in their biological make-up to behave in this way.' Examine arguments for and against this view.

Psychological explanations for crime

The psychological approach to the study of crime focuses on the mind of criminals. The belief that human behaviour is governed by processes that occur in the mind was based upon the pioneering work of Freud. He shifted attention away from innate biological or genetic explanations of human behaviour and directed attention at unconscious conflicts or tensions that take place within the psyche of an individual. In particular, he asserted the importance of childhood experiences in repressing desires in the unconscious mind as explanations for later personality disorders.

His approach gave rise to psychoanalysis as the means to uncover the underlying forces governing human behaviour. The aim of this approach was to unlock and bring to the surface unconscious mental processes thereby revealing repressed experiences and traumatic memories. It was designed to give the patient a clear insight into his or her disorder and provide the basis for corrective treatment.

Although Freud's approach was compatible with many aspects of the positivist criminology, psychoanalysis involved an element of subjective interpretation of what the patient revealed during psychoanalysis that went beyond the normal positivist reliance on scientific observation.

Hans Eysenck also considered that human behaviour was shaped by psychological factors, but unlike Freud he believed that personality was influenced by biological and social factors rather than childhood experiences.

Eysenck believed that individuals had two key dimensions to their personality: extrovertism and neuroticism. A criminal was typically viewed as being extrovert, with an enhanced desire for stimulation and a lower level of inhibitory controls. This resulted in a personality that was difficult to condition and hence to socialise and was directed to the pursuit of excitement and pleasure regardless of the punishment that might result from this behaviour.

Offender profiling

Aspects of a criminal personality may be revealed through various factors that include the type of crime committed, the circumstances under which it was carried out and the methods that were used to conduct it. The practical use to which this information may be put is offender profiling, which involves seeking to establish the characteristics of an offender based upon gathering detailed knowledge of the offence and other relevant information. The use of this approach was pioneered in the 1970s by the Federal Bureau of Investigation in the USA and was subsequently popularised in the UK by the television programme, *Cracker*.

New psychology

Psychological approaches to an understanding of crime were developed by the 'new' psychology of the 1970s and 1980s. The determinism associated with positivist criminology was replaced with an approach whereby crime was viewed as an activity that occurred as the result of a rational person making choices. In common with all psychological positivism, this approach was criticised for concentrating on the individual and ignoring the wider social system that might exert influence over an individual's behaviour.

Taking it further 4

Outline the key factors that Sigmund Freud and Hans Eysenck contributed towards an understanding of criminal behaviour.

Crime and its social setting

Sociology offers a further set of explanations for the occurrence of crime. Sociologists turned attention away from the human body or mind as the explanation for this behaviour and instead focused on social context as the key issue that influenced human behaviour.

In this section we focus on a number of theories that emphasise the importance of the social setting in which crime occurs. All of these suggest that adverse social circumstances have a direct or indirect bearing on the commission of crime.

Emile Durkheim and anomie

Durkheim was a leading figure in sociological positivism. He argued that crime emerged against the background of social upheaval. Durkheim developed the concept of *anomie* to describe a situation in which the behaviour of individuals seeking to achieve their personal goals was not effectively governed by established rules of social conduct: instead, a state of social indiscipline had arisen.

Durkheim's concept of anomie was initially put forward in 1893 and was subsequently developed in 1897. He believed that anomie occurred in two separate sets of circumstances. The first was concerned the period of transition from one society to another, from feudalism to capitalism. The old social order and its methods of enforcing social control broke down but the new social order and rules to regulate the behaviour of its members were not fully developed. He referred to this as a transition from a mechanical to an organic society.

The second period of social development in which anomie occurred was in an organic society undergoing rapid social change or upheaval, which Durkheim associated with the boom and slump of capitalist economies. Here, anomie described the situation in which a society's established rules of conduct were unable to regulate an individual's behaviour, which instead was motivated by an 'every man for himself' attitude towards the attainment of personal goals.

Durkheim also considered whether crime played a useful or harmful role in society. He believed that social cohesion was influenced by the division of labour and consequent specialisation of tasks within it. He argued that a mechanical society was characterised by little division of labour, and consequent uniformity in the work and beliefs of most of its members. The solidarity of this society was maintained by the pressure for uniformity exerted by the majority against the minority who adhered to different standards of behaviour. In a society in which consensual values were adhered to by most of its members – which he asserted was a key feature of a mechanical society – crime was both normal but also useful in that it was a spur to progress, challenging the *status quo*.

The situation was, however, different in an organic society. Here individuals pursued a wide range of different goals and social solidarity rested on a mutual acceptance of the legitimacy of diverse aims underpinned by the law which defined acceptable and unacceptable methods to achieve them. However, rapid social change could destroy the mechanisms that maintained social equilibrium and promoted social solidarity. In societies experiencing this form of upheaval anomie was viewed as a pathological state, giving rise to crime that, in extreme cases, could result in anarchy and the total destruction of that society.

As a positivist, Durkheim focused attention on the individual whose actions was influenced by social processes. His emphasis on the social origins of crime was adapted by other theorists, whose work we discuss below.

The Chicago School, social disorganisation and environmental criminology

The Chicago School focused on environment and sought to explain why crime seemed to be a constant feature of certain neighbourhoods or localities. They made a key contribution to criminology by developing the concept of *social disorganisation*.

Two of the key members of this school were Clifford Shaw and Henry D. McKay, who mapped the areas of a city that were inhabited by juvenile delinquents aged between ten and 16 years. They employed methodologies that combined official data, such as crime statistics, with information from other sources such as life histories and participant observation. They concluded that there was a definite spatial pattern to crime in urban locations whose make-up was characterised by concentric circles. Juvenile delinquents were particularly identified with a specific geographic area within a city and this pattern was constant across historical periods, resulting in the existence of perennial high crime areas (Shaw and McKay, 1942). This was termed 'zone two' or the 'zone of transition', which circled the non-residential business zone (zone one or the 'loop'). It exhibited the characteristics of social disorganisation.

Zone two was characterised by rapid population change, dilapidation and conflicting demands made upon land use, which was evidenced by housing being pulled down to make way for new businesses. New immigrants would initially settle in this location, as rented residential property was cheapest here, but would move outwards into the other residential zones when they could afford better living standards. They would then be replaced by further immigrants. The development of the city was viewed as operating according to a process of evolution that was depicted as 'natural'.

Criticisms of the Chicago School

There are several problems with the work of the Chicago School. Their reliance on crime statistics to provide information on the distribution of crime within a city focused their attention on lower social classes and thus ignored criminal activities committed by persons in higher social categories. This methodology also disregarded the manner in which control agencies such as the police service could influence crime statistics.

The suggestion that crime zones arose as the result of the *natural* evolution of the city has also been questioned by suggestions that these were *artificially* created. Decisions by local authorities (for example, to create 'sink' estates) and building societies (to refuse granting mortgages in certain 'red-lined' areas) may create areas in which a disproportionate number of criminals and delinquents lived.

Taking it further 5

For what reasons did the Chicago School suggest that crime and delinquency was a constant feature of certain urban locations?

Environmental criminology

The importance attached by the Chicago School to spatial pattern of crime was subsequently developed in the latter decades of the twentieth century into environmental criminology. This focused on a range of factors that had a bearing on criminal behaviour, which included the design and layout of neighbourhoods as well as the habits of those who were the victims and perpetrators of crime. Practical applications of this approach include crime mapping, which can form the basis of interventionist strategies, and crime prevention initiatives that seek to design out crime, which we consider later in this chapter.

Social strain

Strain theory was also based on the view that human behaviour was determined by the social structure. Robert Merton was a leading social strain theorist whose ideas were originally put forward in 1938. He adapted Durkheim's concept of anomie, arguing that it did not, as Durkheim contended, arise during periods of social disintegration but was a condition that more constantly affected members of the working class. It arose from a mismatch between the culturally induced aspirations to strive for success (which he asserted in western societies was the pursuit of wealth) and the structurally determined opportunities to achieve this goal: in other words, social strain was caused when a person was unable to achieve the goals that society established as a benchmark of success because of the position that he or she occupied within that society – social inequality was thus seen as the key reason for deviancy. Additionally, whereas Durkheim believed that an individual set his or her own success goals subject to the constraints imposed by society, Merton contended that these and the means to achieve them were set by society.

Robert Merton

Merton suggested that there were a number of behavioural patterns that individuals could exhibit in reaction to the culturally approved goals of the society in which they lived and the institutionalised ways of achieving them. These were:

- *Conformity*. This entailed accepting society's success goals and the approved means to attain them. Merton believed that most people behaved in this conforming way and conformity was a feature of stable societies.

- *Ritualism*. An individual could adhere to the culturally accepted goals of society, even though he or she did not think that these were likely to be attained through conventionally approved ways. A person in this situation continued to adhere to the approved means to attaining these goals but was likely to experience feelings of despair (although he or she did not necessarily turn to crime).

- *Innovation*. An individual prevented from obtaining society's success goals by legitimate means might attempt to achieve them by abandoning the 'rules of the game' and attain them by criminal methods.

- *Retreatism*. In this case an individual abandoned both the culturally accepted goals of society and the conventional means of securing them. Behaviour that embraced the use of drugs or alcohol might be adopted by a person who adopted a negative form of deviancy and effectively decided to 'opt out' of society.

- *Rebellion*. An individual unable to achieve society's success goals and the approved means to achieve them might reject them and replace the goals with new objectives which were achievable. These were often associated with a cause or an ideal ranging from membership of street gangs to association with a terrorist cause.

Subcultural theorists

Subcultural theorists combined Merton's strain theory (which explained individual deviancy) with the Chicago School's ecological theory (which was concerned with collective deviancy). Whereas Merton argued that delinquency arose from a mismatch between society's goals and the means that were available to an individual to achieve them, subculturalists focused on how groups of people responded to the inability to attain society's goals. They asserted that this situation resulted in the emergence of deviant values that were embraced by groups of people and constituted a delinquent subculture.

Albert Cohen was a leading exponent of subcultural theory. He argued that working class boys experienced inner tensions in a society that was dominated by middle class values. The school was seen as an important forum in which this 'status frustration' occurred. They could choose to conform to these values or they could rebel against middle class norms of behaviour and engage in delinquent actions. This latter situation resulted in the emergence of a delinquent subculture in which society's values were rejected and new ones were substituted in their place.

The delinquent actions that arose from the deviant subculture were not necessarily designed to secure economic or financial rewards but were especially concerned with achieving status and prestige among the delinquent's peers, that resulted in him acquiring self-esteem that was denied by mainstream society. Subcultural theories have been put forward to explain the behaviour exhibited by delinquent gangs or more loosely organised juvenile associations such as peer groupings.

Learning theories

Below is a brief exploration of the two key aspects of social learning theories: differential association and opportunity theory.

Differential association

The most important social learning theory applied to criminal behaviour was the concept of differential association, developed by Edwin Sutherland. This theory emphasised the importance of socialisation, and suggested that inadequate socialisation from parents would result in the behaviour of children being influenced by other role models such as peer groups. Differential association theory argued that the techniques of committing crime and the motives and rationalisation of attitudes that were favourable towards breaking the law were aspects of a learning process and occurred when people were subject to an excess of definitions favourable to the violation of the law over definitions that supported rule-abiding behaviour.

This theory asserted personal contact to be the fundamental source of criminal behaviour and further implied that the actions of an individual were the unavoidable (or determined) product of their personal experiences. However, other social learning theorists such as Daniel Glaser emphasised the importance of individual choice in deciding whether to identify with a criminal subculture, thus giving rise to a theory of differential identification.

This helped to explain why, in areas of social inequality, some people embraced deviant forms of behaviour whereas others did not.

Aspects of social learning theory have also been applied in examining the impact that external influences such as books, films and television may have on an individual's learned behaviour. This approach has formed the basis of accusations (albeit supported by little 'hard' evidence) alleging that the violent and sensational depiction of crime by the media has resulted persons copying these actions occurring in real life.

Opportunity theory

Opportunity theory drew on Merton's strain theory and Sutherland's concept of differential association and was concerned with the legitimate and illegitimate ways of achieving success in society. According to this theory, the legitimate opportunity structure was mainly available to upper and middle class youths whereas working class juveniles, finding the legitimate route to success blocked, were more likely to rely on illegitimate ways to achieve success within society.

Opportunity theory further attempted to explain why varying forms of delinquent subculture were evidenced in different areas. The explanation centred on the balance struck in particular communities between the legitimate and illegitimate ways to achieve success in society. It was asserted that lower class juveniles who were denied the possibility of achieving success through legitimate means would form gangs whose behaviour was dependent on the kind of illegitimate opportunities that were locally available to them. Three scenarios were identified:

- *The crime-oriented gang*. This consisted of a juvenile gang whose main activities were stealing. It was associated with an area in which there was a high degree of tolerance towards crime, thus existing alongside (and perhaps orchestrated by) more hardened adult criminals who served as role models for disaffected youths and could arrange for the disposal of goods that had been stolen by them. In these areas, juvenile crime was characterised by a relatively high level of organisation.

- *The conflict gang*. This gang was especially characteristic of socially disorganised neighbourhoods. The absence of effective restraints on the behaviour of young people (including the lack of criminal opportunity structures that were characteristic of areas where crime-oriented gangs existed) resulted in violence that might take the form of warfare in that rival gangs vied with each other for control (and the status that derived from this) of an area.

- *Retreatism*. Those who failed to achieve success in society through legitimate or illegitimate means might embrace a more passive rejection of society and its values, often characterised by drug-taking. This activity was more loosely structured than the delinquency of crime and conflict gangs, and could entail individual as opposed to group responses to the inability to achieve success.

Taking it further 6

Strain theory has been criticised for making assumptions that a high level of agreement existed within society about desirable objectives, and a tendency to ignore the deviancy of those who did not suffer from inequality.

A more significant objection, however, concerned whether social strain did, in fact, give rise to deviant subcultures that indicated a rejection of society's mainstream values.

Evaluate the concepts of:

● techniques of neutralisation (Sykes and Matza, 1957)
● subterranean values (Matza and Sykes, 1961)
● drift (Matza, 1964)

in connection with the assertion that social strain resulted in the emergence of deviant subcultures that indicated a rejection of the mainstream values of society.

The state and criminality

In this section we discuss a range of theories whose common features include rejecting the assumption that society is based on consensual values. This view forms the basis for expanding the focus of criminology, which becomes concerned less with explaining why people commit crime and concentrates instead on how crime is defined and who has the power to declare acts to be criminal.

This new approach shifts the focus of criminological study onto the power relationships in society and how these are maintained by the process of criminalisation. Crime is viewed not as an objective reality but as a social construction whose definition is constantly adjusted in response to actions that those who wield power in society judge to be threatening to their position.

New deviancy

Key aspects of strain theory were developed by a new criminological school that emerged during the 1960s: new deviancy (or interactionism). This shifted attention onto the various factors that were involved in determining whether an act was judged to be deviant (their focus was on deviancy rather than on crime) rather than seeking to explain why the act occurred. The key features of this approach were:

● *To reject the existence of consensual values*. New deviancy asserted that society functioned in the interests of the powerful who were able to foist their attitudes throughout society because of the control they exerted over the state's ideological apparatus (such as religion, education and the mass media), its political system and its coercive machinery (especially the police and courts). Thus the moral, cultural and political values of the dominant class(es) became adopted throughout society – creating an illusion of consensual values which in reality did not exist.

- *To suggest that deviancy was socially constructed.* Deviancy was viewed as behaviour that was defined as 'bad' or 'unacceptable' by a powerful group of people who controlled the operations of the state, and who were able to utilise their power to stigmatise actions of which they did not approve. This suggested that crime and deviance were based upon subjective considerations and value judgements. This led Becker to suggest that deviancy was the consequence of the application by others of rules and sanctions directed at an 'offender': the deviant was a person 'to whom that label has successfully been applied, deviant behaviour is behaviour that people so label' (Becker, 1963: 9).

- *To emphasise the impact of labelling on those to whom it was applied.* This aspect of new deviancy had initially been put forward by Edwin Lemert (1951), who argued that individuals who were labelled became stigmatised and a self-fulfilling prophecy arose whereby they might seek to live up to their designation and engage in activities they would have otherwise avoided. Lemert distinguished between primary deviance (an act labelled as deviant) and secondary deviance (caused by the labelling of the primary act). He suggested that social reaction was the prime factor producing deviance, since an individual's internalisation of the social stigma attached to the label 'deviant' had an adverse effect on that person's self-perception and subsequent patterns of behaviour, possibly forcing them to associate with others who had been similarly stigmatised. In this sense it could be argued that social control leads to deviance. This was opposed to the conventional assertion that crime or deviancy resulted in social control.

Criticisms and consequences of new deviancy and labelling theory

New deviancy viewed criminalisation as a mechanism of social control. The argument that the actions of an individual were of less importance than how society reacted to them emphasised that similar acts might be treated differently, determined by factors such as who committed them and where. This was compatible with the view that crime was not an activity primarily or exclusively carried out by the working class but could also involve members of higher social classes.

However, this approach was also criticised. Its emphasis on why and how individuals were defined as deviant, and how the application of this label affected their subsequent actions, was at the expense of a failure to discuss the initial causes of their behaviour. Additionally, the fact that it viewed behaviour as deviant only when it was officially labelled as such implied that there was no consensus whatsoever within society on values and standards of behaviour. New deviancy also assigned a passive role to those who were labelled as deviant, whereas those who undertook actions of this nature may regard their actions in a positive way, perhaps as deliberate protests directed against society and its values. There was also very little objective evidence to support the theories of new deviancy: it could be, for example, that recidivism among many ex-offenders was largely due to lack of skills or opportunities rather than the stigma of this label.

There are a number of consequences of labelling theory:

- It gave rise to suggestions that certain types of activity identified as criminal should be de-criminalised to avoid the negative consequences associated with labelling.

- It implied that crime and deviance are activities that are 'natural' or 'normal' to those who carry them out and possess no inherent negative qualities until these are bestowed upon them by the processes of making and enforcing rules to prohibit such behaviour.

- It poses the question as to how actions come to be labelled as 'criminal' or 'deviant' and who has the power to do this. There are several views concerning this. Phenomenological explanations emphasise that reality is constructed out of social reaction. Thus definitions of crime or deviance arise as the product of a dialectic process whereby individuals interact with their social world. Liberal explanations view definitions of crime and deviance as consensual, reflecting popular perceptions of right and wrong. Alternatively, conflict theorists suggest that definitions of crime and deviance are the outcome of a process of political and social conflict. Pluralists root this conflict in the competition between interest groups seeking control of the policy-making agenda, whereas Marxists see it as the inevitable product of inequality born of the class structure in capitalist society whereby actions that pose a threat to the economic dominance and political power of the bourgeoisie are labelled 'criminal'.

- It helps to explain why definitions of crime and deviance are not permanent designations but change over periods of time. This may result in criminalising actions that were formerly tolerated, or the decriminalisation of those that were previously disapproved of. Prohibition between 1920 and 1932 in the USA is an example of the former and the UK 1968 Abortion Act (which legalised abortions under certain circumstances) an example of the latter.

Conflict theories

Labelling theory focused on the way in which the definition of deviance was constructed and its subsequent impact on the behaviour of those labelled as deviant. However, labelling theorists failed to offer any detailed investigation of the way in which social reaction was underpinned by the power relationships that exist within society. Conflict theorists addressed this issue. They reject the notion of society being consensual and view inequality as the key explanation of criminal behaviour. Below we identify some of the key aspects of conflict theory.

Marxism

Marxists agreed with the new deviancy school that society did not operate in a consensual manner, but tried to explain why this was so. According to Marxists, society was comprised of classes. Social relationships were viewed as reflecting the 'relations of production' that entailed a minority owning the means of production and a majority selling their labour. Exploitation and social inequality were seen as inevitable features of capitalist society. The economy was viewed as the basis on which all other institutions were constructed: the state and its institutions were primarily concerned with serving the interests of those who owned or controlled the means of production and in particular to ensure that conditions existed for the accumulation of capital needed both to buy labour and to invest in order to increase profits.

There are two key aspects of Marxist criminology.

- *The maintenance of social order through criminalisation.* Marxists directed attention to the mechanisms of state control that ensured the continuance of what they asserted was an essentially unjust social system. Thus the criminal whose actions challenged private property ownership and threatened to undermine the work ethic, the striker whose actions eroded profit margins, or the rebellious underclass that jeopardised social harmony, were examples of groups whose actions were likely to become vilified by the media, criminalised by the law, subjected to special attention by the police and treated harshly by the sentencing policy of the courts. This view rested on the belief that law was rooted in the class and power structure of society, and emphasised the manner in which those in positions of power could apply the label of 'criminal' to whole groups of people who posed a threat to the existing social order. According to such an analysis, criminalisation was primarily directed against the lower classes and actions such as white collar crime that do not essentially threaten the underpinnings of the capitalist state were likely to be viewed more leniently.

- *Crime is based on economic inequality.* Marxist criminology viewed the economic system and the unequal property relations that this generated as the root cause of crime, although there were diverse views as to why economic inequality caused crime. These included arguments that crime was an expression of class conflict rooted in the exploitative nature of class relations; that crime was a protest or rebellion by the poor against the social structure that prevented them from acquiring material possessions, or that the poor and powerless were forced into crime in order to survive.

Criticisms of Marxist criminology

Marxist criminology has been criticised for failing to encompass crime that is not obviously underpinned by economic motives. However, it has been suggested that juvenile aggression might be explained by underlying economic factors such as unemployment, whereby young males whose economic status prevents them from fulfilling their socially constructed gender roles (especially that of provider) display their masculinity through acts of violence.

Marxist criminology has also been criticised for tending to glamorise criminal actions by depicting them as subversive acts directed against capitalism and its underlying values, in particular the work ethic and the sanctity of private property ownership. Marxist criminology is also compatible with the view of crime as a mechanism of wealth redistribution, imbuing the criminal with the characteristics of Robin Hood, who is said to have robbed the rich to give to the poor. In reality, however, much crime is not of this nature and the victims are often the poorer and weaker members of society.

Radical and critical criminology

Marxism provided the ideological underpinning for radical (sometimes referred to as 'new') criminology that emerged during the 1960s. This first arose in the USA against a background of popular protest in connection with issues such as civil rights and opposition to the Vietnam war, which highlighted the lack of power and alienation of the lower classes. In the UK, radical criminology was initially most forcefully expressed in *The New Criminology* by Taylor, Walton and Young (1973), and whose second work (published in 1975) was entitled *Critical Criminology.*

Radical criminology synthesised labelling theory and Marxist criminology to provide a comprehensive conflict theory. It directed attention at the impact of wider social processes on the behaviour of individuals, asserting that the root causes of crime were located 'in the class-based and patriarchal nature of contemporary societies' (Mooney, 2005). Radical criminology highlighted the manner through which the state maintained the rule of the elite by its ability to define conflicting actions or values as 'criminal'. An important aspect of radical criminology was its focus on the process of criminalisation.

The terms 'radical' and 'critical' are frequently used interchangeably but the term 'critical' is more widely used. The main concern of critical criminology is the power structure of society and how this is maintained, rather than why people commit crime. Critical criminology was based on the belief that capitalist society was not consensual but, rather, was based upon social and economic inequalities, and it sought to provide an understanding of society's underlying power relationships.

Although critical criminology seeks to expose the nature of society's underlying power relationships there is no single view as to the source of power that may derive from factors that include class division, gender and race.

Left realism

This term was coined by Jock Young and represented a left-wing attempt to wrest the initiative away from the Conservative governments that dominated British politics in the 1980s and 1990s in connection with their exploitation of popular worries concerning the escalation of crime and disorder and the apparent inability of society to stem this tide. It represented a division in critical criminology between those termed 'left realists' and those described as 'left idealists'.

Left realism rejected the arguments based upon Marxist criminology that emphasised criminalisation as an essential activity utilised by the capitalist state to sustain itself. Whereas 'left idealism' emphasised the essentially coercive way in which the state secured conformity by all of its citizens through its use of the process of criminalisation, left realism asserted that most of the problems arising from criminal behaviour were experienced by the poor, which justified the left taking the problem of crime seriously. Left realism placed considerable reliance on obtaining evidence of 'ordinary' people's experiences of crime, especially through the use of social surveys (such as the Islington crime surveys, the results of which were published in 1986 and 1990) in order to design practical policies to reduce the level of crime, especially as it impacted on working class communities.

The process of criminalisation

Conflict theory viewed criminalisation as a key mechanism for securing the maintenance of the existing social order. It was the means to control the dissent of those who adopted a rebellious stance towards the values or institutions of capitalist society, and the targeting of these rebels helped to divert attention from the inherent unfairness of that system. They, rather than inequalities in the distribution of wealth and power, were depicted as the key social problems that society needed to address.

However, in a liberal democratic political system, social control achieved through punitive actions would only be successful if these had a considerable degree of public support. Drawing from a number of criminological perspectives, in particular labelling and conflict theories, the concept of moral panics has been advanced to explain how widespread popular endorsement for a law and order response to social problems that threatened the position of the ruling elite could be created.

Taking it further 7

What is a moral panic and how does this secure social control?

The media and crime

The media (especially television and newspapers) exerts an important influence on popular perceptions of the nature and extent of crime. Since many people lack first-hand experience of crime, the media is an important source of information regarding criminal behaviour.

However, the media does not necessarily provide an accurate portrayal of these events. It will focus its attention on crimes that are 'newsworthy'. This ensures that crimes of a sexual or violent nature receive prominent coverage (often in a sensationalised fashion) whereas other crimes are relatively underreported. This may thus convey a misleading picture to the public regarding the nature and extent of crime and those who are victims of it.

The media may also have a political axe to grind. This may reflect the views of its owners or of the political party that it supports. This means that stories favourable to this viewpoint receive high-profile coverage to the detriment of stories that fail to substantiate this political opinion. Thus a newspaper wishing to support a tough line with criminals is likely to highlight problems that in their opinion have arisen through the use of community penalties (such as further crime carried out by offenders that in their opinion have been treated leniently) and disregard stories evidencing the success of such responses to crime.

There is, however, debate as to whether the media seeks to manipulate public opinion in connection with its coverage of crime or whether it seeks to reflect the views of large numbers of members of the general public.

Conservative criminology

The need to support the existing social order is a key concern of conservative criminology as well as conservative political thought. The social order may be threatened by actions that include moral misbehaviour as well as the more traditional forms of criminal activity directed against persons or their property.

Unlike positivist approaches, this perspective sees no essential difference between a criminal and non-criminal, as all human beings are thought to possess the potential to act in an unsocial manner. However, most people do not do so as their powers of self-restraint are sufficient to overcome any temptation to surrender to their inborn instincts. Those who yield to temptation are deemed responsible for their actions, which are allegedly based on free choice and driven by moral failings such as greed. Conservative criminology emphasises the importance of social structures and processes to educate or coerce individuals into overcoming their potential to commit actions that threaten the social fabric. This includes the family unit in addition to the institutions of the criminal justice system.

'Right realism'

The recent practical application of conservative criminology was associated with 'right realism' in the UK and America. This emerged out of the economic crisis of the 1970s in which governments responded by cutting public spending and promoted a philosophy that encouraged people to take responsibility for their own welfare. This new right political philosophy of individualism was compatible with the view that the responsibility for crime rested with the individual, and was not connected to shortcomings in the way in which society failed to adequately help its poorer and underprivileged members through the provision of employment and other benefits arising from social welfare policies.

Right realism, also incorporated socio-biological explanations for crime. Some American studies equated race and intelligence, suggesting that the social circumstances of black and Latino Americans was caused not by discrimination but by the 'fact' that they were innately less intelligent.

Taking it further 8

Identify the key approaches to crime that were associated with new right criminology in the UK. What consequences did this approach exert on subsequent criminal justice policy?

Feminist criminologies

The study of female crime was traditionally a neglected area of criminology. The main reasons for this situation included the relatively low number of female offenders, the nature of the crimes they committed (female crime being especially identified with property crime such as shoplifting rather than the more 'spectacular' crimes of most interest to males who dominated the discipline of criminology) and the tendency for female criminals not to re-offend.

Accordingly explanations of female crime remained rooted in theories derived from late nineteenth century biological positivism, which attributed female criminality to impulsive or irrational behaviour caused by factors that included hormonal changes derived from biological conditions such as menstruation and childbirth. This implied that women could not be held responsible for their criminal actions which lacked meaning for those who carried them out.

A key development associated with feminist criminology was the publication of *Women, Crime and Criminology* (Smart, 1977). However, there is no coherent set of beliefs guiding feminist analysis, and the terms 'feminist criminologies' or 'feminist perspectives within criminology' have alternatively been used. In addition to seeking to establish the causes of female criminality, feminist approaches have also sought to investigate other aspects of women's interaction with the criminal justice system. Below we briefly consider the key themes associated with feminist criminologies.

Female criminality

One aspect of feminist criminology is concerned with investigating the causes of female criminality, thus remedying the perceived deficiencies of mainstream (or what is often termed 'malestream') criminology. This approach broadly accepted the underlying principles and methodology of conventional criminology, but suggested that it could be improved by making more use of female researchers and the inclusion of greater numbers of females in survey samples.

This has resulted in investigations that analyse the trends and patterns of female crime both as a discrete subject and also in comparison with male criminality. The 'discovery' of girl gangs was one aspect of this approach which has also examined the social circumstances in which females and males commit crime and the factors that motivate female criminality.

Women as perpetrators of crime

Feminist studies have also examined the manner in which the criminal justice system treats women who have committed crime. Earlier studies had argued that victims were less willing to report female offenders and the criminal justice system was accused of operating in a manner that was overly protective towards women offenders who allegedly benefited from the application of what was termed 'male chivalry' (Pollak, 1950, Mannheim, 1965). Although evidence of favourable bias has been raised in some studies relating to areas such as sentencing policy, it was not conclusive. A key difficulty was the virtual impossibility of finding a set of male and female offenders in identical circumstances (in areas such as previous convictions, family responsibilities and income). Thus any apparent leniency towards women offenders may derive from the nature of their crimes or their previous criminal record rather than favourable treatment by criminal justice professionals.

On the other hand, the criminal justice system has been accused of discriminating against women by the application of what is termed 'double deviance'. This suggested that women offenders were more harshly treated within the criminal justice system because they were judged according to two criteria – the nature of the offence they had committed, and the extent to which they had deviated from conforming to the roles that society expected women to perform.

One aspect of this argument is that women whose crimes constituted a rejection of the mothering characteristics of 'nurture' and 'protection' (such as Myra Hindley and Rosemary West) would be treated severely, especially when they used violence. However, as with arguments related to male chivalry, the evidence supporting double deviance is not conclusive.

Women as victims of crime

Radical feminism focuses on female oppression by males and has underpinned many criminological studies. These highlight women as the victims of crime such as rape, domestic violence and child abuse.

Oppression of this nature is argued to be re-enforced by the gendered way in which the law and the operations of the criminal justice process are administered. This may be illustrated by the way in which the criminal justice system has traditionally responded to female victims of crime, especially in cases of sexual misconduct by a male towards a female. The police may be reluctant to believe a woman's account of the episode and the courts may accept what is viewed as the 'socially acceptable' attribute of masculinity as an implicit or explicit defence of male actions or as a mitigating factor for their behaviour. This has resulted in conviction rates for rape being extremely low in England and Wales.

Crime as a product of gender

Some aspects of feminist criminology seek to explain how gender roles that are socially constructed influence the levels of both male and female criminality. This perspective suggested that the low level of female offending could be explained by pressures placed on women to conform to the role of housewife and mother, in which the family unit played a key role. This suggested that female criminality is influenced by the values and attitudes learned by (or enforced on) girls as part of the socialisation process and also by the limited opportunities available to them to commit crime.

The argument that socialisation might explain low levels of female criminality can also be applied to provide an understanding as to why male rule-breaking is at a higher level. Girls are subject to a greater degree of control within families than boys, which limits their opportunities to commit crime. Additionally, girls are pressurised by the educational system and the media to conform to their social role and are subjected to a range of informal sanctions to stop them acting improperly. Boys, on the other hand, learn attitudes such as toughness and aggression, which tend to be more compatible with anti-social behaviour and criminality.

The view that female criminality was constrained by the limited opportunities available to women to commit it was developed by the 'liberation of crime' thesis associated with some aspects of feminist criminology. This suggested that the extent and variety of women's criminal involvements would increase as they became more socially equal.

A move away from positivist methodologies

Some feminist criminologies have employed different methodologies than those associated with traditional, especially positivist, criminology. This has entailed a move away from quantitative methodologies to ethnographic methods utilising qualitative approaches, which has sought to provide an understanding of women's experiences at the centre of criminological studies (see Chapter 4 for a definition of these terms). One product of this approach has been a number of ethnographic accounts that seek to provide offending women with an opportunity to explain 'their side of the story' – their background, why they committed crime and how they were treated within the criminal justice system.

Criminology in the postmodern age

The impact exerted by economic and social change on the nature of society is a key concern of sociological study, which during the nineteenth and twentieth centuries sought to provide an understanding of the processes that resulted in the transition from traditional society to modern society and to analyse the consequences of this change and key characteristics of modern society.

Further social, economic and cultural changes that took place during the latter decades of the twentieth century have given rise to a society that has sometimes been depicted as different in nature from the one that preceded it and has been described as a 'late' or 'post' modern. Late modern society emerged against the background of a wide array of factors that included the emergence of a global economy, the erosion of the autonomy of the nation-state, a shift in employment from manufacturing to service industries (giving rise to a society dominated by consumerism) and the development of new forms of communications technology that embraced transport and the electronic mass media.

Late modern society also gave rise to new political ideologies that were especially associated with the individualist creed put forward by 'new right' politicians in the USA and the UK. Their espousal of free market economic policies had particular consequences for the role of the state, social welfare policy, law and order and the concept of community. The new political order also evidenced the emergence of issues such as environmental concerns that were not as obviously underpinned by the traditional class struggle that characterised modernist political debate, and were often played out by social movements and pressure groups as opposed to the traditional political parties.

Criminology was considerably affected by the events associated with late modernity. The changes that took place in this period resulted in the emergence of new forms of criminal enterprise (such as credit card fraud and cyber crime and crimes conducted at an international level such as money laundering, people and drug trafficking and terrorism) which often required an international response.

Additionally, late modern society witnessed new methods of responding to crime. What has been termed 'new penology' placed particular emphasis on the management of risk rather than the reform and rehabilitation of offenders as being a key role of criminal justice agencies. Key changes in the processes of crime control have been identified in David Garland's key work, *The Culture of Control*, first published in 2001.

These changes embrace a number of key areas that include an emphasis on retribution as the key rationale for punishment in which prison has assumed pride of place in the state's penal policy armoury, an emphasis on crime prevention and community safety, and a host of managerialist initiatives that seek to provide enhanced efficiency and value for money on the part of the crime control agencies. Concern has especially been directed at the behaviour and habits of young people (such as disorder and anti-social behaviour, alcohol consumption and drug-taking) as responses to popular emotions based upon a wide range of insecurities and which have tended to exacerbate social exclusion.

What has been termed postmodern criminology rejects the approaches associated with modernism that sought to put forward universal explanations for criminal behaviour and instead asserts the existence of a multiplicity of explanations that may be derived from individuals attaching different meanings to similar actions. It embraces the belief that there is no such thing as an act that is inherently criminal and contends that crime is a social construction which underpins social inclusion and exclusion. The methodology through which criminal behaviour is studied is typically multi-disciplinary, reflecting the view that this behaviour cannot be understood from the standpoint of one academic discipline or single theoretical perspective.

The cultural context within which persons embrace forms of behaviour that the state and criminal justice agencies may define as criminal or deviant is a key concern of cultural criminology. This approach was influenced by subcultural theories (discussed above) and views relationship to the means of consumption as exerting a central role in shaping human behaviour. The belief that a person's behaviour is shaped by their relationship to the means of consumption suggests that factors such as style of dress, drinking habits and tastes in music are key defining factors to secure mainstream social acceptability or to justify social exclusion.

This approach views crime and the agencies associated with crime control as cultural products to be consumed (in particular to obtain excitement) and attention is paid to the meaning that specific cultures and subcultures attach to behaviour that the criminal control agencies may define as criminal or deviant and to the manner in which crime and punishment is constructed by the interaction between these two sets of actors.

White-collar, middle-class and corporate crime

The theories concerned with crime that have been discussed above concentrate on providing explanations for crimes committed by working class people. This preoccupation with lower class crimes implies that crimes committed by the more 'respectable' members of society do not constitute a significant form of criminal activity. Such a view was, however, challenged by critical criminology, which asserted that 'different social groups are treated differently for behaviour which is objectively identical' (Fattah, 1997: 177). For example, benefit fraud and tax evasion both entail a loss of revenue for the state but the former (which is identified with poorer persons at the lower end of the social scale) is proceeded against more vigorously.

Definition, scale of activities and prosection of white-collar, middle-class and corporate crime

The traditional focus adopted by criminologists on working class crime was challenged in the 1940s by Edwin Sutherland. He pioneered the concept of white-collar crime, which he defined as 'a crime committed by a person of respectability and high social status in the course of his occupation' (Sutherland, 1949: 9).

This definition covered a broad range of activities and also raised numerous problems, which included the definition that should be given to key terms employed by Sutherland such as 'respectability' and 'high social status'. This has led to his initial definition being refined to embrace three forms of activity:

- *White-collar crime.* The term 'occupational crime' may also be used to describe activities that seek to advantage the person who commits it at the expense of his or her employer or the employer's customers. This person may be of any social status, thereby including 'blue-collar' occupational crime.

- *Corporate crime.* This is sometimes referred to as 'organisational crime' and typically involves a form of collective rule-breaking designed to advance the goals of a commercial concern. The term embraces a number of wrongdoings, which include causing pollution, health and safety violations, unfair trade practices and the deliberate selling of faulty goods, all of which are designed to maximise the profit of a company.

- *Middle-class crime.* This refers to crime committed by persons of respectable status but committed outside of a workplace. Examples of this include insurance fraud and tax evasion.

White collar and corporate crimes traditionally have a low visibility in official crime statistics but some criminologists have asserted both the large scale of these activities and the problems that they pose for society. Sutherland drew attention to the financial cost of white-collar crime (Sutherland, 1949: 12), and more recent estimates suggested that the annual cost of white-collar crime in the USA was $415 billion, compared to the $13 billion annual estimated cost of street crime (Barkan, 1997).

Loss of life may also be occasioned by activities typically associated with business corporations. At Bhopal, India, in 1984 the release of methyl isocyanate into the atmosphere resulted in several thousand deaths and many more injuries. Violations of safety regulations are a regular cause of accidents and fatalities at work. Consumers may also suffer from business practices that place profits before health and safety concerns.

It is widely assumed that there is an official reluctance to prosecute white-collar, corporate and middle-class offenders, and that the penalties meted out are inadequate when they are proceeded against. This situation poses a number of problems. The image of apparently respectable entrepreneurs, financiers, businesspeople and politicians acting improperly may destroy popular trust in finance, commerce and government, and legitimise other forms of criminal activity on the grounds of 'what's good for them is also good for me'.

Taking it further 9

'The scale of white-collar, corporate and middle-class crime is such that society should take it more seriously than is currently the case.' Discuss.

Explanations of white-collar, corporate and middle-class crime

The study of white-collar and corporate crime has been neglected in traditional criminology, which is most concerned to provide an understanding of the causes of male, working-class crime. However, some of the theories discussed above may be capable of being adapted to explain the causes of white-collar, corporate and middle-class crime. These include the following.

Differential association

Sutherland's theory of differential association was based on social learning theory and argued that criminal behaviour was learned in a social setting. Although this thesis can be applied to all crime, it was designed to explain white-collar crime (Sutherland, 1939), viewing the workplace as the social setting in which new employees were directly educated into criminal activity by other employees (if this was endemic to the organisation).

Marxist and critical criminologies

Marxist criminology proposes that white-collar, corporate and middle-class crime does not pose a fundamental threat to the capitalist economic system, and in particular, corporate crime may be driven by the worthy capitalist objective of maximising profits. This may explain why the process of criminalisation has not been traditionally directed at those who carry out such activities. Critical criminology particularly links crime committed by all social classes to the individualist creed initially put forward by new right politicians, arguing that this has bred a 'dog eat dog' attitude in which individuals seek wealth or profits regardless of the effect their activities have upon others.

Anomie theory

The transition to monopoly capitalism during the first half of the twentieth century could be linked to Durkheim's anomie theory in the sense that this development created a sense of normlessness in which the newly created large-scale commercial enterprises outstripped the capacity of existing laws and regulations to control their activities.

Merton's theory of anomie may also be adapted to explain white-collar and corporate crime, which emphasises the importance of innovation to attain success goals. Although he associated this approach with the actions of those at the lower end of the social ladder, it could also be adapted to account for attempts by those higher up the social scale to maintain or improve their social status. Corporate crime may be seen as a deviant response to the strain experienced by an individual to succeed in a corporate setting when confronted with obstacles that prevented the attainment of such goals such as increasing the profits of the organisation. Although these criminal actions directly advantage the organisation rather than the individual, the latter may also directly benefit from rewards such as bonuses or promotion.

Individual choice

Conservative criminology can be applied to suggest that impulses such as greed may account for white-collar, corporate and middle-class crime. This perspective also views crime as a rational activity that could be pursued to advance the interests of an individual, a company, or both.

Crime prevention

Crime prevention assumed increased significance after 1980. Its importance grew on the back of the 'nothing works' pessimism of the 1970s (Martinson, 1974) and perceptions during the 1980s that crime was escalating out of control, evidenced by rising crime rates and falling detection rates. This questioned the effectiveness of 'conventional' solutions to crime (such as increasing the resources made available to the police service and imprisoning larger numbers of offenders).

There is a close relationship between the theories that attempt to explain why crime occurs and the suggested methods of preventing it. Brantingham and Faust (1976) identified three broad approaches to crime prevention:

- *Primary prevention*. This focuses on the environment within which crime occurs. It suggests that crime can be prevented by reducing the opportunities that enable it to be committed.

- *Secondary prevention*. This method targets those deemed to be most likely to embark on criminal activities, and forms the basis of programmes seeking to divert those perceived to be most at risk of offending.

- *Tertiary prevention*. This approach is directed at known offenders, and seeks to prevent crime by stopping them from re-offending.

These approaches underpin practical policies that are designed to prevent crime: situational and social methods of crime prevention.

Situational methods of crime prevention

Situational crime prevention methods are associated with the introduction of various forms of interventions (often of a physical nature) to alter the conditions within which crime occurs. The aim is to influence the decisions that criminals might make regarding the commission of crime.

Situational crime prevention draws from a wide range of theoretical criminological perspectives. It is especially associated with the theory of rational choice, which echoed some aspects of classicist criminology. This viewed the criminal as an economic actor who weighed the potential gains of a criminal act against its possible costs. It is also influenced by routine activities theory, which suggested that the probability that certain types of crime (namely 'direct contact predatory violations') would occur at any specific time and place was the result of the convergence of likely offenders, suitable targets and the absence of capable guardians (Cohen and Felson, 1979: 589). Situational methods of crime prevention seek to create an environment to discourage the actions of potential criminals.

Below we consider some of the main policies associated with the situational approach to crime prevention.

Action directed at the target(s) of crime

Situational methods may entail activities that seek to make the target(s) of crime less attractive. There are three aspects of this approach:

- *Target removal.* Objects that may be the focus of criminal activity are removed from the environment to which criminals may have access. Examples include firms paying their employees' wages directly into bank accounts, thus eliminating the possibility of a payroll robbery, or car owners locking their vehicles in garages to make theft more difficult.

- *Target hardening.* The objective is to undertake activities designed to make it more difficult for crime to be committed. It includes a wide range of physical security measures such as burglar alarms, car steering locks and property marking. Although these methods are not totally foolproof, they may make the commission of crime a more complex or lengthy operation, and/or increase the possibility of being caught.

- *Target devaluation.* The aim is to prevent crime through actions that ensure that goods are of use only to their authorised owners and will cease to work if stolen.

Actions designed to enhance surveillance

Situational crime prevention methods may entail activities undertaken within communities to enhance surveillance. It is believed that potential offenders will be deterred by the threat of being seen. The use of CCTV is an important contemporary example of a form of physical intervention designed to facilitate an improved degree of surveillance.

Taking it further 10

Analyse the role performed by CCTV in contemporary crime prevention work.

Redesigning the physical environment

The concept of defensible space (Newman, 1972) highlighted the relationship between the physical environment and crime. This suggested that urban crime could be partly explained by the breakdown of social mechanisms that once kept crime in check, arising from the virtual disappearance of small-town environments that framed and enforced moral codes. This made it virtually impossible for communities to come together in joint action. Newman put forward a solution that centred on reconstructing residential environments to foster territoriality, to facilitate natural surveillance and re-establish access control. This approach is frequently referred to as 'designing out crime' and has underpinned initiatives that include the widescale redesigning of housing estates.

Taking it further 11

Examine the strengths and weaknesses of situational methods of crime prevention.

Social methods of crime prevention

Social crime prevention is based upon the belief that social conditions have a key bearing on crime. This approach embraces measures that aim to improve social conditions, strengthen community institutions and enhance recreational, educational and employment opportunities. Unlike situational methods of crime prevention (which tend to focus on opportunity reduction), social approaches seek to tackle crime 'at its roots'.

Social crime prevention has been pursued through a number of initiatives that are often delivered through locally-oriented multi-agency approaches. The approach does, however, suffer from a number of deficiencies. In particular, critics have asked two questions:

- *Does it work?* One difficulty associated with social crime prevention is that evaluation has not always been rigorously conducted. This may mean, for instance, that perceptions of youth clubs helping to divert young persons from crime are based upon faith rather than empirical evidence.

- *If it works, why?* Social crime prevention typically embraces a range of actions that are pursued simultaneously. It is thus difficult to ascertain whether specific measures or the overall package of them are crucial to preventing crime.

Community safety

This section focuses on community-oriented crime prevention activities that are now placed under the umbrella of community safety. Schemes of this nature may be delivered in a number of ways, often utilising both situational and social approaches, thereby blurring the distinction between the two approaches to crime prevention described above. Community crime prevention is based upon the work of the Chicago School, seeking to tackle aspects of social disorganisation that resulted in crime and delinquency, and thereby aiming to revitalise community life.

The empowerment of those living in socially disadvantaged areas has been a theme of more recent initiatives of this nature, seeking to create an environment in which behaviour is regulated by internal informal controls rather than through the actions of external crime control agencies such as the police.

Community-oriented crime prevention initiatives

Community-based crime prevention initiatives involve both situational and social methods of crime prevention and have a long pedigree. They include neighbourhood watch, safe neighbourhood units and a wide variety of multi-agency initiatives. The multi-agency (or what we now term 'partnership') approach entails joint action by a number of different organisations (which may be public, private or voluntary sector bodies) that were designed to prevent crime within specific localities. This approach is based upon a belief that crime can be most effectively prevented by various bodies working together rather than leaving the entire burden of crime-fighting in the hands of the police.

A major catalyst to increase the level of community involvement in crime prevention work was the publication of a report prepared by the Home Office Standing Conference on Crime Prevention, chaired by James Morgan, in 1991. This was set up to monitor the progress made in the local delivery of crime prevention through the multi-agency approach. The report stated that 'the local authority is a natural focus for coordinating, in collaboration with the police, the broad range of activities directed at improving community safety' and argued that 'the lack of a clear statutory responsibility for local government to play its part fully in crime prevention has clearly inhibited progress' (Home Office, 1991: 19–20).

The Morgan Report further introduced the concept of 'community safety' as opposed to crime prevention, arguing that the latter term suggested that crime prevention was solely the responsibility of the police. Partnership was thus seen as the appropriate direction on which future policy of this nature should be based. The new designation asserted the important role that communities should play in crime prevention strategies and sought to stimulate greater participation from all members of the general public in the fight against crime. It would also enable fuller weight to be given to activities that went beyond the traditional police concentration on 'opportunity reduction' methods of crime prevention, and would encourage greater attention to be paid to social issues (Home Office, 1991: 13, 20–1)

Developments initiated by post-1997 Labour governments sought to build on the approach proposed in the Morgan Report. The 1998 Crime and Disorder Act gave local government a major role in this area of work through the establishment of Crime and Disorder Reduction Partnerships. This role was re-enforced by Section 17 of the legislation, which imposed a statutory duty on agencies that included local government and police authorities to 'do all that it reasonably can do to prevent crime and disorder in its area', in relationship to the performance of its other responsibilities.

The 1998 Act thus transformed local government into a major player in the area of fighting crime and a resource upon which the police could call, which meant that crime prevention would thus increasingly be waged through the use of multi-agency initiatives, some of which have been managed by charities such as NACRO and Crime Concern.

Taking it further 12

Critically assess the work performed by Crime and Disorder Reduction Partnerships.

Administrative (or mainstream) criminology

Administrative criminology emerged within the Home Office (or from research which it commissioned) in the 1980s and was concerned with putting the study of crime and deviance to official practical use.

Administrative criminology is influenced by classicist criminology, rational choice theory and (especially in connection with research into victimisation) routine activity theory. The latter suggested that certain crimes conformed to a systematic pattern, the understanding of which could be used to prevent the individual suffering further offences. Neither of these theories addressed the reasons why individuals commit crime, but focused on ways of more effectively managing the problem.

Two key aspects of administrative criminology are:

- *To focus on offences rather than on offenders*. It abandoned attempts (based on positivism) to discover why offenders committed crime and instead sought to predict future patterns of criminal behaviour from a detailed analysis of crimes committed in the past. It utilised developments such as crime pattern analysis at a local or national level to identify where certain types of offences took place and to facilitate a targeted police response.

- *To further crime prevention schemes*. A major concern of administrative criminology was crime prevention, particularly situational methods involving alterations to the environment in order to limit opportunities for criminal activities to be committed. It included approaches such as CCTV, neighbourhood watch and multi-agency approaches. Administrative criminology has also been associated with studies of victimisation, especially repeat victimisation.

Administrative criminology was compatible with the new right political thrust of Conservative governments, with the emphasis on individual enterprise and self-reliance rather than on state action as the basis on which criminal behaviour could be restrained.

References

Barkan, S. (1997) *Criminology – A Sociological Understanding.* Upper Saddle River, NJ: Prentice Hall.

Becker, H. (1963) *Outsiders: Studies in the Sociology of Deviance.* New York: Free Press.

Brantingham, P. and Faust, F. (1976) 'A Conceptual Model of Crime Prevention', *Crime and Delinquency,* Vol. 22, pp. 130–46.

Brunner, H., Nelen, M., Breakefield, X., Ropers, H. and van Oost, B. (1993) 'Abnormal Behaviour Associated with a Point Mutation in the Structural Gene for Monoamine Oxidase A', *Science,* No. 262, pp. 578–80.

Cavadino, M. and Dignan, J. (1992) *The Penal System: An Introduction.* London: Sage.

Cohen, A. (1955) *Delinquent Boys: The Culture of the Gang.* Chicago: Chicago Free Press.

Cohen, L. and Felson, M. (1979) 'Social Change and Crime Rate Trends: A Routine Activity Approach', *American Sociological Review,* Vol. 44, No. 4, pp. 588–608.

Cohen, S. (1980) *Folk Devils and Moral Panics,* 2nd ed Oxford: Martin Robertson.

Fattah, E. (1997) *Criminology: Past, Present and Future: A Critical Overview.* Basingstoke: Macmillan.

Garland, D. (2001) *The Culture of Control.* Chicago: University of Chicago Press.

Glaser, D. (1956) 'Criminality Theories and Behavioural Images', *American Journal of Sociology,* Vol. 61, pp. 433–44.

Hall, S. (1980) *Drifting into a Law and Order Society.* London: Cobden Trust.

Hall, S., Critcher, C., Jefferson, T., Clarke, J. and Roberts, B. (1978) *Policing the Crisis: Mugging, the State, and Law and Order.* Basingstoke: Macmillan.

Home Office Standing Conference on Crime Prevention (1991) *The Local Delivery of Crime Prevention Through the Partnership Approach.* London: Home Office (Morgan Report).

Jacobs, P., Brunton, M. and Melville, M. (1965) 'Aggressive Behaviour: Mental Subnormality and the XYY Male', *Nature,* 25 December, pp. 1351–2.

Lemert, E. (1951) *Social Pathology.* New York: McGraw-Hill.

Mannheim, H. (1965) *Comparative Criminology.* London: Routledge and Kegan Paul.

Martinson, R. (1974) 'What Works? Questions and Answers About Prison Reform', *Public Interest,* Vol. 34, pp. 217–27.

Matza, D. (1964) *Delinquency and Drift.* New York: John Wiley.

Matza, D. and Sykes, G. (1961) 'Juvenile Delinquency and Subterranean Values', *American Sociological Review,* Vol. 26, pp. 713–19.

Merton, R. (1938) 'Social Structure and Anomie', *American Sociological Review,* Vol. 3, pp. 713–19.

Mooney, J. (2005) 'It's the family, Stupid: Continuities and Reinterpretation of the Dysfunctional Family as the Cause of Crime in Three Political Periods', in R. Matthews and J. Young (eds) *The New Politics of Crime and Punishment.* Cullompton, Devon: Willan Publishing.

Newman, O. (1972) *Defensible Space: Crime Prevention Through Urban Design.* London: Architectural Press.

Pease, K. (1997) 'Crime Prevention', in M. Maguire, R. Morgan and R. Reiner (eds) *Oxford Handbook of Criminology,* 2nd ed. Oxford: Clarendon Press.

Pollak, O. (1950) *The Criminality of Women.* New York: A. S. Barnes.

Shaw, C. and McKay, H. (1942) *Juvenile Delinquency and Urban Areas.* Chicago: University of Chicago Press.

Smart, C. (1977) *Women, Crime and Criminology: A Feminist Critique.* Boston, MA: Routledge and Kegan Paul.

Sutherland, E. (1939) *The Professional Thief.* Chicago: University of Chicago Press.

Sutherland, E. (1947) *Principles of Criminology.* Philadelphia: Lippincott.

Sutherland, E. (1949) *White Collar Crime.* New York: Dryden.

Sykes, G. and Matza, D. (1957) 'Techniques of Neutralisation: A Theory of Delinquency', *American Sociological Review,* Vol. 22, pp. 664–70.

Taylor, I., Walton, P. and Young, J. (1973) *The New Criminology.* London: Routledge.

Taylor, I., Walton, P. and Young, J. (1975) *Critical Criminology.* London: Routledge.

Walklate, S. (1996) 'Community and Crime Prevention', in E. McLaughlin and J. Muncie (eds) *Controlling Crime.* London: Sage.

2   The criminal justice process – an overview

This chapter seeks to provide a broad overview of the key agencies engaged in the operations of the criminal justice process in England and Wales. Specifically it examines:

- The key criminal justice agencies – their historical development, structure and organisation, and accountability of the key agencies that comprise the criminal justice system.

- The processes and procedures that are involved in bringing offenders to justice.

- The variety of views that explain why society punishes and the mechanisms that it uses to do this.

- How abuses of power and mistakes committed by key personnel in the criminal justice system can be righted.

- Victimology and reforms to the operations of the criminal justice system affecting those who suffer from crime.

- Common themes affecting the contemporary operations of the criminal justice process.

Further reading

This chapter contains a number of questions designed to encourage you to take further the brief outline of a topic that has been provided. To do this you will need to undertake further reading from some introductory books. These include the following.

Braithwaite, J. and Strang, H. (eds) (2001) *Restorative Justice and Civil Society.* Cambridge: Cambridge University Press.

Cavadino, P. and Dignan, J. (2007) *The Penal System: An Introduction*, 4th ed. London: Sage.

Davies, M., Croall, H. and Tyrer, J. (2005) *Criminal Justice*, 3rd ed. Harlow: Pearson Education.

Gibson, B. and Cavadino, P. (2008) *The Criminal Justice System,* 3rd ed. Winchester: Waterside Press.

Hudson, B. (2004) *Understanding Justice: An Introduction to Ideas, Perspectives and Controversies in Modern Penal Theory*, 2nd ed. Buckingham: Open University Press.

Johnstone, G. (2002) *Restorative Justice: Ideas, Values, Debates.* Cullompton, Devon: Willan Publishing.

Joyce, P. (2006) *Criminal Justice: An Introduction to Crime and the Criminal Justice System.* Cullompton, Devon: Willan Publishing.

Marsh, I. (2004) *Criminal Justice.* London: Routledge.

McLaughlin, E. (2007) *The New Policing.* London: Sage.

Newburn, T. (2007) *Criminology.* Cullompton, Devon: Willan Publishing.

Ramsbotham, D. (2005) *Prisongate – The Shocking State of Britain's Prisons and the Need for Visionary Change.* London: Free Press.

Reiner, R. (2000) *The Politics of the Police*, 3rd ed. Oxford: Oxford University Press.

Rowe, M. (ed.) (2007) *Policing Beyond Macpherson: Issues in Policing, Race and Society.* Culompton, Devon: Willan Publishing.

Rowe, M. (ed.) (2008) *Introduction to Policing.* London: Sage.

Scott, D. (2008) *Penology.* London: Sage.

Slapper, G and Kelly, D. (2006) *The English Legal System,* 8th ed. London: Routledge-Cavendish.

Tonry, M. (2004) *Punishment and Politics: Evidence and Emulation in the Making of English Crime Control Policy.* Cullompton, Devon: Willan Publishing.

Whitfield, D. (2001) *Introduction to the Probation Service,* 2nd ed. Winchester: Waterside Press.

Further useful sources of up-to-date information on the policies and procedures of criminal justice agencies can be found in their annual reports, which are available online from the agencies' websites (see Chapter 3); and reports prepared by Parliamentary Committees, in particular the Home Affairs Committee and the Justice Committee (see Chapter 3).

The role of the criminal justice system

The criminal justice system consists of a collection of agencies that are responsible for upholding the law in the interests of all citizens. Specifically it is concerned with:

- The prevention, investigation and detection of crime.

- The gathering of evidence in connection with criminal activities.

- The arrest, charging and trial of offenders.

- The punishment of those found guilty of a criminal act.

- The delivery of the sentence handed out by a court.

- The provision of support to prevent offenders from re-offending.

- Ensuring that the needs of victims are adequately catered for.

The nature of the justice that is delivered can be evaluated from a number of perspectives: the extent to which procedural safeguards that are designed to safeguard the rights and liberties of the subject are adhered to by the criminal justice process (procedural justice); the extent to which the outcomes of the process provide equality of treatment for all members of society (substantive justice); and the extent to which key decisions are based upon a dispassionate application of established processes and procedures, as opposed to extraneous factors that rely on negotiations and interpersonal relationships that are fashioned between the key actors in a specific criminal justice intervention (negotiated justice).

The key criminal justice agencies: historical development, structure, organisation and accountability

The criminal justice system comprises a number of agencies whose operations are discussed in this section. The actions of these agencies are controlled by a number of government departments that exercise responsibility for criminal justice policy. The chief agencies are:

- The Home Office

- The Ministry of Justice

- The Attorney General's Office.

Other departments may also exercise some functions, most notably the Department for Communities and Local Government. There are examples of functions being shared, in particular in the area of youth justice. This is currently the responsibility of the Ministry of Justice and the Department for Children, Schools and Families.

The police service

Basic facts of the police service

The role of the police (as stated in 1829 by Metropolitan Police Commissioner Sir Richard Mayne in his instructions to the newly formed Metropolitan Police) is to prevent crime, protect life and property and pre-serve public tranquillity. To these functions we may add others: enforcing the law, bringing offenders to justice (which until the creation of the Crown Prosecution Service included the prosecution of offenders) and 'befriending the public'. The latter responsibility entails performing a wide range of activities that have little to do with law enforcement but involves answering requests by the public for assistance, whatever the nature of the problem. We refer to this as the 'service function' of policing and it performed an important role in securing widespread popular consent for policing in its formative years in the nineteenth century. In more recent years there have been attempts to scale down activities of this nature on the grounds that they distracted from the 'real' (or core) tasks of policing.

England and Wales has no unified police service – instead we have 43 sepa-rate police forces. Additionally there are eight in Scotland and one in Northern Ireland. Each is headed by a chief constable (the term 'Commissioner' is used in London in connection with the Metropolitan Police Service).

In England and Wales, police forces are divided into a number of territo-rial areas. These were formerly referred to as *divisions*, although the term *basic command unit* is now commonly used by many forces. Divisions/BCUs are usually under the control of a chief superintendent although the Metropolitan Police Service utilises the term *commander* for an officer performing this function.

Police work is carried out by a variety of personnel. In 2008 there were approximately 140,000 police officers in England and Wales. In addition to police officers, police work is performed by a number of other officials, most importantly the Special Constabulary and Police Community Support Officers (PCSOs). The Special Constabulary (which was created by the 1831 Special Constables Act) consists of members of the general public who vol-unteer their services to their local force. They receive training and possess police powers. There were 14,000 of these in England and Wales in 2008.

PCSOs were created by the 2002 Police Reform Act. They are paid to perform police tasks at neighbourhood level, especially routine patrol work. They have fewer powers than regular police officers, although since December 2007 all PCSOs across England and Wales possess a common set of core powers that were drawn up by the Home Secretary. In 2008 there were 16,000 PCSOs in England and Wales.

The police service also includes police support staff. In 2008 there were 76,000 persons employed in this capacity in England and Wales.

The costs of policing are paid for by central government grants (primarily in the form of a general grant which is supplemented by a number of spe-cific grants) and from money obtained from the council tax levied by local authorities. The proportion of central to local government finance varies considerably across England and Wales but it is a growing source of fund-ing. The amount of police spending financed through the council tax precept has doubled in real terms between 2001 and 2006/07.

Historical development

The increase in crime and disorder associated with the growth of towns following the industrial revolution resulted in the reform of policing: the archaic parish constable system (in which police work was carried out by unpaid volunteers who operated in small geographic areas, the parishes) was abandoned in favour of a new system in which police officers were paid a wage and whose work was organised around the geographic boundaries of towns or counties. The first modern police force in England and Wales covered London and was created by the 1829 Metropolitan Police Act. Subsequent legislation (the 1835 Municipal Corporations Act, the 1839 Rural Constabulary Act and the 1856 County and Borough Police Act) resulted in the eventual creation of modern police arrangements throughout England and Wales.

In London control over policing was exercised by the Home Secretary. This situation existed between 1829 and 1999 when the Metropolitan Police Authority was set up under the provisions of the 1999 Greater London Authority Act. However, to avoid the unpopularity associated with a system of policing that was controlled by central government, elsewhere in England and Wales a considerable degree of influence was wielded by local people. In towns local control was exercised by the Watch Committee (a committee of the council) and in rural areas by magistrates (and after the 1888 Local Government Act by a Standing Joint Committee of the county council composed of magistrates and county councillors).

However, as the nineteenth century progressed, the extent of local control over policing was influenced by two key developments: the role performed by the Home Office and the responsibilities carried out by chief constables.

The 1856 County and Borough Police Act provided a degree of central government financial support towards the costs of policing (which was initially equivalent to one quarter of the money spent on the pay and uniforms of police officers). Previously outside of London the cost had been borne by ratepayers. However, this grant would be paid only if a force was certified to be conducted in an efficient manner. This was judged by inspectors whose task was to visit each and every force and assess efficiency. This provided the Home Office with an important lever to control aspects of police affairs (such as the number of officers who were employed) that had previously been determined locally. The control facilitated by the inspectors (nowadays referred to as Her Majesty's Inspectorate of Constabulary) was extended in other ways during the nineteenth century, for example by Home Office circulars.

Chief constables also began to play an increased role in police force affairs during the nineteenth century. As the tasks of policing became more numerous, it proved impossible for detailed control to be exerted by committees of local councils. Increasingly, therefore, chief officers assumed a more active role in controlling the work performed by the forces that they headed. The concept of constabulary independence was put forward to justify this development.

The tripartite system of responsibility for police affairs

By the end of the nineteenth century (outside of London), the responsibility for police work was shared between committees of the local council, the Home Office and chief constables. This three-way division of responsibility was termed the *tripartite* system. However, it had developed in a piecemeal fashion and there was no clear indication as to where the functions of one stopped and those of another began. This led to occasional areas of conflict, especially between chief constables and local government committees.

In order to resolve this problem, the 1964 Police Act formalised the tripartite division of responsibility for police affairs and allocated specific responsibilities to the Home Office, chief constables and newly created committees tied to the structure of local government. These were initially termed *police committees* and latterly were referred to as *police authorities*.

However, this legislation failed to provide a total solution as to who exercised responsibility for each and every specific function associated with policing, and disputes between police authorities and chief constables occurred in areas that included Greater Manchester and Merseyside during the early 1980s. The disputes concerned whether police authorities or chief constables should determine police priorities.

The 1994 Police and Magistrates' Courts Act

After 1979, central government also became concerned about the way in which the responsibility for police affairs was divided. Crime, law and order assumed a major role in domestic politics in this period, and the government needed to ensure that the police service operated in an efficient manner and that the law and order concerns of the government were reflected in the actions undertaken by the police service.

To ensure that this was the case, the 1994 Police and Magistrates' Courts Act was passed. Its key innovations included giving the Home Secretary the power to draw up what were initially referred to as *key national objectives* (the term *ministerial priorities* was later used) accompanied by performance targets to assess their attainment. Although important tasks were allocated to chief constables and to police committees (thereby preserving the tripartite division of responsibility for police affairs), this reform ensured that henceforth much police work would be determined by central government rather than by chief constables.

Further responsibilities were added by the 2002 Police Reform Act. This resulted in the production of a National Policing Plan, the first of which (covering the period 2003–2006) was published in 2002. It is prepared by the

Home Secretary in consultation with Association of Chief Officers (ACPO) and the Association of Police Authorities (APA) and constitutes an attempt to provide the police service with strategic direction. The Plan contains the government's priorities for the service, performance indicators to assess their attainment and plans for new developments. Police work is also guided by additional plans relating to specific areas of activity.

Important changes to the composition and role of police authorities were introduced by the 2006 Police and Justice Act. The requirement that magistrates should sit on police authorities was removed and these bodies acquired new functions including the requirement to hold the chief officer to account for the exercise of his or her functions and those of his or her subordinates.

Taking it further 2

The 1994 Police and Magistrates' Courts Act was underpinned by the principles of new public management. Analyse the ways in which this legislation reflected the concerns of new public management. To what extent have these reforms resulted in a more centralised police service controlled by the Home Office?

The Serious Organised Crime Agency (SOCA)

The decentralised system of policing, the development which was briefly charted above, worked reasonably effectively when crime was mainly a local activity. However, the pattern of crime altered after 1945 and became increasingly organised at national, and now international, level. Contemporary crime of this nature is characterised by activities that include drug trafficking, people trafficking and international terrorism.

It was inevitable that police structure and organisation would have to adapt to these new forms of criminal enterprise. Initially the police service responded with the formation of regional crime squads whose role was to counter the organised (and in many cases violent) crime that emerged during the 1960s, epitomised by the 1963 Great Train Robbery.

Further reforms were developed during the 1990s when the National Criminal Intelligence Service and the National Crime Squad were set up. These two units operated at national level and – along with personnel from other agencies including those drawn from HM Customs and Excise and the Home Office who dealt with issues that included drug trafficking and organised immigration crime – were amalgamated to form the Serious Organised Crime Agency (SOCA), which was created by the 2005 Serious Organised Crime and Police Act. The Assets Recovery Agency became part of SOCA in 2008.

SOCA is an executive non-departmental body sponsored by the Home Office. It is controlled by a Board consisting of 11 persons, including a chair and director general, both of whom are appointed by the Home Secretary. It has been described as an English version of the American FBI. Although it operates throughout the UK it cooperates with the Scottish Crime and Drug Enforcement Agency and the Northern Ireland Organised Crime Taskforce.

Much of SOCA's work is concerned with gathering and evaluating intelligence. It is a civilian agency, although some of its employees (numbering around 4,200 in total) possess the powers of constables or customs or immigration officers.

Its key role is to prevent and detect serious organised crime, and to carry this out it possesses a number of important powers. These include compulsory powers of investigation whereby SOCA can force witnesses to answer questions and provide documents or other forms of information, thereby undermining the criminal justice system's tradition of voluntary witness cooperation. This is to some extent offset by provisions contained in the 2005 Act regarding providing immunity from prosecution for a criminal who gives evidence and statutory plea bargains.

The agency's budget in 2006/07 was £457 million.

Taking it further 3

Analyse the developments that resulted in the creation of the Serious Organised Crime Agency in 2005. What dangers are posed by this body?

Crown Prosecution Service (CPS)

Basic facts of the CPS

The CPS is an independent authority that carries out criminal prosecutions on behalf of the state. It was created by the 1985 Prosecution of Offences Act and is headed by the Director of Public Prosecutions. The Attorney General is responsible to Parliament for its conduct.

Initially the CPS was organised into 31 areas, but in 1993 this was reduced to 13. Perceptions that this structure made cooperation with the police difficult resulted in a reorganisation in 1999 whereby the CPS areas coincided with those adopted by police forces in England and Wales (save that one area embraces all of London covering the area of two police forces: the Metropolitan Police Service and the City of London Police). Each of the 42 areas is headed by a Chief Crown Prosecutor.

In 2008, the CPS employed around 8,000 staff in England and Wales, of whom approximately 2,700 were lawyers, who conduct the prosecution work of the CPS. This amounts to over 1.3 million cases each year, most of which are heard in magistrates' courts. CPS lawyers frequently prosecute cases in magistrates' courts and they liaise with the barristers the CPS buys in (on a fee basis) to prosecute the more serious cases that are heard in the Crown Court. In more recent years the CPS has directly employed some barristers (termed Crown Advocates) to conduct some of these serious cases.

In 2007/08 the operating costs of the CPS amounted to around £632 million.

The introduction of new policing arrangements in England and Wales in the early years of the nineteenth century was not accompanied by the establishment of a prosecution authority. Accordingly, all prosecutions were conducted either by private persons or the police. The creation of the office of the Director of Public Prosecutions (DPP) in 1879 introduced a new element into prosecution policy, but its powers were limited and the police (advised by lawyers but whose advice was neither independent nor binding) carried the great majority of prosecutions. For this reason magistrates' courts were commonly known as 'police courts'.

One difficulty with the dual role played by the police in conducting investigations and mounting subsequent prosecutions was that this might give them a vested interest in securing a positive outcome. This situation might result in pressure being applied to a suspect to admit guilt with the consequent possibility that a miscarriage of justice might arise. Accordingly the two tasks were separated by the 1985 legislation.

The Crown Prosecution Service reviews case files prepared by the police and decides whether to proceed or to discontinue with them. In arriving at decisions of this nature, CPS lawyers are guided by the Code for Crown Prosecutors prepared by the DPP, which lays down guiding principles relating to decisions regarding prosecution. These emphasise the following:

- There should be a realistic prospect of securing a conviction (the evidential test).

- The public interest should be served by pursuing a prosecution.

If the CPS decides to pursue a prosecution, it then determines what precise charge should be brought, following guidelines contained in the Code for Crown Prosecutors. Legal guidance is prepared by the CPS to aid those who prosecute cases.

The operations of the CPS are fashioned by specific CPS public service outcomes and targets. Additionally the agency is required to contribute towards meeting the criminal justice system's Public Service Agreements. The attainment of these measures is the collective responsibility of the CPS Board, which is chaired by the DPP.

Taking it further 4

What criticisms have been made of the operations of the CPS and how successfully have these been resolved?

The probation service

Basic facts of the probation service

The origins of the present probation service date from the 1907 Probation of Offenders Act, which placed probation work on a statutory footing by introducing probation orders and empowering courts to appoint and pay probation officers whose role was to *advise, assist* and *befriend* those who had been sentenced. Probation was available to all courts and applied to most offences provided that the offender agreed to the process and also consented to abide by standard conditions that included maintaining regular contact with the probation officer. In 1925 the appointment of at least one probation officer to each court became a mandatory requirement.

Initially, the probation service had a local orientation. It was administered through 54 areas, each governed by a Probation Committee composed of magistrates, judges, local authority representatives and local persons. The Probation Committee's role was to manage the service provided in their area. However, the role of the Home Office increased after 1936 through the establishment of a Central Advisory Committee, which provided for services that included inspection and training.

The structure of the service was significantly affected by the 2000 Criminal Justice and Court Services Act. This legislation established a unified National Probation Service for England and Wales, which was set up in April 2001. Its operations were conducted through 42 areas, which coincided with those used by the police service and the CPS. These areas are grouped into ten regions across England and Wales.

Further changes affecting the structure of the service were made by the 2007 Offender Management Act, which provided for the creation of Probation Trusts to buy services related to probation supervision, tackling offending behaviour and providing for other forms of specialist support. This has resulted in the service in England and Wales being currently administered by six Probation Trusts and 36 Local Probation Boards.

In 2008 the probation service employed around 21,000 staff, over 80 per cent of whom performed operational roles. Its budget for 2004/05 totalled £872 million.

The probation service's work has been affected by numerous changes in the latter half of the twentieth century. Work performed in prisons assumed considerable importance after 1966 and the introduction of parole in 1968 extended the work of probation officers to the supervision of offenders following their release from prison. New court sentences such as the introduction of community service orders by the 1972 Criminal Justice Act added to the work of probation officers who were responsible for supervising these sentences. Towards the end of the 1990s the service's focus on working with individual offenders was supplanted by the emergence of accredited programmes to which offenders would be directed by probation officers on the basis of a standardised risk assessment programme termed OASys (Offender Assessment System).

The current key roles of the probation service are to supervise offenders over 18 years of age who have been given community-based sentences. These provisions are now governed by the Community Order, which was established by the 2003 Criminal Justice Act and allows numerous requirements to be imposed upon an offender such as residence, curfew, unpaid work and treatment for drug and alcohol abuse. By the early years of the twenty-first century this amounted to supervising around 200,000 persons per year. The service performs a number of additional tasks that include preparing pre-sentence reports (around 250,000 per year) and working with the victims of violent or sexual crime.

The probation service was also affected by the formation of the National Offender Management Service (NOMS) following the 2003 Carter Review. This agency is discussed more fully below.

Taking it further 5

Evaluate the significance of changes made to the operations of the probation service since the late 1960s.

The legal system

Basic facts of the legal system

The legal system is the arena in which those charged with a criminal offence are prosecuted and, if found guilty, sentenced.

The legal system is controlled by the Ministry of Justice. This is headed by a Secretary of State who has the additional title of Lord Chancellor. He is accountable to Parliament for the work performed by the legal system.

There are two tiers of criminal courts in England and Wales: the magistrates' courts and the Crown Courts. The former are concerned with minor (or 'summary') offences and the latter with serious (or 'indictable') offences. A third category of offences (those that are 'triable either way') can be heard in either court, with the defendant being able to decide where the case is heard.

The least serious criminal cases (those that can be tried summarily) are heard in magistrates' courts. There are two types of magistrates. Those termed 'lay magistrates' are members of the general public who volunteer for judicial work which they perform on a part-time basis. They serve in magistrates' courts (sometimes referred to as Courts of Petty Sessions). Traditionally these officials were appointed by Local Advisory Committees, although the 2003 Courts Act established one Commission of the Peace for England and Wales, divided into 101 local justice areas. On 31 March 2008 there were 29,419 magistrates in England and Wales, who try around 95 per cent of all criminal cases. They typically officiate as a 'bench' of two or three magistrates, aided by a legally trained Clerk to the Justices.

In addition to lay magistrates there are a small number (around 180) who have been trained as a solicitor or barrister and who serve on a full-time basis and try cases by themselves. These were historically referred to as 'stipendiary magistrates' but the 1999 Access to Justice Act retitled them as District Judges (Magistrates' Courts).

The powers of magistrates is set out by the 2003 Criminal Justice Act, which gave them the ability to impose a prison sentence of up to 12 months (a reform whose implementation has been delayed) and/or a fine of up to £5,000.

Crown Courts deal with the more serious criminal cases – those that are triable on indictment. They are presided over by a judge and the verdict is decided by a jury. Their work is carried out by around 650 circuit judges and over 1,300 recorders and assistant recorders.

Crown Courts sit in around 90 locations in England and Wales. They were formerly divided into six circuits, but are now organised into seven regions. Crown Courts are divided into three tiers according to the seriousness of offence. Tier 3 deals with the less serious indictable offences presided over by a circuit judge or a recorder. Crown Courts, the High Court of Justice and the Court of Appeal collectively constitute the Supreme Court of Judicature.

Above the Crown Courts is the Court of Appeal, where appeals from the Crown Court are heard. It is staffed by around 40 Lord Justices of Appeal and the highest court of the land is currently the Judicial Committee of the House of Lords, staffed by the 12 Lords of Appeal in Ordinary (usually known as the Law Lords). The Court of Appeal and the House of Lords hear both civil and criminal cases. The 2005 Constitutional Reform Act provided for the replacement of the judicial functions of the House of Lords by a new body, the Supreme Court. It is intended that this will commence work in October 2009.

The personnel of the legal system

Professionals in the legal system consist of solicitors and barristers. Solicitors are required to have a degree in law (or a non-law degree and a one years conversion course) and to undertake a postgraduate legal practice course. This is followed by a one year period of traineeship in a solicitor's office (formerly known as 'articles').

Barristers require a degree in law followed by a one year bar vocational course. Following this, they undertake a period of training (termed pupillage) with an established barrister. Barristers are members of one of the four Inns of Court.

Solicitors are more numerous than barristers. In 2005 there were around 97,000 solicitors and 14,500 barristers in England and Wales. Traditionally solicitors deal directly with members of the public who have a legal problem while barristers appear in court defending or prosecuting an accused person. Elite members of the legal profession are Queen's Counsel, traditionally exclusively drawn from barristers, although since 1997 solicitors have been eligible for appointment.

The appointment of judges

Judges were traditionally appointed by the Lord Chancellor's Department (now termed the Ministry of Justice). Historically they were appointed from the ranks of barristers, but an increased number of solicitors have been appointed since the 1990s. Reforms that were initiated in the 1990s required vacancies for all but the most senior judicial appointments to be advertised. Applicants were required to possess relevant experience for the post for which they were applying (as laid down by the 1990 Courts and Legal Services Act). Traditionally 'soundings' were taken for those who applied for selection, whereby serving members of the judiciary were asked for their opinion on the candidate's suitability for appointment. Following this a shortlist was drawn up and interviews were held. Successful candidates are appointed either directly by the Lord Chancellor or by the monarch on the Lord Chancellor's recommendation.

Problems which included the social unrepresentative nature of judges resulted in reforms to the appointments procedure, whereby the 2005 Constitutional Reform Act established a Judicial Appointments Commission for England and Wales to recommend appointments to the judiciary to the Lord Chancellor.

Once appointed, judges enjoy security of tenure. The Court of Appeal may overturn sentences given out by Crown Court judges, but only the Lord Chancellor is able to reprimand, suspend or dismiss lower level judicial appointees. Since the passage of the 1701 Act of Settlement the senior judiciary (consisting of High Court Judges, Lord Justices of Appeal and the Lords of Appeal in Ordinary) can be removed only by an Address of both Houses of Parliament to the monarch.

Her Majesty's Courts Service

The management of the courts service is the responsibility of Her Majesty's Courts Service. This was established under the provisions of the 2003 Courts Act, which unified the administration of around 650 courts, replacing the previous situation whereby magistrates' courts were administered by 42 independent local committees and a central Court Service administered the remaining courts: Crown Courts, county courts, the High Court and Court of Appeal. HMCS is an executive agency of the Ministry of Justice and is responsible for providing administration and support to magistrates' courts and Crown Courts (and also to the Court of Appeal, the High Court, county courts and the probation service). It manages the courts and their caseloads, develops initiatives to improve people's experience of appearing in court and ensures that penalties handed out by the courts are enforced. The HMCS is divided into 25 areas which are grouped into seven regions.

New arrangements entered into in 2008 resulted in the Lord Chancellor and Lord Chief Justice assuming responsibility for the governance, resourcing and operation of the courts.

In addition to Crown Courts and magistrates' courts, there are a number of other courts, some of which are briefly referred to below.

Coroners' courts

The role of a coroner's court is to hold inquests in cases where there is a reasonable suspicion that a dead person may not have died from natural causes or where a person has died in prison or in police custody. Juries may be used whose power is limited to declaring that a death arose from 'unlawful killing', misadventure or accident.

International courts with jurisdiction in the UK

A number of international courts also have jurisdiction in the UK. These include the European Court of Human Rights (based in Strasbourg), which investigates complaints by either states or individuals alleging that a breach of the European Convention of Human Rights has occurred. The 1998 Human Rights Act incorporated this Convention into UK law, which means that UK courts are empowered to consider allegations of this nature. However, the European Court can still be asked to adjudicate if it can be argued that the national legal system has failed to offer a legal remedy concerning the grievance complained against.

Additionally, the European Court of Justice (based in Luxembourg) adjudicates on cases where it is alleged that EU legislation has been ignored or has not been properly implemented by a national government or where there is confusion regarding its interpretation.

Tribunals

A wide range of tribunals exist. These may be used to settle a dispute between two private parties or to adjudicate on a dispute between a citizen and central or local government. Examples include industrial and employment tribunals. Their operations are governed by the 1971 Tribunals and Enquiries Act (which was amended in 1992) and since 2001 a unified tribunal system has existed, with all appointments being the responsibility of the Lord Chancellor.

The youth justice system

Historically, children were treated as 'small adults' and subject to the same criminal justice procedures. The penalty of execution for a child or young person was ended only by the 1908 Children Act. The age of criminal responsibility (below which a child cannot be charged with a criminal offence regardless of its seriousness) was set at eight years by the 1933 Children and Young Persons Act. It was subsequently raised to ten years by the 1963 Children and Young Persons Act.

Young offenders above the age of ten but below the age of 18 are treated in a different way from adult offenders.

The 1908 Children Act set up a separate system of juvenile courts to deal with offenders aged 15 and below. These courts were renamed Youth Courts by the 1991 Criminal Justice Act and their jurisdiction was extended to deal with those aged 10–17. Magistrates who serve on these courts are drawn from a specialist Youth Court Panel.

Tension has historically existed as to what was the main concern of a youth justice system. Was it to serve the interests of society by ensuring that young offenders were punished for their crimes; or to safeguard the welfare of the young person by providing measures that would avoid a repetition of the offending behaviour? For this latter reason interventions have often sought to avoid a custodial sentence in favour of community-based alternatives.

An important development affecting the youth justice system came with the establishment of Youth Offender Teams in the 1998 Crime and Disorder Act. These were designed to provide a multi-agency (or partnership) approach towards juvenile crime and their role included assessing young persons and their offending behaviour, determining what intervention was required and developing and supervising intervention programmes. YOTs prepare pre-sentence reports in connection with criminal proceedings against juveniles and supervise community penalties imposed by the courts.

Additionally, each local authority was required – in consultation with other agencies – to draw up a strategic plan for youth justice work in its area. The youth justice system is coordinated by a Youth Justice Board, whose role includes monitoring the standards of YOTs in connection with YJB performance targets.

The prison service

Basic facts of the prison service

The role of the prison service is contained in its mission statement, which states that Her Majesty's Prison Service serves the public by keeping in custody those committed by the courts. The prison service's duty is to look after those in custody with humanity and help them lead law-abiding and useful lives while in prison and after release. Additionally, the Ministry of Justice's objective for the prison service seeks the effective execution of the sentences of the courts in order to reduce re-offending and to protect the public.

The prison service is an executive agency of the Ministry of Justice (which sets key performance indicators' for the prison service), headed by a director general. Most prisons are in the public sector but there are a small number of privately managed prisons. Prisons are grouped into ten regions (with Wales forming the eleventh).

In 2008 there were around 25,000 prison officers in the 126 public sector prisons in England and Wales and approximately a further 2,400 in the 11 private sector prisons.

On entry into a prison, prisoners are given a security category (A, B, C or D). Categories A, B and C are housed in closed prisons; category D are placed in open prisons. Similar categorisations apply to both male and female prisoners. The prison population in October 2008 stood at 84,328 (78,999 males and 4,325 females). The interests of prisoners are safeguarded by independent monitoring boards (one for each prison) and the Prison and Probation Ombudsman. The Prison Inspectorate has also traditionally exerted influence over the manner in which establishments treat prisoners.

The budget for the prison service in 2007/08 was £2,057.5 million, most of which was provided by NOMS (see below).

The role performed by prisons in the criminal justice system has been subject to constant development and change. Here we consider the key developments.

Prisons initially existed as institutions to house those awaiting sentence or the implementation of it (either execution or transportation) or to hold debtors and those guilty of relatively minor crimes. Under the influence of late eighteenth and early nineteenth century evangelical reformers (such as Elizabeth Fry and John Howard) and utilitarian thinkers (such as Jeremy Bentham) prisons assumed a new purpose as institutions that could alter the attitudes and behaviour of criminals. The 1779 Penitentiary Act was an important benchmark in this change in the purpose of prisons.

Towards the end of the nineteenth century a further new approach, that of rehabilitation, emerged as a key function of prisons. The difference between reform and rehabilitation was that the latter implied that the state should play a more active role to bring about changes affecting those offenders who wished to mend their ways.

The Gladstone Report of 1895 was a key development in promoting the role of prisons as rehabilitative institutions. The report was based upon the belief that prisoners were sent to these institutions *as* punishment rather than *for* punishment, and it brought about changes to prison conditions, including the abandonment of the use of the crank and treadmill. Although the deterrent role of prisons was not totally set aside, it was balanced by placing a similar emphasis on the objective of the rehabilitation of convicted offenders. The report argued that prison discipline and treatment should be designed to maintain, stimulate or awaken the higher susceptibilities of prisoners, to develop their moral instincts, to train them in orderly and industrial habits, and whenever possible to turn them out of prison better men and women, both physically and morally, than when they came in. Its key provisions were incorporated into the 1898 Prisons Act.

The emphasis placed on prisons as mechanisms to secure the rehabilitation of prisoners gave rise to the 'treatment model' that was viewed as the main aim of prisons during the twentieth century. Government policy as late as the 1950s continued to assert that the constructive function of prisons was to prevent those committed to their care from offending again.

However, the individualist philosophy that Conservative governments promoted between 1979 and 1997 had implications for the attitude adopted towards those who broke the law. The existing emphasis on rehabilitation, derived from the treatment model, gave way to what is termed the 'justice model'. This new approach sought to ensure that punishment was underpinned with a retributivist objective and was reinforced by a political goal to 'get tough with criminals'.

The Conservative belief that the public required evidence that the government was pursuing a punitive approach towards those who committed crime ensured that prisons were at the forefront of their thinking. Locking up offenders provided tangible proof that criminals were being caught, and was the key feature of an approach summarised by the then Home Secretary, Michael Howard, in the phrase 'prison works'. This caused prison numbers to increase: the prison population rose above 50,000 in January 1994, reached 56,000 by the end of July 1996 and stood at 60,000 on the eve of the May 1997 general election. This was due to a change in government policy concerning imprisonment rather than to any dramatic rise in crime. The increase in prison numbers had a direct impact on the prisoners' environment, since it resulted in overcrowding.

Policy changes were also introduced which affected conditions within prisons. The emphasis placed on the rehabilitation of individual prisoners by the treatment model was replaced by a harsher, 'decent but austere' environment that could be presented as additional proof that those who committed crime were being appropriately punished for their wrongdoings. Changes affecting prison conditions that were introduced by Conservative governments in the 1990s included new and increased powers for prison governors, random mandatory drug tests (MDTs) brought in throughout the prison service in 1996, and the introduction of the incentives and earned privileges scheme (IEP) whereby good behaviour by a prisoner would be rewarded and bad conduct would receive punishment.

However, the emphasis placed on tough regimes was balanced by reforms seeking to make the prison regime fairer to its inmates. A major riot and siege in Strangeways Prison, Manchester, in 1990 resulted in a report by Lord Woolf in which he argued that there was a need for a balance to be struck within prisons between security, control and justice (Home Office, 1991: 17).

The Woolf Report (1991)

Lord Woolf argued that justice required prisoners to be treated fairly and humanely. To achieve this he proposed a number of reforms, which included:

- The introduction of a national system of accredited standards for prisons.

- The establishment of a prison ombudsman as an ultimate court of appeal to safeguard prisoners' interests.

- The end of the practice of 'slopping out' through the provision of access to sanitation by all inmates by 1996.

- Improved links with families (which might be achieved through the use of local prisons) coupled with more prison visits and the liberalisation of home leave and temporary release provisions.

- The introduction of contracts for each prisoner outlining their expectations and responsibilities and the improvement of conditions for remand prisoners, including lower security categorisations.

▶

The government responded to this report with a white paper that endorsed some of these recommendations, particularly those related to contracts for prisoners, accredited standards and the establishment of an ombudsman. Following the publication of the report, prisoners were given access to telephones (which enabled them to maintain contact with families, which was seen as an aid to rehabilitation) and the practice of 'slopping out' finally ended in English prisons on 12 April 1996.

Nonetheless, a number of high-profile escapes in the early 1990s resulted in renewed emphasis being placed on security. This objective was directed by the 1995 Learmont Report, which viewed custody as the primary purpose of prisons. Recommendations included bringing all prisons up to minimum standards of security by strengthening perimeter fences and installing close-circuit television; replacing all dormitory accommodation with cells; introducing electronic and magnetic locking systems; and making visitor searching more rigorous. This report was criticised for placing security considerations above the obligations of the prison service to treat prisoners humanely and to seek their rehabilitation.

Post-1997 Labour governments have continued with many aspects of their predecessors' policies and prison numbers have continued to rise. There have, however, been certain differences. Jack Straw (Labour's Home Secretary 1997–2002) was especially concerned to ensure that prison regimes were constructive.

The constructive nature of prison regimes is especially delivered by the provision of 'purposeful activities'. This term describes a wide range of pursuits, which include prison work, education and training courses, physical education, programmes to tackle the causes of criminal behaviour such as alcohol and substance abuse, anti-bullying initiatives, family visits, and the taking of responsibilities in prison gardens and workshops (Home Affairs Committee, 2005). These are designed to provide prisoners with constructive use of their time while in prison. They are also integral to the maintenance of order within these institutions and an essential aid to the rehabilitation of inmates when released.

Subsequent home secretaries have focused on the extent to which released offenders commit further crime, and the need to reduce recidivism was a key purpose for the creation of the National Offender Management Service in 2004 (see below).

Taking it further 6

Analyse and explain why prisons have traditionally found it hard to secure the rehabilitation of offenders.

Young offenders

Children and young persons who commit a serious crime can be subject to a custodial sentence. Specific custodial regimes for young offenders initially took the form of borstals, which were set up by the 1908 Crime Prevention Act. These initially catered for those aged 16–20 (raised to 21 in 1936). Borstals were replaced by youth custody centres by the 1982 Criminal Justice Act and by young offenders institutions in the 1988 Criminal Justice Act (catering for those aged 15–21).

In addition to YOIs there are other institutions to cater for those below the age of 18 whose crimes merit a custodial sentence. These are secure training centres (handling young offenders up to the age of 17) and local authority secure children's homes. The latter are for boys aged 12–14 and girls aged 12–16, although some vulnerable boys aged 15 and 16 may be accommodated within them.

In 2008 there were four secure training centres, 15 secure children's homes and 18 young offender institutions.

The National Offender Management Service

NOMS is an executive agency of the Ministry of Justice and operates through nine regional offices in England and one office in Wales. Each English region is headed by a Regional Offender Manager (titled Director of Offender Management in Wales) whose role includes commissioning services, developing a regional delivery plan to reduce re-offending and to coordinate regional and local partnerships.

NOMS originated from a proposal made in the 2003 Carter Report and was set up in 2004 with the objectives of punishing offenders and reducing the level of re-offending. The latter objective would be achieved by what the 2004 white paper referred to as the 'end to end' management of offenders. This entailed coordinating the operations of the prison and probation services to ensure that the interventions commenced in prison would be continued when the offender was released.

The Parole Board

Basic facts of the Parole Board

The 1967 Criminal Justice Act introduced a procedure whereby prisoners in England and Wales could be released before they had served the full sentence ordered by a court. This system of early release was named 'parole' and the person released into the community would be subject to supervision by a probation officer. The eligibility criteria for release were initially determined by this legislation and amended by subsequent measures, most notably the 1991 Criminal Justice Act.

The status of the Parole Board as an executive non-departmental public body was conferred by the 1994 Criminal Justice and Public Order Act. This became sponsored by NOMS following this agency's creation. However, following an Appeal Court Judgment in 2008 (the Brooke case), which argued that it was insufficiently independent of the executive branch of government to meet the requirements of Section 5(4) of the European Convention of Human Rights, from 1 April 2008 the Board became sponsored by the Access to Justice Group contained within the Ministry of Justice.

In 2007 the Parole Board consisted of 168 members. Most of these were part-time appointments drawn from professionals working in a wide range of areas relevant to the work of the Board: the legal system, psychiatrists, psychologists, probation officers and criminologists. There were also a number of independent members. The Board also employs a small number of support staff. In 2008/09 its budget was £8.36 million and it dealt with in excess of 25,000 cases in 2006/07.

The 2003 Criminal Justice Act established new arrangements for the automatic release of many prisoners, limiting the role of the Parole Board to determine the release of two categories of prisoners.

The first category was those serving indeterminate life sentences (whether these were mandatory, discretionary or automatic) and also those serving the newly-created indeterminate sentence for public protection. In all of these cases, the trial judge stipulates a minimum period of time (termed a 'tariff') that the prisoner must serve in custody, and it is for the Parole Board to assess whether, having completed this term, it is safe for the inmate to be released into the community. The criteria adopted to assess this relates to the likelihood of further offending behaviour and whether this would cause serious harm to members of the public. If this course of action is adopted, life licence conditions are set as requirements to which the released prisoner must adhere.

The second category of prisoner that relates to the work of the Parole Board is those serving determinate sentences. These include discretionary conditional release prisoners serving determinate sentences of over four years for offences committed before 4 April 2005 and those given extended sentences for public protection for offences committed after 4 April 2005. The Parole Board assesses whether, having completed the minimum time the prisoner is required to spend in custody, it is safe to release him or her into the community. If the inmate is released, parole licence conditions are set as requirements to which the released prisoner must comply.

The Parole Board also considers the cases of prisoners in both of these categories who breach their licence conditions. The Board makes recommendations to the Secretary of State regarding the recall of indeterminate life sentence prisoners and considers the cases of determinate sentenced prisoners whom the Secretary of State has recalled. In the case of both categories of prisoners who have been recalled, the Parole Board determines whether subsequent re-release into the community is an appropriate course of action.

Victims of crime may also influence the decisions of the Parole Board. The 2004 Domestic Violence, Crime and Victims Act enabled the victim to make representation to the Parole Board – via the Offender Manager – regarding the conditions that should attach to an offender's licence upon release. Further, following the 2006 Criminal Justice Review, victims of serious crime have been able to voice their views to the Parole Board regarding the offender's release or transfer to open conditions. The mechanism to do this is the Victims' Personal Statement, which was introduced in 2001.

Bringing offenders to justice

A key function of the criminal justice system is to ensure that those who commit crimes are appropriately dealt with. This section briefly examines the processes and procedures that are involved in bringing offenders to justice.

The police service

A person who is suspected of having committed a criminal act for which he or she can be arrested will be taken to a police station and asked questions concerning the offence. Suspects will be advised as to why they are being arrested and formally cautioned. Historically suspects could refuse to answer all questions put to them by the police (this was known as the right of silence), but since the enactment of the 1994 Criminal Justice and Public Order Act they are warned that their defence may be harmed should they not mention anything during questioning which they later rely on in court as part of their defence.

The powers of the police

In order to carry out their duties, police officers are charged with a number of powers. Many of these originally derived from common law, giving support to the view that a police officer was simply a 'citizen in uniform'. However, police officers were also provided with powers through Acts of Parliament. Initially these tended to be limited to specific geographic areas, so that police powers lacked a national framework. This situation was remedied with the 1984 Police and Criminal Evidence Act (PACE), which provided for a national raft of police powers. This legislation gave police officers the following powers:

- Stop and search
- Enter and search of premises
- Arrest
- Detain a person in custody.

The usage and conditions under which these powers can be exercised and what the police can and cannot do when implementing them is further regulated by detailed PACE Codes of Practice. There are currently eight Codes of Practice, introduced in February 2008.

PACE is not the only source of police powers. Powers derived from common law also remain (such as breach of the peace) but these were reduced in number following the enactment of the 1984 legislation. Additionally a considerable volume of legislation augments police powers both in the areas of activity referred to above (especially stop and search) and in other areas (including the regulation of road traffic).

Since the enactment of the 1998 Human Rights Act, police officers are also required to ensure that their actions accord with the European Declaration of Human Rights (including interpretations handed down by the European Court of Human Rights).

The Police complaints machinery

The actions of police officers are regulated in two ways:

- The law (in particular the 1984 Police and Criminal Evidence Act and the Codes of Practice made under this legislation – but other legislation may apply too).

- The Code of Professional Standards for Police Officers: this was introduced in 2006, replacing the former Police Code of Conduct (previously known as the Police Disciplinary Code).

Complaints made by members of the general public against an individual police officer are dealt with by the police complaints machinery. Complaints regarding *police policy* remain less satisfactorily regulated, although some legislation does provide for this. This includes the 1974 Health and Safety legislation: in 2007 the CPS undertook proceedings against the MPS alleging that the force had failed to provide for the health, safety and welfare of Jean Charles de Menezes who was shot dead in a London underground station by armed police officers on 22 July 2005.

A standardised system for dealing with complaints was introduced by the 1964 Police Act. This system was developed by three subsequent Acts: the 1976 Police Act (which set up the Police Complaints Board), the 1984 Police and Criminal Evidence Act (which replaced the Police Complaints Board with the Police Complaints Authority) and the 2002 Police Reform Act (which replaced the Police Complaints Authority with the Independent Police Complaints Commission). The latter Act was especially significant as for the first time it enabled complaints against the police to be investigated by persons other than police officers.

> ### Taking it further 7
>
> Evaluate the effectiveness of the way in which complaints against police officers have been investigated since 1976.

Treatment by the police

The procedure governing the way in which those detained in custody are treated in police stations is laid down in Codes of Practice drawn up under the provisions of the 1984 Police and Criminal Evidence Act. These regulate:

- How long a person can be held for questioning before being either released or formally charged.

- The right of that person to legal representation.

- Arrangements governing the tape recording of interviews held in police stations.

While in the station, the suspect is under the charge of a custody officer (usually a sergeant) who has specific legal responsibility for all persons being held in a police station.

When questioning has ended the police have a number of options. They may release the suspect, or they may formally caution him or her. A caution (which is given by a senior officer) is an alternative to prosecution and is issued for a wide range of offences (including violence against the person) for an accused person aged 18 and over provided that he or she admits to the offence. It is not a formal charge but is placed on a person's record and may count against them should they subsequently be charged with another offence. The system of cautions is governed by the 2003 Criminal Justice Act, which established *simple* cautions and *conditional* cautions, the latter containing provisions that have to be met in order to avoid a prosecution. Cautioning is similar to the system of reprimands and warnings that may be handed out to offenders aged 10–17 under the provisions of the 1998 Crime and Disorder Act.

Alternatively, the police may decide to charge the suspect with an offence or to release him or her on police bail so that further enquiries can be made.

If a person is charged he or she may be detained in custody and taken to a magistrates' court at the earliest opportunity, or be released until a magistrates' court hearing can arranged. If the latter course of action is adopted, the person can be released on police bail. This procedure is governed by the 1976 Bail Act and enables limitations to be placed on a suspect's movements. The 2003 Criminal Justice Act enables police bail to be granted to a person who has been arrested without the need to take them to a police station.

The Crown Prosecution Service (CPS)

Persons who are charged by the police with having committed a criminal act are referred to the CPS.

The work of the CPS has been described earlier in this chapter. The main task of CPS lawyers is to review files submitted to them by the police arising from an investigation and to determine whether to proceed with (or discontinue) a criminal prosecution. They also determine what charge should be preferred.

When it was initially formed (in 1986) the CPS suffered from a number of problems, including suspicion by the police that its insistence that there should be a reasonable chance that prosecution would lead to a conviction had the effect of releasing without charge persons the police believed to be criminals. For this reason, many police officers dubbed it the 'Criminal Protection Service'. However, reforms proposed by Lord Justice Auld (2001) were incorporated into the 2003 Criminal Justice Act which created the legal framework to transfer the responsibility for charging from the police to CPS lawyers. This resulted in CPS staff being placed in police stations to advise the police at the outset regarding the most appropriate course of action. Other reforms (including the alignment of CPS and police force boundaries) have also improved the relationship between these two services.

Persons charged by the CPS will be taken to a court where their guilt or innocence will be determined. Criminal cases are initially referred to a magistrates' court which will either try the case itself or refer the matter to a Crown Court. If the latter course of action is preferred, the magistrates will decide whether to remand the accused person in custody until the case can be heard or to release them on bail.

A person who has been charged with an offence (the *defendant*) will be asked to plead guilty or not guilty. If the latter plea is made, the prosecution is required to prove the person's guilt 'beyond all reasonable doubt'. Courts in England and Wales use the adversarial system of justice in which the prosecution and defence set out to persuade the court of the validity of their own case and to undermine the arguments put forward by their opponents.

In a magistrates' court the magistrates determine guilt or innocence: in a Crown Court the jury decides this. If guilt is determined, the person is sentenced by either the magistrates or, in a Crown Court, the judge. The sentence is determined by legislation and also by proposals drawn up by the Sentencing Guidelines Council which was established by the 2003 Criminal Justice Act.

Sentences may consist of fines for the least serious offences or be community-based or custodial for more serious ones. Community-based sentences are governed by the 2003 Criminal Justice Act, which provided for a new community order that gave sentencers a wide range of options (termed 'requirements') that included unpaid work, curfew, supervision and electronic monitoring. Community orders are implemented by the probation service or (in the case of young offenders) by the Youth Offending Team.

Custodial sentences are served in prisons, or in a range of alternative institutions for those below 21 years of age. The time to be spent in custody is determined by the trial judge. If the offender is sentenced to life imprisonment, the trial judge will stipulate what is known as a 'tariff' – the minimum time that the prisoner must remain in prison. At the end of this time, the prisoner is eligible to be freed – but the decision whether to do so or not is made by the Parole Board.

Summary justice

Summary justice is usually equated with trials that take place in a magistrates' court for the more minor criminal offences. However, in recent years summary justice has also been associated with fixed penalties meted out by police officers and other public officials without the involvement of the courts. Termed 'pre-court summary justice' (Morgan, 2008: 8), it is directed at a wide range of disorderly actions and minor forms of criminal behaviour.

Fixed penalty notices

A wide range of responses that do not involve the courts have long been available for minor offences. These include police cautions for adults and reprimands and final warnings for those aged 10–17 years. The 1988 Road Traffic Act introduced fixed penalty notices for a range of minor traffic offences and this approach was built upon in the 2001 Criminal Justice and Police Act which introduced penalty notices for disorder (PNDs).

PNDs are on-the-spot fines (currently of £50 or £80) handed out (usually by police officers) to those who have committed various forms of anti-social behaviour or minor criminal actions, such as theft to the value of £200, or criminal damage to the level of £500. PNDs can be challenged (in which case the offender may be taken to court or the PND may be dropped) but if the offender fails to pay the fine, it is raised and becomes enforced by the courts.

There are a number of advantages derived from PNDs, which include enhancing the degree of public confidence in the criminal justice system as a result of speedy and visible response to low level crimes and disorder. Also, removing crimes of this nature from the courts enables them to concentrate on more serious forms of criminal behaviour.

However, this approach has been criticised for 'net widening', as minor offenders (especially younger people) can become criminalised for actions that would previously not have merited any intervention from criminal justice practitioners, thereby running the risk that increased levels of criminalisation will enhance the degree of social exclusion and anti-social behaviour. Other objections relate to the extent to which those who take decisions and dispense this form of summary justice are adequately accountable for their actions.

Taking it further 8

Juries are an important feature of Crown Courts. Assess the strengths and weaknesses of trial by jury.

Restorative justice

A key objective of restorative justice is to enable the person who has broken the law to repair the damage that has been caused to the direct victim and to society at large by his or her criminal behaviour.

This is usually achieved in a forum in which the criminal and victim are brought face to face so that the victim can explain the harm that the criminal act has caused him or her and the person who has committed the wrongdoing can apologise, explain the circumstances that brought about the criminal act, and agree to take steps to make amends for the harm that has been caused. These meetings take several forms and frequently adopt some type of conferencing format where the victim and wrongdoer are joined by other family and community members and criminal justice practitioners.

A key advantage of restorative justice is that crime is no longer viewed as an impersonal act that has breached an abstract legal code, but is seen as an act that had caused genuine harm to a real person. It enables the victim and wrongdoer to speak for themselves and each give their account of the incident. The main intention of this process is that the offender can be more readily reintegrated into society than would be the case if she or he merely received punishment for their actions which, in the case of a custodial sentence, may result in long-term or permanent exclusion from society.

There are, however, problems with this approach. Those who support a retributive response to crime criticise restorative justice for being too soft an option: a person who says 'sorry' (whether they mean it or not) may escape the more severe sentence that their actions merited. Also, victims may not wish to face those who have harmed them. There is also the danger that wrongdoers who are subjected to conferencing procedures may resent the process and refuse to cooperate with it. One way in which restorative justice functions is to make the wrongdoer feel ashamed of their actions and thus emotionally susceptible to making amends for them. However, if the lawbreaker does not genuinely feel that his or her actions were wrong, the process will not produce positive outcomes.

Taking it further 9

Evaluate the strengths and weaknesses of restorative justice.

Miscarriages of justice

The term 'miscarriages of justice' is generally understood to refer to persons who have been convicted of an offence they did not commit. Errors of this nature may arise for several reasons, such as:

- Professional misconduct (which historically included improper pressure being placed on a suspect by the police to confess to a crime he or she had not committed, or the planting of evidence on a suspect by the police to ensure a watertight case).

- Inadequacies on the part of defence lawyers.

- Failure by the prosecution to disclose information to the defence that might prejudice the former's case.

- The reliance on expert testimony which turns out to be erroneous.

Mistakes of this nature have resulted in some infamous miscarriages of justice in which persons have served lengthy prison sentences for crimes they did not commit. These include the case of Stefan Kiszko, who was imprisoned for the rape and murder of a schoolgirl in 1975. He served 16 years in prison; the Court of Appeal freed him after medical evidence proved that it was medically impossible for him to have committed the crime for which he had been sentenced.

Miscarriages could also arise through errors that occurred during the trial (for example, the trial judge had misdirected the jury). Although these could be corrected by the Court of Appeal quashing a Crown Court verdict and/or ordering a re-trial (or the Crown Court overturning the verdict of a magistrates' court), the Appeal Court's intervention would depend on a case being referred to it, which is not automatic.

Towards the end of the twentieth century a number of reforms were introduced in an attempt to avoid miscarriages of justice. These included the introduction of tape recording of interviews at police stations under the 1984 Police and Criminal Evidence Act, and legislation under the 1996 Criminal Procedure and Investigation Act that related to the disclosure of evidence by the prosecution.

Allegations that a miscarriage of justice had occurred were historically handled by the Home Office. However, the process was slow, secretive and decisions tended to support the original verdict. The 1993 Royal Commission on Criminal Justice proposed the establishment of an independent body to examine allegations that a miscarriage of justice had occurred and this was provided for by the 1995 Criminal Appeals Act. This legislation set up the Criminal Cases Review Commission (CCRC) to take over the work previously performed by the Home Office in connection with miscarriages of justice.

The CCRC is empowered to receive complaints directly from individuals or their representatives (such as solicitors) regarding either a wrongful conviction or an inappropriate sentence. The CCRC will normally intervene only when a case has been through the established appeals process and in the case of alleged wrongful conviction there also has to be new evidence that was either not available or was not disclosed at the original trial. If the CCRC feels that a miscarriage may have occurred, a caseworker will examine the matter further. If the caseworker agrees with this assessment, the CCRC will refer the case back to the Court of Appeal which may uphold or quash the original sentence.

> ## Taking it further 10
>
> Evaluate the initiatives undertaken in the latter years of the twentieth century to provide an effective remedy against miscarriages of justice.

Victims

In addition to attempting to ascertain why people commit crime, criminology is concerned with those who suffer as a consequence of it. The study of victims of crime is referred to as victimology. There is, however, no uniform approach to the study of those who have experienced crime.

Criminologists have adopted a range of approaches in connection with victims. These range from studies that attempt to identify the characteristics of victims of crime (seeking to examine, for example, whether victims, their habits and their lifestyles are in some way different from those who do not experience crime), to examinations that embrace various forms of victimless crime (including white-collar and middle-class crime). Some approaches go beyond the consideration of criminal acts and consider the impact that social factors such as poverty have on those who become victims of their social circumstances. The latter approach acknowledges that victimisation may arise from the discriminatory operations of the criminal justice system and those professionals who work within it (arising, for example, in connection with those who experience abuses of power).

Victims of crime play an integral part in the criminal justice process, since the state's intervention against those who break the law is usually triggered by those who have directly suffered as a result of the criminal act reporting the matter to the police.

Traditionally, however, the concerns of victims of crime did not receive prominent attention in the criminal justice process. Relatively few of the offences that are committed ever reach court and the attrition rate (the gap between crimes committed and convictions obtained) is especially high for serious crimes that include sexual violence. However, in recent years a number of developments have occurred that seek to ensure that the criminal justice system caters more adequately for those who have suffered as a result of crime. These include:

- *The National Association of Victims Support Scheme.* This was developed in the 1970s and covered all of England and Wales by the mid 1990s. It is now organised by the charity Victim Support and provides emotional support and practical help to those who have suffered as the consequence of crime.

- *The Victims' Charter.* This was published in 1990 and sought to make all agencies within the criminal justice system more responsive to the needs of victims. The charter (which was re-drafted in 1996) set out more than

50 standards as to how victims should be treated and what information they should be provided with at every stage of the criminal justice process. The charter emphasised the need to keep victims informed regarding the progress of a case and to pay regard to their interests when taking key decisions such as whether or not to charge an offender or whether or not to proceed with a prosecution. Other pronouncements such as the CPS's Statement on the Treatment of Victims and Witnesses have reinforced aspects of this charter and since 1995 the probation service has been required to take a victim's account of the impact that a crime has had on him or her when preparing pre-sentence reports.

- *The Victim Personal Statement Scheme*. This was introduced in 2001 to give the relatives of murder victims the opportunity to put on record the anguish caused to them by the crime and how it affected them physically, emotionally, psychologically and financially.

- *CPS procedures*. The commitment of the CPS to victims of crime is contained in the 2005 Prosecutors' Pledge and the 2006 Code of Practice for Victims of Crime. Other CPS initiatives include the Direct Communication with Victims Scheme, the Victim Focus Scheme and the No Witness No Justice initiative. The latter involved the CPS and police introducing Witness Care Units across England and Wales. A witness care officer provides a single point of contact for victims to ensure that information regarding the case and relevant support is provided to meet the needs of both victims and witnesses.

- *Reforms to the law*. A number of reforms have been introduced in an attempt to provide justice to victims of crime. The 1988 Criminal Justice Act introduced the principle that allowed the Attorney General to appeal against an excessively lenient sentence. The 2003 Criminal Justice Act made it possible for the prosecution to bring forward evidence that related to a defendant's previous bad character under certain circumstances. The 2003 Sexual Offences Act sought to address the very low conviction rate for violent sexual crimes: only around 5 per cent of allegations of rape made to the police lead to a successful conviction. Its provisions included redefining the act of rape and providing a clearer definition as to what constituted consent to a sexual act. However, the most significant reform affects the historic principle of double jeopardy.

Double jeopardy

Double jeopardy prevents a person being tried a second time for an offence of which they have previously been acquitted by a court. It was designed to prevent the unfairness and harassment that may arise if the state repeatedly and relentlessly pursued a person they wish to see convicted.

There are, however, imperfections with this rule; in particular, guilty persons may escape rightful punishment if new evidence subsequently emerges. The enhanced use of DNA profiling and cold case review has increased the possibility of this situation arising.

The weakness of double jeopardy was highlighted following the breakdown of a private prosecution brought by the parents of the murdered teenager Stephen Lawrence against three of those whom they alleged had killed him. The technical acquittal of two of these persons in 1996 meant that they could not be re-tried for this offence should new evidence subsequently arise.

Reforms to the double jeopardy rule have been introduced to deal with problems of this nature. The 1996 Criminal Procedure and Investigation Act made it possible for the prosecution to appeal for a re-trial under a limited range of circumstances that included evidence of jury tampering. This procedure has never been successfully used.

However, the 2003 Criminal Justice Act made it possible for a person to be re-tried for a range of offences that include murder, rape, kidnapping and armed robbery if 'new and compelling evidence' emerged following the first trial. The procedure entails the DPP referring the matter to the Court of Appeal who must overturn the original acquittal in order for a new trial to be authorised.

In 2006 Billy Dunlop became the first person to be convicted under this procedure for the murder of Julie Hogg in 1989, having previously been acquitted of the crime.

Common themes

This section seeks to refer to some of the main themes that have influenced the conduct of the criminal justice process in recent years.

Discretion

Discretion refers to 'the freedom, power, authority, decision or leeway of an official, organisation or individual to decide, discern or determine to make a judgement, choice or decision, about alternative courses of action or inaction' (Gelsthorpe and Padfield, 2003: 1). Discretion entails the ability of a criminal justice practitioner (such as a police officer, a magistrate or a judge) to exercise their judgement in relation to a situation they are confronted with.

Historically, discretion covered a wide range of circumstances. These included the ability of chief police officers to determine the priorities for the police force that they commanded; a decision by a police officer to arrest a person for a minor misdemeanour or to handle the matter in some other way; the determination by a CPS lawyer as to whether or not to prosecute an offender and what charge should be brought; and the options that a magistrate or a judge exercised in relation to sentencing a person who had been found guilty of a crime.

A key problem with discretion is that it can be used in a discriminatory manner which may be based upon personal bias and prejudice. It also may result in unequal treatment for persons who have committed similar offences. Thus in recent years, discretion by criminal justice practitioners has been limited.

The 1994 Police and Magistrates' Courts Act enabled the Home Secretary rather than chief constables to set the priorities for police forces, and the discretion exercised by police officers in connection with stop and search powers has been brought under more rigorous monitoring procedures commencing with the 1984 Police and Criminal Evidence Act.

Magistrates and judges also exercised a considerable degree of discretion with regard to sentencing. The Appeal Court would sometimes issue sentencing guidelines but interventions of this kind were not comprehensive. Sentencing guidelines were also produced by the Magistrates' Association, in association with the Lord Chancellor's Department, for the use of magistrates' courts.

More rigorous limits to sentencing discretion were imposed by the 1997 Crime (Sentences) Act; later amendments were made by the 2000 Powers of the Criminal Courts (Sentencing) Act. This legislation imposed a range of mandatory sentences on those who had been convicted of crimes of violence, drug trafficking and domestic burglary. Further limits on sentencing freedom were developed by the Sentencing Guidelines Council, established by the 2003 Criminal Justice Act, whose role was to develop a coherent approach to sentencing. Sentencing guidelines are regarded as binding on all courts, and sentencers are required to give reasons should they depart from them.

Diversity

Accusations that the criminal justice system operated in a racially discriminatory manner were frequently made in the latter decades of the twentieth century. Specific allegations were made in connection with the police service (in particular the use of powers such as stop and search in a way that stereotyped young black males as criminals yet failed to adequately protect minority ethnic communities when they were the victim of crimes such as racial violence).

The perception that black people in particular were over-policed and under-protected underpinned the negative views that these communities had of the police service, a negativity that sometimes boiled over into serious episodes of disorder such as occurred in 1981 and 1985. The role of the police as gatekeepers of the criminal justice system had further discriminatory consequences, one of which was the high proportion of black and minority ethnic persons who received custodial sentences.

Attempts were made to respond to criticisms of this nature. Lord Scarman's report, produced in 1981, following a wave of disturbances across England, made a number of recommendations that were designed to improve the relationship between the police service and minority ethnic communities, many of which (including monitoring stop and search powers, reform of the police complaints procedure and the requirement that the police consult with local communities) were embodied in the 1984 Police and Criminal

Evidence Act. However, this failed to stem criticisms that the police service operated in a racially discriminatory manner.

The issue was forcibly placed on the criminal justice policy agenda following the racist murder of the black teenager Stephen Lawrence in 1993. The failure of the Metropolitan Police Service to secure a conviction for this murder sparked criticism and resulted in the incoming 1997 Labour government appointing Sir William Macpherson to chair an inquiry as to what had gone wrong.

Sir William's report in 1999 produced a scathing indictment of the way in which the murder investigation had been handled. However, in addition to condemning it as professionally incompetent, he argued that the police service was institutionally racist. He defined this term as:

> the collective failure of an organisation to provide an appropriate and professional service to people because of their colour, culture or ethnic origin. It can be seen or detected in processes, attitudes and behaviour which amount to discrimination through unwitting prejudice, ignorance, thoughtlessness and racist stereotyping which disadvantage minority ethnic people. (Home Office, 1999: 28)

His report then put forward 70 recommendations designed to address the problems he had identified. The vast majority of these applied to the police service but other criminal justice agencies were included too, thus providing an agenda for the reform of discriminatory practices in the criminal justice system for the early years of the twenty-first century.

Taking it further 11

Analyse the effectiveness of reforms put forward by Sir William Macpherson's 1999 report to eliminate institutional racism from the police service.

Joined-up government

Traditionally the agencies within the criminal justice system operated very much in isolation. Each had their own roles to perform and this bred outlooks that were not necessarily shared by the personnel in other agencies: for example, the police and probation service were likely to have different attitudes towards those who broke the law: attitudes that were based on the different functions each performed in the criminal justice process, whereby one was primarily concerned with protecting the public and the other with the welfare of the law-breaker. This situation was also reflected in the structure and organisation of the key criminal justice agencies, all of which used different organisational boundaries within which to perform their tasks.

The 1997 Labour government vigorously pursued initiatives in multi-agency (now termed 'partnership') working. There have been several developments to bring about this change, some of which are listed below.

- *The 1998 Crime and Disorder Act.* This legislation established multi-agency Crime and Disorder Reduction Partnerships, and also multi-agency Youth Offender Teams to deal with crimes committed by young people. The police service, local government, probation service and the health service played key roles in both of these joined-up initiatives.

- *Public Service Agreements.* These were introduced in the 1998 Comprehensive Spending Review. They consist of objectives whose delivery requires joint working by a number of central government departments. The measurement of these objectives is assessed by outcome-based performance indicators.

- *Common organisational boundaries.* Key criminal justice agencies have adopted the same operational boundaries. For example, since 1999 the organisation of the police service into 43 areas is now mirrored by the Crown Prosecution Service (although this has 42 areas: London is treated as one whereas there exist two police forces in that locality – the Metropolitan Police Service and the City of London Police force). Common organisational boundaries facilitate joint working arrangements, one example of which is joint police/CPS Criminal Justice Units (referred to as Integrated Prosecution Teams) which provide for the integration of these two agencies in relation to issues such as the preparation of case files, the management of magistrates' courts cases and in connection with witnesses.

- *The Office for Criminal Justice Reform (OCJR).* This was set up in 2004 to coordinate the work of the three central government departments that exercise responsibility for the operations of the criminal justice agencies: the Home Office, the Ministry of Justice and the Office of the Attorney General. The National Board is responsible for attaining the criminal justice system's Public Service Agreements and to do this it sets delivery targets for the 42 Local Criminal Justice Boards that were set up in 2003. These are composed of local agencies responsible for delivering criminal justice system targets: the police, the CPS, magistrates' and Crown Courts, YOTs, and prison and probation services.

- *The creation of NOMS.* This was established in 2004 to secure a joined-up approach by the prison and probation services and other public, private and voluntary sector organisations to secure the task of reducing the rate of re-offending.

- *Strategic plans.* These are an important aspect of Labour's new managerialist reforms, and a key role of the OCJR is to exercise overall responsibility for the content, resourcing and delivery of the criminal justice strategic plan. The criminal justice strategic plan 2008–2011 establishes how the agencies of the criminal justice system in England and Wales will work together to deliver a criminal justice system that is effective in bringing offenders to justice, especially in serious offences; engages with the public and inspires confidence; places the needs of victims at its heart; and provides simple and efficient processes.

LSPs and LAAs

The 2000 Local Government Act placed a duty on local authorities to pre-pare community strategies. *Local Strategic Partnerships* were subsequently developed to advance this objective. These bring together a range of public, private, voluntary and community bodies that operate at local authority level with the aim of securing coordinated activity to improve the economic, social and environmental aspects of an area.

Local Area Agreements were introduced in 2005 and consist of written agreements between central and local government that seek to improve the quality of life of local authority residents through joint working of public, voluntary and private sector bodies in the local authority area. LAAs established the desired outcomes to be achieved by joint working arrangements, the indicators through which progress in attaining this end would be measured and the services and projects that were designed to deliver improvements.

The 2007 Local Government and Public Involvement in Health Act provided for LSPs to become the main vehicle through which the government's Sustainable Community Strategy would be advanced. In order to achieve this, the strategic goals of LSPs would be delivered through LAAs.

Technology

Information technology brings a number of advantages to the operations of the criminal justice system. It reduces the time that practitioners need to devote to paperwork and form-filling and also facilitates the speedy exchange of information both within criminal justice agencies and between them. It has important implications for joined-up government both within individual agencies and between them.

The Bichard Enquiry (2004), which followed the murder of Holly Wells and Jessica Chapman in Soham, drew particular attention to the absence of information-sharing within the police service. This gave rise to a number of developments to facilitate this objective, including the IMPACT Nominal Index (INI) which enables individual police forces to share information they have gathered locally. The INI provides pointers as to where those looking for information might find it. It was intended to be developed to provide direct access to information through the mechanism of a police national database. However, problems with the nature of data stored by individual forces have impeded the progress of this reform.

Technology also performs an important role in enabling criminal justice agencies to share with other agencies the information they have collected, thus advancing the objective of a joined-up and streamlined criminal justice system. Traditionally agencies collected their own data and did not share it with others, but sharing information at an offender's point of entry into the criminal justice system is crucial to ensure appropriate responses and to avoid harm both to the offender and to others.

Developments to achieve joined-up information sharing across criminal justice agencies have been implemented. XHIBIT is a computer system used in Crown Courts that provides information relating to court hearings and case details to a range of key stakeholders that include the police, Crown Prosecutors and witnesses. A similar development was planned to in the National Offender Management Information System (NOMIS). It was intended that a development termed C-NOMIS would promote joined-up data sharing across the prison and probation services' databases and enable a large number of criminal justice staff concerned with offender management to have access to this information. Spiralling costs required this project to be scaled down and what is now termed NOMIS has been rolled out only within the public sector prison service.

References

Gelsthorpe, L. and Padfield, N. (eds) (2003) *Exercising Discretion: Decision-Making in the Criminal Justice System and Beyond.* Cullompton, Devon: Willan Publishing.

Home Affairs Committee (2005) *Rehabilitation of Prisoners.* First Report, Session 2004–05, HC 193. London: TSO.

Home Office (1991) *Prison Disturbances 1990: Report of an Inquiry by the Rt Hon Lord Justice Woolf (part I & II) and His Honour Judge Stephen Tumim (part II)*, Cm 1456. London: HMSO (Woolf Report).

Home Office (1995) *Review of Prison Service Security in England and Wales and the Escape from Parkhurst Prison on Tuesday 3rd January 1995*, Cm 3020. London: HMSO (Learmont Report).

Home Office (1999) *The Stephen Lawrence Inquiry: Report of an Inquiry by Sir William Macpherson of Cluny*, Cm 4262. London: TSO (Macpherson Report).

Morgan, R. (2008) *Summary Justice: Fast – But Fair?* London: Centre for Crime and Justice Studies.

3 Criminology sources

Information related to the study of criminology can be obtained from a wide range of source material. The aims of this chapter are:

- To distinguish between primary and secondary source material.

- To identify some of the key sources from which information regarding criminology and the criminal justice system can be obtained.

- To outline the importance of the Internet as a tool of criminological research.

- To provide information of key Internet resources relevant to the study of criminology.

Primary and secondary sources

The sources you will use in the study of criminology fall under two broad headings: primary and secondary material.

Primary sources consist of a variety of original documents. Criminal justice studies in particular make wide use of 'official' material (such as parliamentary debates, Acts of Parliament, reports from Parliamentary Select Committees, various forms of publications from government departments, in particular the Home Office and Ministry of Justice) and material produced by groups and organisations that are concerned with a particular aspect of criminal justice, such as the Prison Reform Trust, Liberty or Statewatch (fuller reference to these and similar bodies is contained later in this chapter).

Other primary sources include autobiographies, diaries and memoirs written by criminal justice practitioners or by those who have been on the 'receiving end' of criminal justice (such as offenders or ex-offenders), and interviews published in formats such as journals and newspapers.

In addition to primary sources contained in documents, criminologists frequently compile their own primary material derived from methods such as interviews and personal letters.

Secondary sources consist of material that is not entirely based upon original sources. Typically, it is based upon an author's assessment and interpretation of a range of primary sources, from which views, opinions and reasoned arguments can be formulated related to the issue that is the subject of the author's investigation. Secondary sources enable a rounded evaluation of a topic to be presented, but this is reliant on the author providing an accurate and impartial assessment of key material. Issues such as bias and professional competence may undermine the reliability of secondary source material.

At undergraduate level, the majority of sources you will use will consist of secondary material. Below the key categories of source material are discussed.

 # Books

A wide variety of books are useful in the study of criminology, and some of the key categories of literature of this nature are discussed below.

Text books

Text books encompass a wide subject area and are particularly useful in the early stages of a criminologist's career. Books of this nature provide a broad level of knowledge and understanding – they constitute the building blocks of criminological study. They are of most use in courses taught up to first year undergraduate level, after which it is expected that students will consult more detailed literature.

Readers

The aim of readers is to provide those interested in criminology with access to key sources that are not always readily available; for example, if they have been published abroad or are out of print. They also generally provide a commentary on each text that is contained in the work, thus giving readers a context within which the discussion is set and perhaps explaining what the author sought to do and why this was important to criminological study.

There are, however, pitfalls with works of this nature: in particular they tend to provide only a portion of the text and important arguments might thus be omitted in the editing that has taken place.

Dictionaries

Criminological books often assume a level of knowledge that the readers do not possess. Accordingly it is helpful to have access to works that define key criminological terms and concepts and explain practices and procedures that are relevant to the operations of the criminal justice process. The dictionaries that are available either tend to focus on one discrete area of crime and criminal justice studies or are of a more general nature, dealing with aspects of study that include the criminal justice system.

Specialised texts

Books of a more specialised nature that deal with a particular aspect of crime or the criminal justice process are indispensable when basic concepts have been understood. Courses taught on the second and third years of an undergraduate course are typically of a specialised nature, giving the student the ability to study an area of interest in some depth. The material covered in text books is developed more fully in specialised works and it is essential that texts of this nature are consulted in order to gain specialised knowledge.

Information on literature

Information regarding books can be found from several sources. Browsing the shelves of bookshops and libraries is a good way to keep informed of up-to-date material. Other sources include those listed below.

Unit outlines

For those enrolled on university courses, unit outlines, in which a lecturer provides details of his or her unit, are a good guide to key literature. The material contained in unit outlines is often updated in lectures (or material associated with lectures such as Web CT).

Publishers' catalogues

Publishers' catalogues are a particularly useful source relating to books that are 'hot off the press'. Criminology is a popular subject and many publishers commission books in this area. However, the main publishers of books on criminology are:

- Willan Publishing
- Routledge
- Sage
- Waterside Press
- Oxford University Press
- Open University Press

Journals

Because journals are published on a regular basis throughout the year, they are able to provide up-to-date information on specialised criminological topics. Two broad forms of journal are available.

Specialist journals

Journals of this nature provide information that is typically highly specialised and written by criminologists who are expert in their field of study. Articles that appear in specialist journals have undergone a process of 'peer review': the author's work is considered by other colleagues who may suggest alterations to the material that has been initially presented. This means that articles in a specialist journal have been carefully considered and vetted by other experts before being published. This is a good guarantee of academic excellence.

The key criminology journals are :

British Journal of Criminology
Community Safety Journal
Crime Prevention and Community Safety
Crime, Media, Culture

Criminal Justice Matters
Criminology and Criminal Justice
Criminology and Public Policy
European Journal of Crime, Criminal Law and Criminal Justice
Policing and Society
Journal of Criminal Justice
Police Journal
Police Practice and Research
Punishment and Society

University libraries tend to keep hard copies of the key journals, but many others are available in electronic format.

Professional journals

Professional journals are typically concerned with highlighting contemporary issues and problems facing those who work in particular criminal justice agencies. The material put forward is not often peer reviewed and often represents the personal views and opinions of the author.

Nonetheless, journals of this nature can be important sources of information for those studying criminology, especially in connection with the workings of agencies within the criminal justice system. The views of senior professionals are likely to contain important insights into current and future policy directions.

The key professional journals are:

Magistrate
Policing
Police review
Policing Today
Prison Service Journal
Probation Journal

Information on journals

Information regarding journals can be found from several sources. Browsing the shelves of libraries is a good way to keep informed of up-to-date material. Other sources include unit outlines, in which a lecturer provides details of his or her unit, for those studying criminology in higher education. Information on journals contained in unit outlines is often updated in lectures (or material associated with lectures such as Web CT).

Television

Crime is a popular issue and programmes related to criminology and criminal justice are frequently aired on television. Programmes including *Dispatches* and *Panorama* frequently show material that is relevant to contemporary criminological issues. Universities have facilities to enable programmes of this nature to be copied for use in classes.

The Internet

The Internet has become a key tool of information on all aspects of criminological study. It contains the two main categories of information:

- *Primary source material.* Documents prepared by a range of official agencies, public bodies and pressure groups whose work relates to criminology and criminal justice are often available online. These include defences, critiques and evaluations of policies associated with crime and criminal justice matters, and ideas on which future policy in these areas is based. Material of this nature is an indispensable tool to contemporary study in criminology and criminal justice.

- *Secondary source material.* Much material, often in the form of articles, is posted by persons with an interest in crime and criminal justice affairs. Articles are sometimes included in editions of online journals (such as the *Internet Journal of Criminology*) and are often written by leading criminologists, providing an important source of ideas and information. Others, are put forward by individuals on an *ad hoc* basis. The key problem with the latter type of information concerns its accuracy. Articles of this nature will not have undergone any process of peer review, which means that there is no guarantee, of the academic worth of the ideas put forward – they might be good, bad, or totally ill-informed and inaccurate. Material of this nature thus needs to be treated with caution.

Key organisations and sources of information

The rest of this chapter provides a list of organisations whose work is relevant to the study of criminology and to the operations of the criminal justice process, together with their website addresses. Bear in mind that web addresses do change and if any given here fails to work, enter the name of the organisation into a search engine.

Acts of Parliament
www.opsi.gov.uk/acts

Much of the work performed within the criminal justice process is governed by Acts of Parliament. Such legislation, may provide for the creation of agencies operating in this process and gives them powers with which to conduct their work. Legislation affecting the criminal justice process is contained in Public General Acts. All from 1988 onwards are available online in HTML and PDF format. Some Acts from 1832 to 1987 are also available in PDF format.

Association of Chief Police Officers (ACPO)
www.acpo.police.uk

ACPO originates from the County Chief Constables Club (formed in 1858) and the Chief Constables' Association of England and Wales (established to represent city and borough police forces in 1896). It assumed its present form in 1948, and the Royal Ulster Constabulary was incorporated in 1970. ACPO consists of the most senior ranks of the police service (chief constables, deputy chief constables and assistant chief constables or their equivalents in the 44 police forces of England, Wales and Northern Ireland, together with the most senior ranks from national policing agencies, the Isle of Man and the Channel Islands and a small number of senior non-police staff). Members numbered 312 in 2005. Initially ACPO served both as a staff association for these senior ranks and also acted as the central focus for the development of police policy. The staff association role was taken over by the Chief Police Officers' Staff Association in 1996, enabling ACPO to concentrate on policy formulation. Its website contains online copies of the annual report since 2000 and ACPO policies on a very wide range of activities and issues concerned with the internal and external operations of the police service.

Association of Police Authorities (APA)
www.apa.police.uk/apa

The APA represents the 44 police authorities in England, Wales and Northern Ireland. This body was established in April 1997 to promote the concerns of these bodies both locally and nationally and to seek to influence police policy. Online material on its website includes responses to consultative documents related to police reform, and material connected with police policy such as stop and search powers and neighbourhood policing. The website provides up-to-date statements on contemporary police issues and the APA's annual report is available from 2002/03.

Attorney General's Office
www.attorneygeneral.gov.uk

The Attorney General's office consists of the Law Officers of the Crown (the Attorney General and the Solicitor General). They perform three main functions: acting as guardians of the public interest (for example, by initiating appeals against unduly lenient sentences or referring a case to the Court of Appeal on a point of law); being the chief legal advisers to the government (exercising responsibility for all Crown litigation); and performing leadership functions in connection with the operations of the criminal justice system. The law officers exercise overall responsibility for the Treasury Solicitor's Department, the Crown Prosecution Service, the Serious Fraud Office, the Customs and Revenue Prosecution Office and Her Majesty's Crown Prosecution Inspectorate.

The website contains material that includes consultation documents, guidelines issued by the Attorney General, key speeches, statistical information on matters such as unduly lenient sentences and the Office's annual report.

Audit Commission
www.audit-commission.gov.uk

The Audit Commission was created in 1983 to regulate the external auditors of local authorities in England and Wales. Its remit was subsequently extended to include a wide range of bodies that spend public money. It seeks to aid those responsible for delivering public services to achieve a high level of quality by attaining the three 'Es' of economy, efficiency and effectiveness. The website contains a range of online reports relevant to criminal justice matters. There is also a community safety section that contains information on issues such as inspections of local community safety services and the police use of resources. It is useful to occasionally check the Audit Commission's website for details of their current investigations.

Bar Council
www.barcouncil.org.uk

The General Council of the Bar was established in 1894 to represent the interests of barristers in England and Wales. It is the governing body of the Bar and seeks to promote and improve its services and functions and represent its interests on all matters related to the profession. It is composed of around 100 barristers who are elected and represent the Inns of Court and interest groups. The Bar Council's website contains online copies of its annual reports since 2001 and a range of material relevant to the operations of the criminal justice process such as consultation papers. Much of the work of the Bar Council is discharged by committees and reports by these (covering issues such as equality and diversity) are also available online. The website contains a link to the Bar Standards Board (**www.barstandardsboard. org.uk**), which deals with the regulation of barristers. This was established in 2006 and has a different membership from that of the Bar Council.

Commission for Equality and Human Rights
www.equalityhumanrights.com

The Commission for Equality and Human Rights was established by the 2006 Equality Act, and replaced the former Equal Opportunities Commission, the Commission for Racial Equality and the Disabilities Commission. Its role is to eliminate discrimination, protect human rights and build good community relations, and discharges this role through enforcing the law, conducting campaigns and influencing good practice within organisations. It also provides advice on equal opportunities policy, which includes guidance on organisations' legal duty to comply. Its website contains a range of publications that are relevant to its work, codes of practice and guidance and the Commission's business plan.

Courts Service
www.hmcourts-service.gov.uk

In 2005 Her Majesty's Courts Service was set up as an executive agency of the Department of Constitutional Affairs (now the Ministry of Justice) to provide for unified organisation and administration of the civil, family and criminal courts in England and Wales. Its website provides online information about the work of the Service, access to Crown Court annual reports since 2000/01 and county court annual reports since 2002/03, HMCS frameworks and guidance to the legal professions, and policy and strategy documents.

Crime and Disorder Reduction Partnerships (CDRPs)
www.crimereduction.homeoffice.gov.uk/regions/regions00.htm

CDRPs (or Community Safety Partnerships) were established by the 1998 Crime and Disorder Act (as amended by the 2002 Police Reform Act) to provide for multi-agency cooperation to reduce the level of local crime and disorder. The legislation placed a statutory obligation on what were termed 'responsible authorities' (initially police forces, local authorities, fire authorities, police authorities, health authorities in Wales and primary care trusts in England) to cooperate in identifying local crime and disorder issues and develop strategies to cope with them. CDRPs worked closely with Drug Action Teams (DATs) and integrated the latter's work in unitary local authorities in 2004.

The mini-site that is dedicated to the work of CDRPs contains information and resources to aid practitioners and a range of publications related to crime reduction.

Crime Info
www.crimeinfo.org.uk

This extremely informative website is operated by the Centre for Crime and Justice Studies at King's College London. It provides up-to-date information on a wide range of topics affecting the study of crime and the criminal justice system, including current publications. The site includes a discussion forum, an interactive exercise in which you can discover what it is like to be a judge, and a topic of the month. Additionally, a highly useful dictionary section provides readily understandable definitions of complex technical terms.

Criminal Cases Review Commission (CCRC)
www.ccrc.gov.uk

This body was established by the 1995 Criminal Appeal Act to investigate suspected miscarriages of justice in England, Wales and Northern Ireland, and determine whether or not to refer a conviction or a sentence to the Court of Appeal. It became operational in March 1997. Its website contains information related to its work, an online case library with information on the cases handled by the CCRC, and for some of these a full copy of the Appeal Court's judgment is available at **www.casetrack.com** (although this is a subscription service). The CCRC website also contains a small publications list, some of which (including the annual report) are available online.

Crown Prosecution Service (CPS)
www.cps.gov.uk

The CPS was established by the 1985 Prosecution of Offenders Act and became operational in 1986. It is responsible for prosecuting persons charged by the police with a criminal offence in England and Wales. Specifically, it advises the police on prosecutions, reviews cases submitted to it by the police and prepares and presents cases at court. It is headed by the Director of Public Prosecutions who is responsible to the Attorney General. Its website includes online annual reports since 2000/01 and business plans, and provides access to material prepared by the 42 CPS areas. It also contains consultations initiated by the CPS that help inform their policy-making in areas that include the prosecution of domestic violence and rape, and access to the annual CPS lecture, inaugurated in 2008. Additionally, the Code for Crown Prosecutors is available online together with CPS guidance on prosecution policy in connection with specific criminal offences including racist and religious crimes.

The work of the CPS is monitored by the CPS Inspectorate, the CPSI (**www.hmcpsi.gov.uk**). The role of the CPSI is to promote improvements in the efficiency, effectiveness and fairness of the prosecution service within the framework of a joined-up criminal justice system, through the processes of inspection, evaluation and dissemination of good practice. Its website includes online annual reports since 2000/01 and reports of thematic and joint reviews, and provides access to reports prepared by the CPS areas and branches.

Europol
www.europol.europa.eu

Officially known as the European Police Office, the creation of Europol was sanctioned by the 1992 Maastricht Treaty. It commenced limited operations as the European Drugs Unit (EDU) in 1994 and became fully operational in 1999. It is based in the Hague (Holland) and is funded by the EU member countries. Its main purpose is to support law enforcement agencies in EU countries by gathering and analysing information and intelligence in connection with terrorism, drug trafficking and other forms of international organised criminal activity. Its website contains online reports on organised crime, specific aspects of serious crime, the annual report and press releases detailing current activities and operations.

Home Affairs Committee
www.parliament.uk/parliamentary_committees/home_affairs_committee.cfm

The Home Affairs Committee is a select committee of the House of Commons that conducts periodic investigations into services administered by, and issues connected with, the Home Office. Many of these are concerned with aspects of the criminal justice process and it is worthwhile periodically investigating this website to see what the Committee is currently examining. Evidence submitted to the Committee during its investigations is published as and when it is presented and is then incorporated into the Committee's final report. To find these, click on 'Reports and Publications', which are available online from the 1997/98 Parliamentary session onwards.

Home Office
www.homeoffice.gov.uk

The Home Office (which was reorganised in 2007) plays a key role in the operations of the criminal justice process and its website provides immediate access to a vast amount of up-to-date information that is available online, including white papers and strategic plans related to Home Office activities. The website is organised into a number of sections and key ones include crime and victims, security, anti-social behaviour, drugs and the police.

Research, Development and Statistics (RDS) is a directorate within the Home Office that publishes a wide volume of information relevant to students of crime and criminal justice, available online at **www.homeoffice. gov.uk/rds**. This includes the British Crime Survey and other crime statistics. It also provides a link to the Home Office Scientific Development Branch (**http://scienceandresearch.homeoffice.gov.uk/rds**) which is concerned with applying technical solution to combat crime.

The Home Office website provides access to the Home Office Research Studies archive, which consists of reports undertaken by or on behalf of the Home Office in the areas over which the Home Secretary exercises responsibility. These are available online from 1969 to 2004.

Home Office Circulars
www.circulars.homeoffice.gov.uk

Home Office circulars provide information on the operations of those aspects of the criminal justice process that are controlled by the Home Office. Circulars give instructions on issues that include the implementation of legislation and policy administered by this department. Circulars are available online from 2003 onwards.

Howard League for Penal Reform
www.howardleague.org

The Howard League is a charity established in 1866. It seeks to reform the penal system through education and campaigns in support of its core beliefs, one of which expresses support for community sentences. In addition to the *Howard Journal for Criminal Justice*, published five times a year, it produces a wide range of material on issues connected with the criminal justice process including prisons, restorative justice, human rights, sentencing and victims. The website provides information on these publications, most of which are available for purchase.

Independent Police Complaints Commission (IPCC)
www.ipcc.gov.uk

This body is responsible for managing or supervising police investigations into complaints made by members of the public against police officers. It can independently investigate the most serious cases of this nature. It was established by the 2002 Police Reform Act and replaced the Police Complaints Authority in April 2004. The website contains material that includes IPCC reports, guidelines and research, an archive of press releases, responses to IPCC reports and consultations, and an annual report that provides information on the operations of the complaints system.

Judicial Appointments Commission
www.judicialappointments.gov.uk

This non-departmental body, composed of 15 commissioners, was established by the 2005 Constitutional Reform Act and its role is to select candidates for judicial office. It does this by making one recommendation to the Lord Chancellor as to who should fill a specific vacancy. The Lord Chancellor may reject this advice, but may not substitute a nominee of his or her choosing. The website contains information related to its selection procedures, current selection exercises, the annual report and statistical information since 2006/07.

Complaints made by candidates seeking judicial office (and also in connection with judicial discipline and complaints) are handled by the Judicial Appointments and Conduct Ombudsman (**www.judicialombudsman.gov.uk**) whose position was also created by the 2005 Constitutional Reform Act. The Ombudsman is independent of both the judiciary and the government and is appointed by the monarch on the recommendation of the Lord Chancellor.

Justice
www.justice.org.uk

Justice is an influential legal and human rights organisation, established in 1957. It seeks to improve the legal system and quality of justice by advocating improvements to all aspects of the operations of the criminal justice process, in particular by promoting human rights in the UK and the EU. It conducts research and issues policy briefings. A list of publications is available on its website. Many of these have to be purchased, although some material is available online, including the Justice Annual Lectures and key articles that appear in its journal, *Justice*.

Justice Committee
www.parliament.uk/parliamentary_committees/justice.cfm

The Justice Committee is a select committee of the House of Commons that is responsible for the policy, administration and expenditure of the Ministry of Justice and for the work carried out by the Law Officers of the Crown, the Crown Prosecution Service and the Serious Fraud Office. The Committee also scrutinises draft sentencing guidelines prepared by the Sentencing Guidelines Council.

The website contains reports since 2002/03 dealing with aspects of the Committee's work, including sentencing, terrorism and legal complaints. It also contains material concerned with the compilation of these reports: oral and written evidence and uncorrected oral evidence.

Law Society
www.lawsociety.org.uk

The Law Society of England and Wales represents solicitors in England and Wales. It was formed in 1825 (replacing the London Law Institution which had been formed in 1823), its charter was granted in 1843, although it did not officially adopt the title of 'Law Society' until 1903. It also seeks to influence the process of law reform. Its website contains online copies of its annual report since 1999/2000 and publications on a range of issues affecting the profession. The website also contains access to the Law Society's online bookshop and a directory of the publications produced by the Law Society Strategic Research Unit that are available for purchase.

The website provides a link to the Solicitors' Regulation Authority (**www.sra.org.uk/consumers/consumers.page**), which acts as an independent regulatory authority for all solicitors in England and Wales, and to the Legal Complaints Service (**www.legalcomplaints.org.uk**), which investigates complaints made against solicitors.

Legal Action Group (LAG)
www.lag.org.uk

LAG is a charity, established in 1972, that works with lawyers and advisers to promote equal access to justice for all members of society. LAG produces a journal, *Legal Action,* which is available by subscription although some material, including editorials and indexes, is available online. The website also contains online reports concerning responses to consultations on criminal justice issues and information on its publications, which cover areas such as crime, criminal justice, human rights, legal aid and the legal profession. These are available for purchase.

Legal Services Commission (LSC)
www.legalservices.gov.uk

An executive non-departmental body sponsored by the Ministry of Justice, LSC's role is to administer the legal aid system in England and Wales. It was created by the 1999 Access to Justice Act and became operational in April 2000. It is responsible for two legal aid schemes: the Community Legal Service (through which civil legal aid and advice is delivered) and the Criminal Defence Service (which funds defence services for those involved in criminal investigations and proceedings). The website contains public information leaflets related to its operations, consultations on LSC policy development, newsletters, the annual report and strategic plan and specialised publications.

Liberty
www.liberty-human-rights.org.uk

This body was established in 1934 and was originally called the National Council for Civil Liberties. It is an important human rights and civil liberties organisation and aims to secure equal rights for everyone and opposes abuses or the excessive use of state power against its citizens. Its activities include lobbying Parliament, providing advice to the public and expert opinion, and conducting research and publishing reports on a wide range of issues that have human rights or civil liberties implications in areas that include ASBOs, young people's rights, terrorism and torture. The website contains online reports, responses to consultations and briefings.

Ministry of Justice
www.justice.gov.uk

This department was formed in 2007, taking over responsibilities formerly carried out by the Home Office and Department for Constitutional Affairs. It is headed by the Lord Chancellor and its main functions relate to the courts, prisons, probation service, criminal law and sentencing. The Ministry of Justice website provides access to a range of online reports and consultation papers on the tasks for which it is responsible. An important one is the annual publication *Statistics on Race and the Criminal Justice System*, prepared under Section 95 of the 1991 Criminal Justice Act, which provides detailed information related to minority ethnic groups as suspects, offenders and victims. The website also contains online publications such as policy reports and circulars related to changes in legislation, and research undertaken by the department related to its operation.

National Association for the Care and Resettlement of Offenders (NACRO)
www.nacro.org.uk

NACRO is a crime-related charity that was established in 1966. It funds a large number of projects that seek to provide ex-offenders, disadvantaged persons and deprived communities with practical help in areas such as education, employment and housing. Detailed information on the services with which NACRO is involved are available online and its website also provides access to the organisation's publications catalogue which covers areas such as youth crime, mental health, race and criminal justice and crime reduction. Some of these are available online while others can be purchased.

NACRO also published the quarterly journal *Safer Society* until February 2008 when it was replaced by *The Community Safety Journal*. This is available by subscription, although aspects of the former journal are available online.

National Audit Office
www.nao.org.uk

The National Audit Office is headed by the Comptroller and Auditor General and is responsible for auditing the accounts of all government departments, agencies and public bodies, and reports to Parliament on the extent to which their use of public money reflects the three 'Es' of economy, efficiency and effectiveness. This includes areas of activity concerned with the criminal justice sector.

The National Audit website contains reports related to investigations that it has conducted itself or which it has commissioned outside research. It also includes briefings that it provides to Parliamentary Select Committees. Online copies of the annual report since 1999 and the corporate plan since 2007 are also available.

National Offenders' Management Service (NOMS)
www.justice.gov.uk/about/noms.htm

NOMS was created in 2004 and is now an executive agency of the Ministry of Justice. It provides a framework to place the prison and probation services into a single correctional service and was designed to oversee the end-to-end management of offenders and to devise interventions and services for offenders in order to reduce re-offending and conviction rates, and to protect the public. Its key function is to commission and deliver services for adult offenders both in custody and in the community.

It is headed by a chief executive who is responsible for strategic policy. A national offender manager controls offender management and national commissioning and nine regional offender managers (and one in Wales) control most of the expenditure of the service. Its website contains a number of online policy and consultation papers, and other useful publications including prison performance ratings, action plans and the annual performance reports of the regions.

National Probation Service (NPS)
www.probation.homeoffice.gov.uk

The probation service was created by the 1907 Probation of Offenders Act. The service was administered through local probation areas until the enactment of the 2000 Criminal Justice and Court Services Act when a national service was created, organised into 42 operational areas. The service aims to protect the public, reduce the level of re-offending, provide for the secure punishment of offenders in the community, ensure offenders are aware of the impact of their crimes on the victims and general public, and to secure the rehabilitation of offenders. Its key responsibilities include supervising offenders serving community sentences and those who have been released from prison on licence with a statutory period of community supervision, and running probation hostels. The NPS website includes online news/updates, bulletins and briefing sections which provide up-to-date information on a wide range of issues affecting the service. It also includes a list of local probation areas and YOTs and access to their websites.

The NPS is inspected by Her Majesty's Inspectorate of Probation (HMIP). HMIP reports directly to the Home Secretary on the performance of the NPS and Youth Offending Teams, in particular on the effectiveness of their work in relation to individual offenders, children and young people which aims to reduce re-offending and protect the public. The HMIP's website (**http://inspectorates. homeoffice.gov.uk/hmiprobation**) contains online reports of inspections of specific probation areas and other activities performed by HMIP.

The probation service and prison service were amalgamated into the National Offenders' Management Service in 2004. The work of this new agency is discussed above.

Office for Criminal Justice Reform (OCJR)
www.cjsonline.gov.uk/the_cjs/departments_of_the_cjs/ocjr/index

The OCJR is a cross-departmental team designed to promote the principle of joined-up government in the criminal justice process by coordinating the relevant activities performed by the Home Office, the Ministry of Justice and the Office of the Attorney General, thereby providing an improved service to the public. The process of reform is driven at national level by the National Criminal Justice Board, which is headed by the same three government departments. The team reports to the Home Secretary, Lord Chancellor/ Justice Secretary and the Attorney General's Department. Its key role is to deliver the Criminal Justice Strategic Plan which it does by providing local Criminal Justice Boards with guidelines and a framework through which to deliver reform.

The OCJR website provides online information on the operations of the criminal justice process and key publications related to the goal of a joined-up approach to criminal justice.

Information related to operations of the National Criminal Justice Board can be obtained from the NCJB website, (**http://lcjb.cjsonline.gov.uk/ ncjb/1.htm/**). Information on the operations of the 42 local boards can be accessed through **http://lcjb.cjsonline.gov.uk**.

Parliament
www.parliament.uk

Key issues affecting criminal justice that require legislation are discussed in the House of Commons and the House of Lords and these deliberations provide excellent sources to enable the pros and cons of measures to be considered. General issues are considered in the Second Reading of Bills and detailed issues are discussed at Committee stage.

Debates in the House of Commons and House of Lords are recorded in the publication *Hansard,* which is available online at **www.publications. parliament.uk/pa/pahansard.htm**. You can then access daily debates (which are concerned with current legislation being considered by Parliament and also provide access to questions by MPs answered orally and in writing and statements made by Ministers); bound volume debates (which provide details of legislation considered in previous Sessions of Parliament); and Standing Committees considering Bills. Online bound volume debates commence in the 1988/89 parliamentary session in the House of Commons and the 1994/95 parliamentary session in the House of Lords. Online debates in House of Commons Standing Committees commence in the 1997/98 parliamentary sessions.

Parole Board
www.paroleboard.gov.uk

The Parole Board was set up by the 1967 Criminal Justice Act and became operational the following year. It became an independent non-departmental board in 1996 under the provisions of the 1994 Criminal Justice and Public Order Act. Its current operations are governed by the 2003 Criminal Justice Act. The Board is responsible for conducting risk assessment as to whether prisoners serving indeterminate sentences and those serving determinate sentences of over four years can be safely released into the community.

The Parole Board's website contains online copies of its annual report since 2002/03 and its three-year corporate plans since 2001/04. The site also contains information leaflets related to the Board's work and policy statements dealing with areas such as risk assessment and race. There is also an online exercise, *'Judge for Yourself'*, relating to a decision to grant parole in a fictitious case.

Police Federation of England and Wales
www.polfed.org

This organisation was established by the 1919 Police Act and has a statutory duty to represent its members (which comprise all officers below the rank of superintendent) on issues related to their welfare and efficiency. Its work includes negotiating on pay and conditions, and campaigning on a wide range of issues affecting the police service. It is also consulted on the formulation of police regulations. Its journal is the monthly *Police* magazine, and editions published since 2005 are available online in the website's media centre. This also contains press releases and reports by the Federation, and Federation news.

Police forces
www.police.uk/forces.htm

There are 43 police forces in England and Wales, and each has its own website. Access to specific force websites can be obtained through the above address, by clicking on the relevant region of the map provided. Online information available includes items such as performance statistics, matters of current importance and news updates to provide for communication between the police force and the public it serves.

The activities performed by police forces in England and Wales are subject to scrutiny by Her Majesty's Inspectorate of Constabulary (HMIC). The office was first established by the 1856 County and Borough Police Act, and the current duties are specified in the 1996 Police Act. Initially, inspectors were required to have a background in policing, but since 1993 a lay element has been introduced. The HMIC website (**www.inspectorates.homeoffice. gov.uk/hmic/inspections**) provides access to online reports concerned with force inspections, inspections of basic command units, thematic inspections and best value reviews of specific activities conducted by individual forces. The annual report of the Chief Inspector of Constabulary (HMCIC) is available online from 1998/99.

Scotland has eight police forces, maintained by either a police authority or a joint board. Online information on all eight forces is available through the Scottish Police Forces website (**www.scottish.police.uk**), including details of individual force organisation and policy and access to annual reports and performance indicators. There is also a link to ACPOS (**www.acpos.police.uk**).

Policing in Northern Ireland is provided by the Police Service of Northern Ireland (PSNI). This force was established as a successor to the Royal Ulster Constabulary in November 2001 as an aspect of the Belfast Agreement. Its website (**www.psni.police.uk**), gives online access to PSNI annual reports and statistical information and an archive of press releases since January 2001. The PSNI is supervised by the Northern Ireland Policing Board, whose website (**www.nipolicingboard.org.uk**), contains a wide range of literature related to policing including the Board's annual report since 2001/02, the corporate plan 2005–08 and the policing plan since 2003–07.

Political parties
www.labour.org.uk
www.conservatives.com
www.libdems.org.uk

Crime is an important political issue that is accorded considerable attention during election contests. Political parties devote much attention to crime and their websites include policy statements that put forward their own intentions in this area and criticise the policies of their opponents. It is worthwhile consulting the websites of the main parties for up-to-date information on their respective anti-crime measures. These are contained in reports and also in speeches and press statements by leading politicians with responsibilities for home affairs and criminal justice matters.

Prison Reform Trust (PRT)
www.prisonreformtrust.org.uk

PRT is a charity established in 1981. It seeks to create a just, humane and effective penal system and to this end offers advice and assistance to a range of persons (including prisoners and their families, prison and probation staff and academics) and conducts research on all aspects of imprisonment.

A considerable amount of material related to imprisonment can be accessed online and the PRT website also contains a list of publications available for purchase, including books, pamphlets, briefing papers and consultation responses. The *Bromley Briefings Factfile*, giving up-to-date statistical information on prisons, is available online. There are links to websites of other organisations whose work is concerned with imprisonment. The PRT issues a quarterly journal, *Prison Report*, which is available to Friends of the PRT (who make an annual gift to this charity).

Prison service
www.hmprisonservice.gov.uk

The main objectives of the prison service are to hold prisoners securely, to reduce the risk of prisoners re-offending and providing safe and well-ordered establishments in which prisoners are treated humanely, decently and lawfully. In order to achieve these aims, the prison service works in close partnership with other agencies in the criminal justice system. The Resources Centre section of the website contains online copies of annual reports (since

2001), the business plan (since 2000/01) and the corporate plan from 2001/04 onwards. It also contains publications and documents on issues such as prison performance standings and ratings and strategy documents. There is also an online prison virtual tour. The bi-monthly *Prison Service Journal* discusses issues of relevance to the prison service. This is a subscription journal, but articles in the most current issue are available online. A complementary publication, *Prison Service News*, is available online, since November 2003.

Separate prison services exist for Scotland and Northern Ireland and their websites contain similar material as for England and Wales. The Scottish Prison Service (**www.sps.gov.uk**) is an executive agency of the Scottish Executive and is responsible for Scotland's 15 custodial establishments. The Northern Ireland Prison Service (**www.niprisonservice.gov.uk**) is an executive agency of the Northern Ireland Executive and controls Northern Ireland's five custodial institutions.

Her Majesty's Inspectorate of Prisons provides independent scrutiny of the conditions for, and treatment of, prisoners and other detainees held in prisons, young offender institutions and immigration removal centres. Contracted out prisons also fall within this official's remit. It is headed by a Chief Inspector of Prisons and seeks to promote the concept of a 'healthy prison' in which staff work effectively to support prisoners and detainees to reduce re-offending or achieve other agreed outcomes. Its website (**http://inspectorates.homeoffice.gov.uk/hmiprisons**) contains online reports of inspections of specific institutions, thematic reviews and research publications. The annual report is available from 1996/97 and the HMIP business plan since 2008/09.

The prison service and probation service were amalgamated into the National Offenders' Management Service in 2004. The work of this new agency is discussed above.

Public Accounts Committee (PAC)
www.parliament.uk/parliamentary_committees/committee_of_public_ac counts.cfm

The PAC was established in 1861, and made permanent the following year. Its task is to examine 'the accounts showing the appropriation of the sums granted by Parliament to meet the public expenditure, and [since 1934] of such other accounts laid before Parliament as the committee may think fit'. Its website contains reports, oral and written evidence and government responses to PAC reports. Reports cover a wide range of subject areas, including those connected with the criminal justice process. These are available online, commencing in the 1997/98 parliamentary session, and it is worthwhile periodically checking this website for details of current investigations into criminal justice affairs.

Scottish Executive
www.scotland.gov.uk

The Scottish Executive constitutes the devolved government for Scotland. The Justice Department of the Scottish Executive is responsible for a wide range of activities concerned with the criminal justice process. These include the police service, the administration of the courts and legal aid. There are two executive agencies attached to the Justice Department: the Scottish Prison Service and the Scottish Courts Service. The website of the Scottish Prison Service (**www.sps.gov.uk**) contains online information concerning headquarters policy statements, and research publications. Copies of the annual report and accounts are available from 1999/2000 and the business plan for 2006–08. The website of the Scottish Courts Service (**www.scotcourts.gov.uk**) provides online access to the agency's business plan 2008/09, the corporate plan 2008–11, the annual report and accounts since 2002/03 and information leaflets related to its work.

Security Industry Authority (SIA)
www.the-sia.org.uk

The SIA was established by the 2001 Private Security Industry Act to manage the operations of the private security industry, to raise standards of professionalism and skill in the private security industry and to promote the spread of best practice. Its website includes general publications, information on specific licensing sectors and financial and strategic information related to the agency. It also contains a number of case studies designed to highlight the benefits arising to companies from the work performed by the agency.

Security Service (MI5)
www.mi5.gov.uk

MI5 was established in 1909 to combat activities undertaken by German spies in Britain. Its role was subsequently extended to counter all covert threats to national security. Until the enactment of the 1989 Security Service Act, MI5 had no statutory basis. The role of MI5 was broadened during the 1990s: in 1992 it was given the lead role of countering terrorism on mainland Britain and the 1996 Security Service Act allocated the agency the responsibility to combat 'serious' crime (which was defined as an offence that carried a sentence of three years or more on first conviction, or any offence involving conduct by a number of persons in pursuit of a common purpose). MI5's website contains much online information on the detailed activities of the organisation, security advice, and material related to the contemporary threats posed by espionage and terrorism to the UK.

Sentencing Guidelines Council (SGC)
www.sentencing-guidelines.gov.uk

The SGC was established by the 2003 Criminal Justice Act and took over the responsibility for formulating sentencing guidelines from the Magistrates' Association and the Court of Appeal. In doing so it takes advice from the Sentencing Advisory Panel on particular offences or categories of offences and other sentencing issues. Its website contains a wide range of online material including guidelines, draft guidelines and consultation papers and research reports related to aspects of crime and sentencing. The SGC's newsletter, *The Sentence*, and its annual reports are also available online.

Serious Organised Crime Agency (SOCA)
www.soca.gov.uk

SOCA was established by the 2005 Serious Organised Crime and Police Act. It is an executive non-departmental body whose main area of work is gathering intelligence in order to combat organised crime. It brought together under one roof a number of existing bodies: the National Criminal Intelligence Service, the National Crime Squad, the investigative and intelligence work performed by HM Customs and Excise in relation to serious drug trafficking and the recovery of criminal assets, and the responsibilities exercised by the Home Office for organised immigration crime. The Assets Recovery Agency was merged with SOCA in 2008.

Its website contains literature related to its operations and work, the annual report from 2006/07 and the annual plan from 2006/07.

Social Exclusion Task Force
www.cabinetoffice.gov.uk/social_exclusion_task_force

This body was originally known as the Social Exclusion Unit and was set up in 1997, within the Cabinet Office. It was transferred to the Office of the Deputy Prime Minister in May 2002, then under its new name was placed back within the Cabinet Office in 2006. Its key aims are to identify priorities for those suffering from social exclusion, to test solutions to tackle social exclusion and to facilitate collaboration across government departments. Much of its work is focused on specific projects.

The emphasis placed by post-1997 Labour governments on tackling the social causes of crime (such as unemployment, family background, substance misuse and low educational attainment) through a joined-up approach at local level has meant that the work of the Social Exclusion Task Force is of considerable importance to criminology. Its website contains a range of documents related to the analysis and implementation of policy to alleviate social exclusion and it has a publications page listing reports written for the former Social Exclusion Unit since 1997.

Statewatch
www.statewatch.org

Statewatch was established in 1991 and monitors state and civil liberties throughout the EU, seeking to identify developments that threaten to encroach or erode civil and political liberties. Its website contains online briefings on issues that include changes/projected alterations to state powers in connection with protest and developments affecting EU-wide policing. It also provides an extremely useful online link to UK legislation of relevance to the concerns of Statewatch. Statewatch publishes *Statewatch Bulletin* and *Statewatch Online* and the website also contains a publications list.

Victim Support
www.victimsupport.org.uk

Victim Support is an independent charity that seeks to help people cope with the effects of crime. It provides counselling, and information on matters such as court procedures and compensation, and also campaigns on behalf of victims and witnesses. It operates through local branches that can be accessed through the organisation's four websites (related to England and Wales, Scotland, Northern Ireland and the Irish Republic). The England and Wales website contains information on the work of Victim Support, which includes leaflets and reports related to specific categories of crime, the annual report and accounts (available since 2000), and the national strategy 2005–08. The magazine *View*, launched in November 2004, is also available online.

Willan Publishing
www.willanpublishing.co.uk

Willan is a specialist criminology publisher whose catalogue covers a very wide range of material in key areas of the criminal justice process, including crime and crime prevention, sentencing and punishment, probation, policing, prisons, youth justice, victims and victimology criminal justice history and criminal behaviour. The website contains full details of current and forthcoming publications and includes a title, author and search facility and secure ordering.

Youth Justice Board
www.yjb.gov.uk

The main purposes of the Youth Justice Board for England and Wales are to prevent offending and re-offending by children and young persons below the age of 18 and to ensure that custodial arrangements for them are safe, secure and address the cause of their offending behaviour. It is an executive non-departmental agency that became operational in September 1998 and performs a number of specific functions, including advising the Secretary of State for Justice on the operations of the youth justice system; monitoring the performance of the youth justice system; purchasing places for children and young people remanded in or sentenced to custody; identifying and disseminating good practice; and commissioning and publishing research.

The website provides up-to-date information on the organisation's activities and gives access to publications related to its work, including Youth Justice Board position papers, and access to key legislation affecting the youth justice system. Many reports and publications are available online, while others can be purchased. The website also includes online copies of the annual report and accounts since 2005/6 and the annual statistics. Free access to the bi-monthly *Youth Justice Magazine* is also available from this website.

The Youth Justice Board website also has information on the operations of the 155 Youth Offending Teams in England and Wales, including guidelines issued by the Youth Justice Board to YOTs on a wide range of policy matters. Online information includes the YOT annual report since 2004 and copies of the programme of inspections into specific YOTs that commenced in 2003.

4 How to conduct criminological research

The aims of this chapter are:

- To distinguish between quantitative and qualitative research.

- To identify key methods associated with each form of methodology.

- To identify good practice in the construction of a questionnaire.

- To discuss the practical application of research techniques in connection with gathering information regarding the level of crime in society.

- To consider the ethical considerations affecting criminological research.

Further reading

Bottomley, K. and Coleman, C. (1981) *Understanding Crime Rates.* Farnborough: Gower.

Bottomley, K. and Pease, K. (1986) *Crime and Punishment: Interpreting the Data.* Buckingham: Open University Press.

Bryman, A. (2008) *Social Research Methods*, 3rd ed. Oxford: Oxford University Press.

Coleman, C. and Moynihan, J. (1996) *Understanding Crime Data: Haunted by the Dark Figure.* Buckingham: Open University Press.

May, T. (2004) *Social Research: Issues, Methods and Process*, 3rd ed. Buckingham: Open University Press.

Approaches to criminological research

In order to understand why a particular problem occurs that is of concern to criminologists (such as why people commit crime, how much crime occurs within society or whether crime 'runs in families') it is necessary to carry out some form of first-hand investigation. There are two broad approaches that can be employed to do this: quantitative and qualitative.

Quantitative methodologies

Quantitative research methods are based upon the gathering of data that is capable of being analysed through the use of statistical methods. The findings produced in this way form the basis of conclusions related to the issue under consideration. The intention of quantitative methodologies is to enable conclusions to be formulated that have a wide application – the findings are regarded as definitive. Quantitative research sometimes adopts a deductive approach whereby a theory or idea is tested to ascertain its accuracy.

Qualitative methodologies

The aim of qualitative research methods is to gather data that seeks to provide an understanding of a criminological issue from the perspective of those who have first-hand experience of it – perhaps as a victim of crime or as a prisoner. The intention of this approach is to enable such people to 'tell their own tale', thus giving the researcher an understanding of the issue from the perspective of an individual who is intimately associated with it.

Although findings drawn from research of this nature may be too specific to justify broader application, they may form the basis from which tentative conclusions can be drawn – an approach that is referred to as inductive.

Key research methods

Findings that relate to issues of criminological concern can be gathered in a number of ways. The key findings may be based on data gathered by quantitative and qualitative research methods. These methods are briefly discussed below.

Documentary research

Much research at undergraduate level, especially in connection with the operations of the criminal justice system, will be based on documentary research. Rather than having to conduct your own fieldwork your work will be based on material that has already been produced.

The documents you can draw upon are derived from a wide range of sources. These include primary data (such as reports prepared by key criminal justice agencies and organisations, autobiographies of key persons associated with criminal justice, select committee reports or parliamentary debates) and secondary data (such as books, journal articles, newspapers and the Internet). Here your aim as a researcher is to digest and evaluate the material and to present findings related to the research topic in a logical and coherent manner.

Documentary research has a number of advantages; in particular it enables 'official' views or the opinions of informed individuals to be analysed without the need to conduct face-to-face interviews (which may sometimes be difficult or impossible to arrange). This research does, however, pose some problems, concerning the accuracy or validity of the views being put forward in documents for instance:

- Is the document written from a biased perspective?

- Does the author have a personal agenda that he or she wishes to put forward that may cloud objectivity?

- Are the contents reliable or even true?

- Is the evidence on which the author's findings are based deliberately manipulated to produce the outcome or views that he or she wishes to put forward?

Problems of this nature are not insurmountable: it is often possible to offset bias by examining documents written from a broad range of sources, so that the researcher can consider a range of diverse opinions and come to an informed conclusion. The status of the person authoring the material may also be a good guide to accuracy and academic worth, assuming, of course, that the document is authentic.

Documents may be subjected to more specific forms of analysis, one method being *content analysis*. This involves analysing the treatment which a document gives to a particular topic. You may, for example, wish to scrutinise the coverage that various newspapers devote to crime and law and order issues within a particular period of time. To do this you might employ quantitative techniques such as frequency counts to find out how often each newspaper mentions matters of this nature. Computer programs may also be employed to conduct this form of analysis.

Surveys

Surveys are identified with quantitative methodologies and are used to gather information from a considerable number of people. They typically seek information on a range of issues that are relevant to the overall topic of the survey.

There are two key matters that those conducting surveys have to address:

- *Whose views are sought?* It is impossible to gain access to all those affected by a particular problem and only a limited number of people can be consulted. These are referred to as a 'sample'. A sample can be constructed in two ways: random and representative. These terms are discussed below.

- *How can the sample be approached to give their views?* A survey is often based on a questionnaire which can be addressed to the recipient in a number of ways: a face-to-face interview, or an interview conducted over the telephone, Internet or through the post. All these approaches have their strengths and weaknesses and are discussed in greater detail below.

Questionnaires

Questionnaires are a common way of conducting surveys. A list of questions is drawn up to which respondents are invited to give their views. Data derived from the views of those completing the questionnaire can then be summarised and form the basis on which conclusions can be drawn.

Research at undergraduate level makes frequent use of questionnaires. However, you should avoid using a questionnaire either to prove what is already known about a criminological issue, or to prove the obvious. For example, we already know that large numbers of persons who receive custodial sentences re-offend once released and there would be no point in constructing a questionnaire whose sole or main purpose was to establish whether this was the case or not. A key reason for using questionnaires is to gather information that established literature may have ignored or downplayed, thereby adding to our store of knowledge and giving your research a degree of originality. This justifies the inclusion of some open-ended questions, since these enable insights to be gathered from the respondents and included in your overall analysis.

Do's and don'ts of questionnaires

Before asking anyone to complete a questionnaire it is important to explain why this request is being made. Researchers should provide a brief introduction explaining who they are, what they are researching and why they are doing so. It is also common to guarantee anonymity to the individual completing the questionnaire. This is especially important if the questions seek to elicit the recipient's first-hand knowledge of the topic under discussion – for example, asking if someone has ever been the victim of domestic violence.

It is also usual for questionnaires to include a section requesting demographic information about the recipient, as this may have relevance for the opinions expressed. This commonly means asking the recipient to record their sex, age and ethnicity.

Statistical techniques make it possible to cross-reference this information with the answers provided, perhaps to ascertain if the views of women differ from those of men or to compare the experiences of minority ethnic and white persons regarding the issue with which the questionnaire is concerned.

A good questionnaire will embrace the following features that include:

- *A brief list of key questions.* It is important to avoid preparing a long questionnaire that will take some time to answer, as this will reduce the number of recipients willing to undertake this task.

- *Questions that can be easily answered by ticking boxes.* Prepare questions that can be answered by 'Yes', 'No' or 'Don't know', or put forward statements that ask the recipient to indicate whether they 'Agree', 'Disagree' or 'Neither agree or disagree'. There are two advantages to this approach (termed 'closed questions'): it speeds up the process of replying (and is thus likely to boost the response rate) and makes the analysis of responses easier since the range of answers can be coded and subsequently analysed through the use of a statistical packages such as SPSS.

A questionnaire should avoid the following:

- *The use of complex questions or technical terminology.* Any complicated wording that may not be readily understood by the recipient will reduce the response rate.

- *Questions that presuppose a particular course of action.* These are termed 'leading questions' and will produce a biased outcome. For example, a question such as, 'Why do you think that the general public has no confidence in community penalties?' presupposes all members of the public hold a negative view towards non-custodial forms of punishment. But this may not be the case.

- *The excessive use of open-ended questions.* These questions invite the recipient to give his or her views on a particular topic. It is acceptable to make very limited use of questions of this nature, since they allow recipients to add their views or insights to the issue under discussion. However, their excessive use greatly slows down the process of analysis: unlike closed questions, the tools of statistical analysis cannot be applied to them. You may therefore have to plough through responses that constitute a series of lengthy essays, which will be very time-consuming.

Taking it further 1

Consider the following questionnaire that has been designed to obtain findings related to victims of crime.

Questionnaire on Victims of Crime

I am a student at the local university writing my final year dissertation on the treatment given to victims of crime. I would like you to complete the following questions. Where appropriate, please place a circle around the answer that applies to you.

The questionnaire is anonymous and the information is solely sought for the purposes of my own research.

Age
What is your age?

Gender
Are you male or female?

Race/ethnicity
What is your racial background ?

Victimisation
Have you been the victim of crime in the past year?

   Yes

   No

Location
If the answer to the above was 'Yes', where did the incident take place and did it occur during the daytime or at night?

....

....

Nature of the crime
What type of crime were you the victim of? Was it serious?

Reporting the crime to the police
Did you report the crime to the police?

Yes

No

Reasons for non-reporting
If the answer to the above question was 'No,' what factor(s) persuaded you not to report it?

The crime was trivial.
I was too embarrassed to report it.
I was too frightened to report it.
I was concerned the police would not take my complaint seriously.
I was worried that there would be bad repercussions for me if I reported it.

Response by the police
If you reported a crime to the police, were you satisfied with their response?

Yes

No

If the answer was 'No', what weaknesses did you encounter?

....

....

Prosecution
If you have been a victim of crime, was the person who carried it out prosecuted?

Yes

No

If the answer was 'Yes', were you satisfied with the way in which the prosecution was handled?

Yes

No

Reform
What changes, if any, do you think should be introduced into the criminal justice system to benefit those who have been the victims of crime?

....

....

Thank you for taking the time to complete this questionnaire.

How would you improve this questionnaire?

See Chapter 7 for suggestions.

Interviews

Interviews entail interaction between the researcher and the subject. They are frequently conducted on a face-to-face basis, although they can be carried out over the telephone or by e-mail. A question or series of questions is put to the subject and responses are recorded by the researcher, either in writing or by recording.

Interviews may assume several formats:

- *Structured.* Interviews of this nature are similar to a questionnaire that is presented on a face-to-face basis. The questions are typically of a closed nature and can be addressed to a wide range of participants whose responses can be subjected to statistical analysis.

- *Unstructured.* These interviews are primarily driven by the subject who is asked by the researcher to provide his or her opinions to an issue or set of issues that the researcher is investigating. The researcher will set the scene for the subject's discussion and intervene perhaps to explore issues that are raised or about which the researcher wishes to investigate, but the key aim is to let the subject give a personal account of the issue under considera-tion. The nature of unstructured interviews means that they can be used only selectively on a small-scale basis.

- *Semi-structured.* This form of interview embraces features of structured and unstructured accounts. Typically a set of closed questions are addressed to the recipient but there is scope to enable both interviewer and researcher to conduct a more detailed investigation of issues related to the topic under review.

Focus groups

Focus groups involve face-to-face contact between a researcher and a group of people. The aim is to discover their views and opinions on an issue of which they all have experience. Although the researcher will have an agenda to focus the discussion, a key intention is to enable the participants to put forward their views and opinions, thus giving the session a conversational slant that is similar to an unstructured interview.

Variants of focus groups (such as citizens' summits and citizens' juries) can be used to ascertain opinions on public policy issues and may vary consider-ably in size. For the purposes of academic criminological research it is likely that the groups used will be smaller in order to prevent them from becoming unwieldy and unmanageable. Other key issues concern how the group is com-posed, the need to ensure that discussions are not dominated by one or two vocal individuals whose views may be unrepresentative of the group, and how the data that emerges from discussions of this nature can be analysed.

Ethnographic methods

Ethnographic research methods are based upon the researcher engaging in a prolonged period of face-to-face contact with a person or persons being studied in order to obtain an understanding of the meaning that the subjects who are being observed attach to their actions. The participant's perspective is at centre stage of the research and the aim of the researcher is to observe – or enter into – the social world of the subject in order to investigate how they make sense of the social situation within which they exist. The data produced in this manner is termed *field research*, and it involves the researcher writing up an account of his or her observations either at the conclusion of the study or on a more regular basis as events unfold.

There are various ways whereby ethnographic methods can be conducted. The researcher may become a member of the community that he or she is studying and participate in its activities. In this case the research is likely to be covert, with the subjects being unaware of the motives of the researcher.

Alternatively, the researcher may attach him or herself to the community and make detailed observations of its actions and activities without joining in any of them. The researcher becomes a 'fly on the wall'. Research of this nature can be either overt (where the researcher provides the true reasons for his or her attachment to the group) or covert (where the researcher gives false reasons for wishing to associate with it). The former approach is referred to as *participant* observation and the latter as *non-participant* observation.

Ethnographic studies form an important aspect of qualitative methodology and are especially useful for obtaining information on groups and organisations whose activities are conducted in a relatively closed environment, out of the gaze or scrutiny of the general public. These methods do, however, pose a number of problems of which researchers should be aware:

- The possibility of personal danger, especially if the 'cover is blown' of a researcher engaged in covert participant or non-participant observation.

- This method of gathering research findings is likely to be time-consuming and costly.

- Reliability: the researcher may lose his or her objectivity by becoming too closely involved and sympathetic to the group with which he or she becomes associated.

- In order to retain credibility with the group being studied, the researcher may engage in activities that are criminal, thus becoming an accessory to a criminal act.

- There are serious ethical issues involved in covert research where this entails data being gathered from subjects without their knowledge or consent.

Key tools of research

This section briefly discusses some of the tools related to the use of research methods that have been outlined above.

Sampling

The methods a researcher employs to gather information on criminological issues, such as questionnaires or interviews, can be directed to only a small number of people. A key issue is, on what basis are those who are to be the subject of research selected for this task?

If, for example, you were seeking to examine why a high proportion of those who receive custodial sentences subsequently re-offend, it would not physically be possible to investigate every individual who committed crime following their release from prison. Some form of selection process would have to be embarked upon in order to make the research project a manageable one.

The total audience to whom your questions could be addressed is known as the *sampling frame*. Depending on the topic that is being researched, documents such as postcode address files, electoral registers and membership lists of organisations or agencies may constitute the sampling frame.

There will be occasions when the sampling frame is less easy to elicit. For example, if you were researching drug use it would be relatively straightforward to compile a list of those convicted of offences related to the use of Class A drugs within a specific time period. Official records of convictions exist that would constitute your sampling frame. It would, however, be harder to compile a list of all those who had used Class A drugs within that time period, whether convicted or not.

The process of narrowing down those contained in the sampling frame into a smaller group of a size that is realistic to approach and whose opinions can be readily evaluated is known as *sampling*. Various methods can be used to produce a sample, and fall into two categories: *probability* and *non probability* sampling. The main methods associated with each are discussed below.

Random sampling

This method is a type of *probability sampling* and is similar to pulling names out of a hat. The names of everyone who is eligible to be included in the research is drawn up in (or taken from) some form of list and a random choice is made from that list in order to produce the sample. The benefit of this approach is that any possible bias on the part of the researcher as to whom he or she might wish to interview is eliminated – the sample is determined by the luck of the draw.

Stratified sampling

This method is a slightly more complex form of random sampling and is used when the researcher wishes to ensure that the views and opinions of specific groups within the overall sampling frame are taken into account. This enables differences between these groups to be incorporated into the findings of the research. For example, a survey of attitudes towards the policing of a particular neighbourhood is likely to benefit from the views of women and of members of minority ethnic communities whose experiences regarding issues such as the police handling of domestic violence, racial violence and the use of stop and search powers may be different from those of white males living in the same area.

In order to achieve this purpose, the overall sampling frame is broken down into a number of sub-groups, the composition of which is determined by the issues that the researcher wishes to investigate (such as age, gender, ethnicity, disability or home ownership). The composition of these sub-groups is selected as is the case with a random sample.

Non-probability sampling

This embraces a number of methods to construct samples so that research is targeted at specific groups or types of subject. Some of these techniques are as follows.

Quota sampling

This commonly used method of market research is often employed in surveys seeking to discover support for political parties. Here the sample is carefully constructed in order to provide a genuine cross-section (a microcosm) of the general public. Thus the sample will contain an accurate reflection of the balance between men and women and will mirror other key demographic features such as ethnicity, age and employment. Depending on the issue that forms the focus of the survey, other factors can also be included. Those conducting the field interviews will typically be asked to select a specified number of persons in each of the designated categories.

Quota sampling is generally regarded as providing a reasonably accurate picture of the views and opinions of the general public on a particular issue and is a widely used method. But it is not totally foolproof: pollsters have, on occasions, failed to accurately predict the outcome of a general election contest in the UK even allowing for a 'margin of error.'

The main problems associated with quota sampling are as follows:

- The person conducting the interview may not precisely follow the guidelines they have been given. For example, if asked to interview a male aged below 25 the interview should terminate when it becomes clear that the person who has been selected for interview is actually aged 27; however, there will often be a tendency to proceed with the interview, especially if the interviewer is finding it hard to find eligible respondents from a particular category. Actions of this nature – especially if replicated – may adversely influence the overall accuracy of the survey.

- The person being interviewed may not give a truthful answer to the questions being posed, or having given an answer they may subsequently alter their opinions.

- The replies given may be in the nature of a knee-jerk response to a particular incident, which fails to give a true impression of longer-term and deep-rooted popular sentiments. For example, a poll regarding the death penalty conducted in the wake of a highly-publicised murder may reveal a high level of support for such an action which is not sustained in the longer term.

Convenience sampling

This method involves constructing a sample from an audience that is readily available to the researcher. Thus a student whose research focus is on students as victims of crime might distribute questionnaires to a group gathered in a University coffee bar, or to his or her housemates, and use the material gathered in this manner as field research to supplement other information that has been gathered.

This method is generally associated with qualitative research and the merits of this approach are the ease of access that the researcher has to the audience (hence 'convenience') and the likelihood of a reasonable response rate. The key problem is that of representativeness: although the views of some students will be gathered using this method, the sample is based on those who happened to be in a specific location at a particular time and their views cannot be taken as valid for the views of the student population as a whole.

Snowball sampling

This method involves a sample that is built up over a period of time whereby one respondent will give the researcher further contacts that he or she can approach. Thus the researcher investigating student experience of crime may start with a student that he or she knows was the victim of crime, and that respondent then provides a further contact, who in turn provides information on others who have suffered in this manner. The advantage of this method is that it gives the researcher access to an audience that he or she might have found difficulty in approaching at the outset of the research.

Like convenience sampling this method is associated with qualitative research and poses a similar problem, namely that the group the researcher constructs is not necessarily representative of all students who have suffered from crime – it merely reflects the views of those to whom the researcher was able to gain access.

Practical applications of research methods

In this section we consider the practical application of some of the research methods discussed above. The chosen topic concerns *gathering information on the level of crime that exists within society*.

Official crime statistics

An important source of evidence as to how much crime exists within society is provided by official crime statistics. These consist of figures collected by individual police forces and forwarded to the Home Office, thus providing information concerning the national trend.

However, these figures do not reveal accurate information concerning the level of crime at any given period, since official crime statistics document only a limited range of criminal activity. The gap between the volume of crime that is actually committed and that which enters into official crime statistics is referred to the 'dark figure' of crime. The explanation for this is found in the process of crime reporting.

The process of crime reporting

A number of stages are involved in translating a criminal act into an official statistic. Each acts as a filtering process, tending to progressively reduce the number of actions that the state takes action against. Accordingly, there is often a large difference between the number of crimes that actually take place and those for which the perpetrator receives some form of penalty. The key stages are discussed below.

Discovery

In order for a crime to enter into official statistics, it is necessary that someone – usually a victim and/or witness – is aware that a criminal act has occurred; that is, the crime has to be 'discovered'. Certain types of crime in which there is no individual victim (such as fraud or tax evasion) may not be easily identified as having taken place. Other crimes may not be noticed by the victim, who may attribute matters such as missing money or other forms of property loss to personal carelessness, as opposed to another's criminal actions.

Reporting the crime to the police

When a crime is discovered, the next stage is to report the matter to the police. Individual victims, however, may not wish to do this. The victim may believe the crime to be too trivial to warrant police intervention, or that the police would be unable to do much about the incident were it reported. Alternatively, the victim may fail to report a crime because they fear that if they do so they will suffer reprisals.

Victims may also fail to report crimes because they believe the criminal justice system will not handle the complaint justly. The courts' poor treatment of women who have been victims of serious sexual attacks, and the consequent reluctance of women to report such crimes, means that official statistics have traditionally underestimated figures for crime of this nature. Embarrassment may be another reason why certain crimes are not reported such as thefts from their clients by prostitutes or their accomplices.

Recording of an incident by the police

Assuming that the police agree with a victim or witness that a criminal act has occurred, the final stage of the process is the recording of the offence. However, this does not automatically happen. The gap between offences reported to the police and what actually enters official statistics, is called the 'grey area' of crime. Decisions concerning whether or not to record a reported crime are dependent on factors such as the individual discretion of a police officer, police organisational culture, and official procedures laid down by the Home Office. These issues are discussed below.

- *Too minor to record.* A police officer to whom a crime has been reported may decide that the offence is a minor one that can be dealt with informally, perhaps by warning a person who has behaved incorrectly. Decisions of this nature may be based upon individual bias or prejudice as to the seriousness of the matter, or upon a view derived from organisational culture. The latter means that minor offences may be disregarded by a popular view within the police service that intervention is inappropriate: an officer who disregarded such peer group pressure may become the subject of derision.

- *'Cuffing'.* The practice of 'cuffing' entails either not recording a crime that has been reported, or downgrading a reported crime to an incident that can be excluded from official statistics. The decision to do this was initially motivated by a desire to avoid the time-consuming practice of filling out a crime report for minor incidents. However, the introduction in 1992 of performance indicators for the police service intensified pressures on the police to avoid recording all offences notified to them. Crime statistics were a key source of evidence of police performance, so increased levels of reported crimes could imply inefficiency. These factors may reinforce the inclination of individual officers not to report crime in the first instance, or of crime managers to discount it later.

- *Willingness of victims to give evidence in court.* The decision to declare an action 'no crime' may be influenced by a police manager's assessment of whether the victim would be prepared to give evidence in court. The perception that victims of domestic violence will ultimately drop such charges is one explanation for the traditional police reluctance to become involved in these matters.

- *Home Office directions.* Police reporting of crime is influenced by directions from the Home Office. The police are required to pass to the Home Office only details of 'notifiable offences'. Since 1999 these have included all crimes that are triable on indictment in a Crown Court, many that are triable 'either way' (that is, either on indictment or summarily, before a magistrates' court) and some summary offences. Thus many crimes (including the great majority of motoring offences) are not notifiable and are therefore excluded from crime statistics. Additionally, what are termed Home Office Counting Rules give guidance on how to handle issues such as discounting recorded crimes (by classing them as 'no crimes') and recording multiple offences. Rules introduced in 1979 required certain types of offences (for example, theft from several cars in a car park) to be recorded as one crime. These rules were altered in 1998 so that one offence was recorded for each victim in these circumstances. The most recent version of these rules was published in 2008, applying counting rules across nine categories of recorded crime.

Changes to the procedures for crime reporting

The use of crime statistics as a measurement of police performance (in particular in connection with the publication of league tables, which compared one force with another) generated pressure on forces to manipulate both the level of crime that had been reported and the detection rates.

In 2000, a report by the police inspectorate (HMIC) found wide variations in the way police forces recorded crimes. It was alleged that offences were sometimes wrongly classified as less serious crimes, that there was inappropriate 'no-criming' of offences after they had been recorded, and there was a failure to record the correct number of crimes (HMIC, 2000).

In 2002 ACPO, with the support of the Home Office, sought to address criticisms of this nature by introducing the National Crime Recording Standard (NCRS). This sought to promote 'greater reliability and consistency in collecting and recording crime data. It requires police services to take an approach that focuses on the victims' perspective and requires all forces to record crimes according to a clear set of principles', in order to 'produce more robust data on police performance for the dual purpose of measuring performance and informing local decision-making' (Audit Commission, 2004: 2, 4).

However, progress towards achieving uniformity in this area was slow. It was subsequently concluded that although there was evidence of 'clear corporate commitment to national standards, with strong leadership and sound policies in place in the majority of forces', there 'remain variations in the quality of crime data between forces. Improvements have not been achieved consistently across the country' (Audit Commission, 2004: 3).

Taking it further 2

'Crime statistics are socially constructed'. What are the consequences of this and does it mean that they contain no information that is valid for criminological study?

Clear up rates

Official statistics also give information concerning the extent to which recorded crimes subsequently result in the apprehension of an offender. This 'clear up' or detection rate is a major means for assessing the efficiency of the police service. However, as with the level of crime, statistics governing clear up rates provide a distorted picture of the operations of the criminal justice system.

The circumstances under which a crime is deemed to be solved (or 'cleared up') are laid down by the Home Office. There are two methods used to determine this: *sanction* and *non-sanction* detections.

A sanction detection is where a person receives some form of punishment for the act they have committed. This can range from a fixed penalty notice, a caution, a charge, a summons or a 'taken into consideration' (TIC).

Non-sanction (or administrative) detections describe situations where the police possess sufficient evidence to charge a person with an offence but choose not to do so. In the past this has been for a number of reasons, including:

- There were practical hindrances to a prosecution, including the absence of witnesses willing to give evidence.

- The offender or key witness had died or was too ill to proceed.

- The offender, having admitted an offence, was under the age of criminal responsibility.

- The police or CPS considered that the public interest would not be served by proceeding with a charge.

From 2007, the scope of non-sanction detections has been reduced to cover only those situations when the CPS declines to prosecute an indictable offence or where the accused person dies.

Alternative studies of criminal activity

Victimisation surveys

Other statistical methods may be used in addition to those adopted to compile official crime statistics. One of these is victimisation surveys.

Victimisation surveys have been used in a number of official studies, such as the British Crime Survey (BCS), first published in 1982. Figures have been published bi-annually since 1992 and annually since 2001/02. Each survey has involved interviewing a randomly selected representative sample of the adults (aged over 16) in private households in England and Wales, gathering information relating their experience of victimisation during the previous year in relation to personal and household crimes.

Since surveys of this nature are unaffected by the changes to reporting and recording practices that affect official crime statistics, they are of greater use than the official figures in providing a measurement of national crime trends. Additionally, the existence of data derived from this source makes it possible to compare statistics for similar categories of crime used by both the police and the British Crime Survey, and in particular to obtain information on crimes that are either not reported or not recorded by the police. This difference is significant. In 2003/04, the BCS estimated that approximately 11.7 million crimes had been committed against adults living in private households, compared to the 5.9 million crimes recorded by the police (Dodd *et al.*, 2004: 8–9).

One historic explanation for this was the way official statistics counted incidents as opposed to victims. As has been noted above, until 1998 official statistics classified an episode with several victims as one incident, whereas victimisation surveys would record it as several, thus suggesting a higher level of crime. Additionally, victims of crimes such as racial violence may be more willing to reveal details of such incidents to those conducting victimisation surveys than to the police – possibly as they lack confidence that the criminal justice system will deal with their complaint justly.

However, a number of problems affect the reliability of victimisation studies. They exclude 'victimless crimes' and are distorted by the impossibility of obtaining a representative sample of victims of different categories of crime, and are influenced by what is termed 'forward and backward telescoping'. (Coleman and Moynihan, 1996: 77–9). These terms refer to the reporting of an incident that occurred outside the period that is being surveyed, or a failure to remember minor incidents that took place during that time. Such studies also rely on the accuracy of a person's perception that a particular act constituted a crime.

It can be concluded that these studies provide only selective information on crime. They generate data on certain crimes but offences such as domestic violence or sexual assault, which are often not reported to the police, are also under-reported in victimisation surveys (Walklate, 1989). The Smith Review (2006) also argued that the BCS should be extended to persons under 16 (a reform accepted by the government) and to those living in group residences in order to obtain a truer picture of the extent of victimisation.

Self-report studies

Some of the problems identified with victimisation surveys may be addressed by self-report studies, which present a further alternative to official statistics for the collection of crime data.

Self-report studies ask individuals to record their own criminal activities. They typically consist of a series of questions, addressed to selected groups, about their personal involvement in criminal or rule-breaking behaviour. These studies are not intended to address a representative sample of the population, and they rely on the honesty of persons responding to the survey who may choose to exaggerate or downplay their involvement in such activities. Yet despite these reservations they can still prove valuable.

They have elicited important information, particularly connected with youth culture, that suggests certain activities such as shoplifting or drug taking are relatively widespread (Mott and Mirrlees-Black, 1993). They have also provided information on victimless crimes and offences conducted within the privacy of a home, such as child abuse. However, they may also secure information on trivial offences that constitute minor infractions of the law not regarded as crimes by those who perpetrate them – such as using a work telephone to make a private call.

A recent study using self-reporting methods was the Crime and Justice Survey, introduced in 2003. This was based upon interviews with around 12,000 people aged 10–65 in England and Wales. Its findings suggested that there were around 3.8 million active offenders (defined as persons who committed at least one offence in the previous year). Those defined as 'serious or prolific offenders' (those who committed six or more offences in the previous year) were said to comprise about 2 per cent of the population, but accounted for around 82 per cent of all crime (Budd and Sharp, 2005).

Ethical considerations

Ethical considerations underpin the conduct of all research, at undergraduate level and beyond. This means that legal and moral obligations are placed upon the researcher to ensure that the personal safety of the researcher and the rights and sensitivities of those who are the subject of research are fully understood and acted upon.

The key ethical considerations that underpin research are as follows:

- The researcher must comply with the law. Researchers should not, for example, engage in criminal actions to gather material or to secure credibility with those whose activities are being studied.

- The methods used to gather research should be morally defensible. When researching into sensitive areas consideration should be given as to how the information required can be gathered using ways that minimise any potential legal risk or accusation of moral impropriety.

- Those participating as the subjects of research should be provided with guarantees of anonymity and confidentiality. These guarantees have implications for the safe storage of data that is collected during a research study.

- The purpose of the research should normally be fully explained to participants, who should also be given an assurance that they can opt out of the study at any time and that any information they have imparted will be removed. Those who opt out must not be placed under subsequent pressure to become involved again in the project.

- Participants should usually have given their express consent to be involved in the research project. There may be exceptions to this, perhaps in connection with covert research, when the researcher may decide that the end result justifies withholding information of this nature to those who are the subject of research.

- Where samples are used, the researcher should ensure that the size of the group is appropriate for the investigation in hand. Unnecessarily large samples should be avoided.

- All risks to the researcher and to his or her subjects should be fully assessed before any research is conducted. Here the key aim is to ensure that the researcher and the subjects of research are not placed in positions of danger arising from the project.

● Care must be taken to avoid any course of action that causes the subject of research unnecessary distress.

Taking it further 3

Much criminological research carries ethical implications that must be considered. What ethical issues arise in the following scenarios? (Suggestions are contained in Chapter 7.)

1. You wish to undertake a study of paedophilia and you intend that one aspect of your research is to study examples of child pornography available on the Internet. What ethical considerations should you consider before embarking on this research?

2. You intend to monitor the activities of an extreme right-wing political organisation. To carry out this research you intend to covertly monitor meetings of this organisation and secretly tape record conversations with leading activists. What ethical considerations arise from this proposed research?

3. You have gathered research in connection with drug taking among school children. They are informed that this is in connection with your final year undergraduate dissertation. Although the self-report questionnaires were completed anonymously, you are able to identify the children involved and decide to pass on to the head teacher information about those who admit to using drugs. What ethical issues does this course of action raise?

4. You are conducting research into domestic violence. A contact you have made in a criminal justice agency provides you with a list of victims who may be willing to participate in research of this nature. You decide to send each person on the list a detailed questionnaire, which includes questions seeking to ascertain the nature of the violence they have experienced. What ethical considerations arise from this proposed course of action?

5. You are conducting research into the sex industry and wish to interview some persons who are involved in this form of activity. To do this, you intend to visit a local red light area in the early hours of the morning and question sex trade workers and their clients. What ethical issues arise from this research proposal?

References

Audit Commission (2004) *Crime Recording: Improving the Quality of Crime Records in Police Authorities in England and Wales.* London: Audit Commission.

Budd, T. and Sharp, C. (2005) *Offending in England and Wales: First Results from the 2003 Crime and Justice Survey*, Home Office Research, Development and Statistics Directorate, Findings 244. London: Home Office.

Coleman, C. and Moynihan, J. (1996) *Understanding Crime Data: Haunted by the Dark Figure.* Buckingham: Open University Press.

Dodd, T., Nicholas, S., Povey, D. and Walker, A. (2004) *Crime in England and Wales, 2003/4*, Home Office Statistical Bulletin 10/04. London: Home Office

Her Majesty's Inspectorate of Constabulary (2000) *On the Record*. London: HMIC Press.

Mott, J. and Mirrlees-Black, C. (1993) *Self-Reported Drug Misuse in England and Wales: Main Findings from the 1992 British Crime Survey*, Home Office Research and Statistics Department Research Findings No. 7. London: HMSO.

Smith, A. (2006) *Crime Statistics: An Independent Review*. London: Home Office.

Walklate, S. (1989) *Victimology: The Victim and the Criminal Justice Process*. London: Sage.

5 The presentation of written work

The aims of this chapter are:

- To identify good practice in the presentation of essays.
- To apply the discussion of good and bad principles in essay writing to specific examples.
- To establish the meaning of plagiarism and how to avoid this.
- To provide information regarding the procedure of referencing.

Essay writing

An essay typically consists of a question or problem that the student is required to consider. The aim of an exercise of this nature is to test the student's ability to digest a range of material related to the essay topic and to present a coherent argument (or set of arguments) that discuss the key issues involved and to do so within the prescribed word limit. For an undergraduate essay this is typically between 1,500 and 2,000 words.

An essay should be coherently presented. It should consist of an introduction, in which the author briefly sets out what he or she intends to discuss, followed by a more detailed consideration of the key issues that the question embraces. The key findings should then be summarised in the conclusion in which the writer puts forward his or her views concerning the essay question based upon a consideration of the main arguments that were contained in the body of the essay.

Finally an essay should contain a bibliography that lists all the sources that have been consulted. Every piece of material cited in the text of the essay must be included in the bibliography, together with other sources that have been used but not referenced.

Essays – good practice

A good essay will display a number of key skills, These are detailed overleaf.

Description and analysis

A good essay requires a balance between description and analysis (or evaluation). There is a place for factual material in any essay but it is important to draw out the significance of the facts and figures that are presented.

Referencing

The information and arguments presented in essays derive from published material. It is essential that all sources that have been used in the construction of an essay are cited both in the body of the essay and also in the bibliography.

A more detailed consideration of referencing is provided below.

Essays – bad practice

A number of key weaknesses in essay writing should be avoided. The main ones are as follows:

One-sidedness

Essays should provide a rounded account of the issues under discussion. It is unlikely that there is only one answer or solution to the problem or issue being discussed and it is therefore important to consider all relevant aspects and then to arrive at a conclusion based on this diverse range of arguments.

The first person tense

The use of the first person tense should be avoided in written work. It is preferable to use the passive tense. 'This essay will discuss . . . .' is preferable to 'In this essay I will discuss . . .'

Self-opinion

Criminology is a highly interesting subject. Many issues that it embraces, such as how society should punish those who have broken the law, are the subject of popular discussion and all individuals have their own views on such matters.

However, when writing essays it is important to realise that what is required is an academic consideration of the subject matter, in which arguments based upon published material are put forward and evaluated. Personal opinions unsupported by factual evidence have no place in an academic essay and must be avoided.

Insufficient references

An essay should display evidence that a range of relevant material has been consulted by the author, and all the material on which the ideas expressed in the essay are based should be cited in the text of the essay and in the bibliography.

Criminology embraces many contentious issues and a wide selection of sources should be consulted in order that a range of opinions – often of a diverse nature – are considered and then evaluated. The use of one or two sources is unlikely to meet this requirement – and the absence of *any* references in the text of the essay may suggest that the account is either one-sided, self-opinionated, or both.

Plagiarism

Plagiarism covers a number of vices that no essay should contain. These include:

- Seeking to pass off material written by someone else as your own by failing to acknowledge the source from which the material was derived.

- Adopting ideas or opinions put forward by someone else as your own by neglecting to cite the origins of these views.

- Copying material without the author's consent and attempting to pass it off as your own.

- Being overly reliant on published material even when the sources used are properly cited. If your essay consists of little more than a string of quotations taken from published material, joined together with the occasional 'and', 'but' and 'however', little in that essay can be judged as your own work. As a rough guide, ensure that no more than 10 per cent of an essay is directly derived from published sources.

Expressed more simply, plagiarism is cheating. It is viewed in a similar way to sneaking notes into an exam, and the penalties can be severe. An essay that contains evidence of plagiarism will normally receive a mark of zero and serial offenders may find that their university careers are prematurely ended.

How is plagiarised work detected?

It is usually quite easy to detect plagiarism. A number of pointers arouse suspicion that work has been plagiarised:

- The tutor reading the essay recognises sources that have not been referenced. He or she has already read the material and knows them not to be the student's own work.

- The text of the essay contains references to material that is not included in the bibliography. This suggests that the writer has not actually consulted this material but has instead obtained this information from other sources.

- The language used in the essay reveals a complexity that is not appropriate to the level at which the essay is meant to be pitched.

- The essay is very disjointed, which often suggests that material has been cut and pasted from published (especially Internet-based) sources.

If the reader's suspicion is aroused, simple detection methods can be utilised. These include:

- Feeding key words and phrases into an advanced Google search. This will reveal the sources from which these words and phrases have been taken, if the work has been plagiarised.

- Feeding the entire essay into the JISC 'Turnitin' plagiarism detection software. The student is required to submit an electronic copy of the essay (this is common in many universities). This process produces a highly detailed report indicating the overall extent (expressed in percentage terms) to which the essay has been obtained from other sources, and also listing these sources. If a considerable proportion of these sources are unacknowledged in the text of the essay, it can be assumed that plagiarism has taken place.

Assessment criteria

The following provides information as to how grades for assessed work and examinations marks are awarded. These begin from a position of excellence and indicate how these high standards can be departed from.

70 per cent and above The work is structured and organised: this means that it has an introduction and conclusion and that the body of the text flows coherently.

All aspects of the question are covered in a detailed and comprehensive fashion and there are no obvious omissions in content. For example, a question concerned with examining the role of policing policies as an explanation for urban disorders since 1980 would need to examine these policies, then move on to discussing other causes (such as deprivation, depravation and political marginalisation) not related to policing.

Key sources that are relevant to the evidence presented are cited. Opinions put forward are justified by reference to a wide range of published authorities.

The balance between description and analysis is biased in favour of the latter, and the evaluation is balanced in the sense that it sees all sides of the issue under discussion. The answer may display the ability to present arguments that challenge the underlying assumptions on which the question is based: for example, a question asking 'To what extent prisons do secure the reform and rehabilitation of inmates?' would need to consider *how* prisons succeed in achieving this goal and also *why* they fail to meet it

60–69 per cent The work is constructed well, having an introduction and conclusion: the body of the text is organised in a logical manner.

The work is not totally comprehensive in its coverage of the subject matter: all key areas of the argument are covered but that there are minor gaps and omissions, although these do not have any substantial bearing on the main issues that are required to be discussed. For example, an essay dealing with the causes of urban disorder since 1980 might refer fully to the main issues (such as policing policies, deprivation, depravation and political marginalisation) but say little or nothing concerning the role of the media or the orchestration of such events.

A number of key sources are quoted to justify the arguments presented but there are some omissions, which means that the full breadth of available information has not been utilised.

The balance between description and analysis is biased in favour of the latter but the analysis is not totally balanced; it may, for example, be a little one-sided, not giving full weight to all academic views relevant to the question. For example, an essay concerned with the rehabilitative and reforming roles of prisons might concentrate on reasons why these objectives are not met and neglect evaluation as to what is done to implement them.

50–59 per cent

The work is reasonably well organised in the sense that it has an introduction and conclusion, but it displays signs of disorganisation in the text of the work. There may, for example, be repetitions or signs of paragraphs not 'flowing' to present a logical and coherent argument.

The answer clearly sees the point of the question but does not deal with it in a comprehensive fashion. Typically, one or two aspects of an argument will be covered in detail but other equally significant issues will be dealt with less fully, if at all. For example, a question dealing with inner-city disorders since 1980 might deal with those that are well documented in the literature (1981 and 1985), to the relative or total neglect of those that have taken place in the 1990s.

A limited range of relevant sources has been utilised but there are deficiencies which thus affect the depth of coverage offered in the essay or the level of evaluation.

The blend of discussion and analysis is biased in favour of the former. For example, the details of a prison riot may be referred to but the significance of this episode and an explanation as to why it occurred and what can be learned from it may be relatively neglected, or the depth of analysis may be deficient, perhaps seeing one side of an argument to the relative or total neglect of another. This results in the answer being unbalanced in its treatment of key issues and arguments.

40–49 per cent The answer is not well organised. Typically it 'rambles' across a range of issues presenting something akin to a shopping list rather than a coherent set or arguments.

The answer is deficient in the coverage of the subject matter. This may involve examining an issue (or issues) relevant to the question but without displaying a broader perspective. Typically an answer will not go beyond responding to the precise wording of the question. For example, an examination of the relevance of policing practices to urban disorder will deal with that issue alone without showing any comprehension that this is only one of many explanations that can be offered for such events.

The coverage of the subject matter is superficial: important areas may be referred to but are discussed in no detail. Typically this results in relevant sources either not being referred to at all or being mentioned in only very limited fashion.

The balance between description and analysis is heavily biased towards the former. Analysis tends to be one-sided and often anecdotal rather than being based on proper evaluation of the arguments presented in key literature.

(Fail) 0–40 per cent The answer is poorly organised. Typically it will discuss issues in a disjointed manner lacking any semblance of logic or cohesion.

The answer either totally misunderstands the question or covers it in a very superficial manner, usually concentrating on one aspect of it to the total neglect of other relevant issues. For example, an essay on the accountability of the security services may mistakenly discuss the accountability of the police.

There is little or no evidence of key sources having been consulted. The essay may be based on anecdotal or 'common sense' arguments not supported by published academic research. Opinions will be conveyed through value judgements, such as 'In my opinion the police are a racist organisation', which are not substantiated by any relevant documentation of sources.

The essay is primarily descriptive. Evaluation, if present at all, tends to be limited in scope and one-sided.

Taking it further 1

Below are two sample essays.

Assume that these are at first year undergraduate level. Your task is to assess them in line with the criteria detailed above.

What marks would you award these two essays? (Comments and suggested marks are contained in Chapter 7.)

Essay 1

You are asked to write a 1,000 word essay on the following topic:

Analyse the arguments for and against the routine arming of the police in England and Wales.

In this essay the arguments for and against the routine arming of the police in England and Wales will be examined and a conclusion as to whether this is a good or a bad idea will be put forward in the light of these arguments.

Police officers in England and Wales have traditionally been unarmed. The concept of minimum force was an important feature of the new system of policing that developed during the early decades of the nineteenth century and was an important aspect in securing the consent of the public to the police. When soldiers had been used to preserve public order they had often used their guns to shoot those engaged in this activity – for example in the Gordon Riots in London in 1780 when around 700 people were killed by the military. There was thus a deliberate attempt to ensure that actions of this nature were not repeated by civilian police officers who were thus unarmed (save for special emergencies when cutlasses – and later pistols – might be issued). This concept was known as 'minimum force' and resulted in the police being armed only with a wooden truncheon which was to be used in situations when they needed to protect themselves.

The image of the unarmed bobby walking the beat displayed the police in a favourable light as persons whose role was to serve the community and secure their aid in combating crime. This image was displayed in a popular television programme, *Dixon of Dock Green*, which ran for 367 episodes between 1955 and 1976. George Dixon didn't need to carry a gun in order to enforce the law in Dock Green. He did it with the cooperation of the public who looked up to him as a figure of authority. However, in recent years pressure has been exerted to arm all police officers. Why is this the case?

The first reason why some have suggested that the police should be armed concerns the nature of contemporary crime. In the latter decades of the twentieth century crime became more violent and gun crime in particular has grown in recent years. Criminals became more organised and more willing to utilise extreme violence to achieve their ends. It makes good sense that since the police are increasingly required to deal with violent criminals they should be given the means to perform their duties to deter and combat crime of this nature. It might be argued that criminals are less likely to use weapons if they know that the police have the means to meet force with force.

One aspect of the increase in violent crime has been the deaths of police officers at the hands of violent criminals. Thus a second reason why the police should be routinely armed is to protect themselves. There has been a large increase in the number of police officers killed by violent criminals in recent years and we need to ensure that they have adequate means to defend themselves when encountering violence.

There are, however, a number of problems with routinely arming the police. Gun crime, although on the increase, is a relatively small proportion of all crime and is often confined to specific geographic locations. It would be costly to train all officers in the use of firearms and as most would use their firearms infrequently, if at all, it is more cost efficient to train only a small number to a high level of proficiency. There is also no evidence that the police themselves see the need, or wish, to be routinely armed. Many fear that carrying a weapon would encourage the use of extreme violence against them and thus increase the number of deaths and serious injuries.

A more serious problem is that the routine arming of the police is likely to increase the number of occasions when officers draw their weapons. Although this may often be justified, there is always the danger that officers may draw them inappropriately, and people who would have previously been arrested end up being shot instead. Additionally accidents do happen and in extreme cases a member of the public ends up being killed. This occurred, for example, in London in 2005.

Following a number of explosions on the London underground (and also on a London bus) on 7 July 2005 that were carried out by suicide bombers in which over 50 people were killed, the police were on a high state of alert to prevent further catastrophes of this nature. On 22 July armed police officers followed a Brazilian man, Jean Charles de

Menezes, onto a train at Stockwell underground station in South London. Believing that he was a suicide bomber he was shot several times and killed. It was later discovered that the dead man had no link whatsoever with terrorism. But as with the death penalty, it is impossible to make amends in situations of this nature. If highly trained firearms officers make such mistakes, it is likely that they will occur more frequently if all officers, trained to less high standards, carry firearms. And, as with the shooting of Mr de Menezes, mistakes of this nature have a bad impact on police–public relations since the public often feel that officers who make such serious mistakes are not held properly accountable for their actions. In this particular incident, the main sanction applied against the MPS was the 1974 Health and Safety legislation: in 2007 the CPS initiated proceedings alleging that the force had failed to provide for the health, safety and welfare of Jean Charles de Menezes on 22 July 2005.

Accordingly, I believe that although violent crime has risen in recent years, we should not routinely arm our police since the disadvantages outlined above outweigh any benefits this is likely to bring in terms of either combating this form of crime or protecting police officers. The police now have access to a wide range of what might be termed 'weaponry' (such as CS spray and pepper spray) and for most issues they are likely to encounter in the course of their working day these are sufficient. An officer doesn't need a gun to deal with a person who is behaving in an anti-social manner or carrying out petty crime. Yet this forms the bulk of police work. Back-up (in the form of rapid response teams) is always available if weapons are required to counter a more violent situation such as a bank hold-up.

Essay 2

Write a 1,500 word essay on the following topic:

> *Evaluate the strengths and weaknesses of the ideas put forward by classicist criminologists concerning the causes of and solutions to crime.*

In this essay I will examine the key ideas put forward by classicist criminologists (in particular Cesare Beccaria and Jeremy Bentham) concerning why crime occurs and what can be done to deter it. I will then examine the strengths and weaknesses of these arguments. First, however, I will discuss the historical context within which these ideas were put forward.

It has been observed that 'Classicism' developed out of the Enlightenment movement of late eighteenth century Europe. Its political expression was liberalism that viewed society as a contract voluntarily entered into by those who were party to it rather than being a structure handed down by God. Government emerged as the result of a rational choice by those who subsequently accorded their consent to its operations, and this belief ensured that the rights of the individual were prominent concerns of liberal and classicist thinking. Crime was viewed as an act that infringed the legal code whose rationale was to safeguard the interests of those who were party to the social contract, especially the preservation of their personal safety and privately owned property. In such a contractual society, the equality of all citizens before the law, and the presumption of the innocence of a person accused of criminal wrongdoing were viewed as cardinal principles to safeguard individual rights and liberties. The state was entitled to intervene in the lives of its citizens only when this would promote the interests of the majority' (Joyce, 2006: 1–2).

Classicist criminology focused on the operations of the criminal justice process and viewed its imperfections as the main source of crime. For the purposes of this essay I will examine the nature of the criminal justice system in England and Wales.

The agricultural and industrial revolutions led to the growth of towns which were viewed by contemporary writers as havens of crime and disorder. The criminal justice system of that period was extremely harsh: 'systems of punishment for much of the seventeenth and eighteenth centuries were bloody and cruel; the rested on ideas of revenge and retribution' (Newburn, 2007: 115). A distinction was drawn between *felonies* (serious crimes) and *trespasses* (minor violations of the law, termed 'misdemeanours'). Following the enactment of the 1723 'Black Act' a large number of felonies carried the death penalty. However, the penalties prescribed by law were not consistently applied: there was an increasing tendency as the eighteenth century progressed to use alternative forms of punishment such as transportation (which had initially been introduced in 1717) rather than the death penalty or for juries to convict criminals of lesser charges to avoid execution.

An additional problem was that the criminal justice system of that period was hopelessly inefficient: this made it unlikely that a person committing a criminal act would be apprehended by the police and processed by the courts.

Accordingly, the focus of classical criminologists was on the criminal justice system. In short, they believed that people committed crime as they perceived that they could 'get away with it'. Accordingly they argued that a reformed system would help to deter crime more effectively.

The key theorists associated with classicist criminology were the Italian, Cesare Beccaria, and the Englishman, Jeremy Bentham. I shall now consider the ideas with which they were associated in more detail.

First, and perhaps most important, classicists argued that crime was an action committed by a rational person. This view was underpinned by two key assumptions – 'that individuals have free will; and that individuals are guided by hedonism, the maximization of pleasure and the minimization of pain' (Walklate, 2003: 16). Classicists believed that a person calculated the benefits that would be derived from undertaking a criminal action and balanced these against the personal costs that it might involve. If the benefits outweighed the costs they would be encouraged to commit a criminal act. Thus 'criminals would be deterred from crime if they calculated that the pain would exceed the pleasure' (Jones, 2006: 108). For example, a person might calculate that robbing a wealthy person in the street would bring large financial reward. He would then consider that it was unlikely that he would be apprehended by the police and even if he was the courts might not insist upon the punishment laid down by law. These uncertainties tipped the balance in favour of committing a crime. Classicist criminologists wished to re-write the equation so that the potential criminal would realise he was likely to be caught by the police and would know in advance exactly what the punishment would be. A second aspect of their thinking, therefore, was that a uniform and consistent response to crime was the most likely development to deter it. They were strongly opposed to the use of discretion, the 'capricious and purely personal justice' (Vold, Bernard and Snipes, 1998: 17) that was dispensed by judges and magistrates since this made for penalties that were not clear at the outset.

Classicists also reacted against the harsh penal codes that existed in many European countries at that time. They believed that popular perceptions that the death penalty was not an appropriate response to many of the crimes that were subject to it was the main reason why the law was inconsistently applied by the courts. Accordingly they argued that the punishment should fit the crime. They focused on the crime and not the person who committed it, and sought to introduce graded penalties related to the seriousness of the criminal act. The intention of these penalties was, however, not to punish but, rather, to deter the commission of the criminal action.

In England and Wales, classicists inspired three important developments affecting the criminal justice system. They were at the forefront of the reform of the penal code (whereby the death penalty was removed from a large number of criminal offences in the early decades of the nineteenth century), and they also promoted police reform. This involved replacing the 'old' policing system that was organised around parishes and delivered by unpaid constables in favour of a new system consisting of paid police officers operating throughout the newly developed towns and cities. This was termed the 'new police' (McLaughlin, 2007: 4). The 1835 Municipal Corporations Act required all large towns to organise a police force and in 1856 this became a mandatory requirement for both town and county.

Classicists were also interested in prison reform. Bentham was an important exponent of this. It was believed that prisons could be a vehicle to ensure that those who had committed crime would learn to make rational choices and thus not repeat their criminal actions in the future. The harsh nature of the prison regime would 'grind rogues honest'. The 1779 Penitentiary Act provided prisons with a mission to reform their inmates and in 1791 Bentham wrote a three-volume work, *The Panopticon*, in which he devised a blueprint for the design of prisons to enable them to bring about the transformation of offenders.

Central to his idea was the principle of surveillance, which provided the potential for prisoners to be observed 24 hours a day. This would encourage them to adopt conforming behaviour.

Having discussed the key ideas associated with classicism and the background against which these ideas emerged, I will finally consider the problems associate with classicist criminology.

Perhaps most importantly, there was no scientific evidence to support their beliefs regarding why crime occurred and how it might best be deterred. It was mere philosophic speculation to suggest that a reformed criminal justice process that was predictable and inflexible in its operations would help to deter actions of this nature. The school of criminological thought that followed classicist criminology, positivism, based its views of scientific (or social scientific) evidence or what has been referred to as the search for 'facts' (Walklate, 2003: 17).

Additionally, classicists placed too much emphasis on the belief that crime was an action carried out by a human being making rational choices. While this might be so for some criminals, it was – and is – not the case for others. For example, crime might be carried out as an impulsive action, taken on the spur of the moment when an opportunity (such as a handbag lying on the seat of a car that has been unlocked) presents itself. It is also possible that criminal actions may be driven by forces beyond the control of those who carry them out which may override their free will and make them do it. As positivists later argued, these forces may be biological, psychological or sociological in origins. Determinism of this nature sharply contrasts with the classicist belief in free will.

It might thus be concluded that although classicists were responsible for initiating a number of important developments affecting the operations of the criminal justice system including the 'just deserts' approach to sentencing (White and Haines, 2004: 30) many of their key ideas that underpinned these reforms were flawed. Accordingly crime continued and paved the way for new schools of thought to put forward different views as to how the problem might be solved.

Bibiography

Walklate, S. (2003) *Understanding Criminology: Current Theoretical Debates*. Buckingham: Open University Press.

Williams, K. (2001) *Textbook on Criminology*, 4th ed., Oxford: Oxford University Press.

McLaughlin, E. (2007) *The New Policing*. London: Sage.

Joyce, P. (2006) *Criminal Justice: An Introduction to Crime and the Criminal Justice System*. Cullompton, Devon: Willan Publishing.

Jones, S. (2006) *Criminology*. Oxford: Oxford University Press.

White, R. and Haines, F. (2004) *Crime and Criminology: An Introduction*, 3rd ed, Oxford: Oxford University Press.

Vold, G., Bernard, T. and Snipes, J. (1998) *Theoretical Criminology*, 4th ed. Oxford: Oxford University Press.

Newburn, T. (2007) *Criminology*. Cullompton, Devon: Willan Publishing.

Other forms of written work

Although essays are an important form of coursework, your written work may be presented in other formats.

Case studies

A case study will typically present a scenario and you will be required to answer questions related to that particular situation.

You might, for example, be asked to consider the case of anti-social behaviour occurring on a run-down housing estate. A profile of the area, of the youths who are causing the annoyance and of those who are suffering as the result of it may be provided. You are asked to assess whether problem-oriented policing or a zero tolerance approach would be the most appropriate course of action to deal with the problem.

In your answer to this case study you should:

- Relate the two styles of policing to the problems that have been identified in the case study.

- Present an analytical account of both styles of policing, identifying what solutions each could put forward to deal with the issues outlined in the case study.

- Provide a reasoned explanation as to what course of action you think would be most preferable, based upon your analysis of the strengths and weaknesses of each style of policing. It is perfectly possible to argue that aspects of both approaches could be utilised in the area; for example, adopting a zero tolerance, law-enforcement approach to ringleaders while at the same time seeking to organise leisure activities to keep some of the youths who are involved in the disorder off the streets and away from the area.

You should not:

- Present a detailed examination of both styles of policing that pays little or no attention to the problems identified in the case study, since the purpose of this exercise is to require you to relate theoretical issues to practical examples.

- Devote excessive attention to providing a profile of the area, the offenders and the victims, which at its worst will consist of little more than retyping the case study scenario: the aim of the exercise is to relate the issues that have been identified to two diverse styles of policing.

- Provide an account that is overly descriptive of these styles of policing, perhaps explaining in great detail the stages and processes that are involved in problem-oriented policing, to the detriment of a thorough evaluation of the strengths and weaknesses of both methods and a conclusion that builds on this analysis.

Book reviews

If you are asked to write a review of a book or a journal article, you should focus on both content and analysis: you need to describe to the reader the main themes and key arguments that are presented in the book, and provide an evaluation of its strengths and weaknesses.

When writing a book review you should seek to strike an appropriate balance between contents and your evaluation of them; in particular you should avoid presenting a detailed blow-by-blow account of the contents of each chapter to the detriment of analysis. Your analysis should consider issues that include the key ideas put forward, but might also extend to matters such as methodology, style of writing (is it reader-friendly?), coherence and presentation.

Reports

Reports are similar to dissertations in that they are typically extended pieces of work that are divided into chapters. The key difference concerns presentation: chapters (or sections) are numbered and are subsequently broken down into discrete areas, which are also numbered.

For example, if you were compiling a report on reforms introduced into the police service in the wake of the 1999 Macpherson Report, your first section might be concerned with discussing some of the main recommendations, each of which would be considered in a separate subsection. This section might be numbered as follows:

1   Main recommendations of the Macpherson Report
1.1   Increased trust and confidence in policing among minority
        ethnic communities
1.2   Definition of a racist incident
1.3   Racism awareness training
1.4   Reforms to discipline and complaints procedures
1.5   Reforms to stop and search procedures
1.6   Recruitment and retention targets

These titles should also appear in your report.

Each paragraph would also be numbered. There are two ways of doing this. If each section contains a number of separate themes, these should be differentiated in the numbering system that you adopt. Using the above example, you will wish to write about the key proposals put forward in the report relating to trust and confidence in the police service. These may be numbered thus:

1.1   Increased trust and confidence in policing among minority
        ethnic communities
1.1.1   Performance indicators to assess the effectiveness of
        initiatives to build trust and confidence
1.1.2   Monitoring of forces by Her Majesty's Inspectorate of
        Constabulary

1.1.3 Establishment of a police authority for the Metropolitan Police Service
1.1.4 Reform to the composition of police authorities
1.1.5 Disclosure of reports by investigating officers relating to complaints made against the police by the public
1.1.6 Reform of the Race Relations Act

However, if the contents of each section are concerned with a single issue, it is not necessary to subdivide the section into a number of subheadings. Instead, each paragraph could be sequentially numbered, 1.1, 1.2, 1.3, etc. The 1999 Macpherson Report followed this format.

Referencing

As indicated elsewhere, referencing is an indispensable aspect of written work. This section seeks to provide more detailed guidance concerning the way in which referencing should be approached.

Why should written work be referenced?

Written work needs to be referenced in order to provide information as to the sources that have been used in its construction. It enables those reading the work to cross-check the information that has been provided.

Thus, the following should be referenced:

- Any direct quotation from a published source: this should be placed in inverted commas in the text of the essay and the source of the quotation should be included in brackets at the end of the material that has been quoted.

- A statement that presents a summary of an idea or ideas obtained from a published source.

- Material that expresses the ideas or opinions that have been obtained from a published source. Even if words are not directly quoted (perhaps because you have paraphrased them – that is, put them in your own words), the source or sources on which the ideas expressed in a portion of an essay are based should be acknowledged in the text of your work.

Facts, opinions or ideas that can be regarded as common knowledge do not need to be referenced. For example, if you do not need a reference:

A jury is used in Crown Courts in England and Wales and consists of twelve persons.

How to reference

Referencing is required in two places:

- In the text of a piece of written work.
- At the end of the work, either in a list of references or a bibliography (see page 136 below).

Referencing in the text of written work

Two systems are used for referencing in the text of a piece of written work: the Chicago system (also referred to as the numeric system) and the Harvard system. The key difference between these two systems relates to the way in which sources are cited in the text of a piece of written work.

The Chicago system uses numbers in the text and the source or note that relates to this number is cited in full either at the bottom of each page or in a section at the end, before the bibliography. If a number of citations from the same source are used, the abbreviation *ibid.* can be used rather than the full reference of the work. If after other references have been cited you then make reference to a source you have previously cited in full, the abbreviation *op. cit.* can be used rather than repeating the full reference to the work.

The Harvard system tends to be more widely used in the UK. Sources are inserted into the text of the essay as and when they arise, at which point they are cited in an abbreviated form:

- Author (followed by a comma)
- Year of publication (followed by a colon)
- Page number(s) (if appropriate)

Full publication details are then provided in the bibliography.

For example, you are writing an essay on organised crime and have used Alan Wright's text as one of your sources. You make reference to his argument relating to difficulties in defining this phenomenon, stating in your essay:

It has been argued that organised crime is a difficult term to precisely define.

You would follow this statement with:

(Wright, 2006: 2–3)

You would supply the full citation in the bibliography:

Wright, A. (2006) *Organised Crime*. Cullompton, Devon: Willan Publishing.

Other issues

* In the text of your written work you should use only the author's surname; if there are several authors with this name, include the first letter of their first name.

* It is permissible for the sake of variation in the text to slightly vary the way in which you cite references. For example:

> Wright (2006: 3) argued that the 1960s were the starting point for extensive debates concerning the meaning and effect of organised crime.

This can alternatively be cited as:

> The 1960s were the starting point for extensive debates concerning the meaning and effect of organised crime (Wright, 2006: 3)

* If a similar argument is made by a number of sources you have consulted, you should include them all in the text of the essay and also in the bibliography. In the text of the written work these should be organised alphabetically rather than chronologically, each source separated by a semi-colon.

* If an Internet source is quoted, the citation in the text of the essay should be:

- Author (followed by a comma)

- Year of publication (followed by a colon)

- The word 'online'.

*When citing from an edited book containing chapters written by various contributors, your citation in the text of the essay should refer to the author of the specific chapter you are using and not the editor(s) of the book.

* If you are citing a source that you have not read yourself, but have found reference to it in a source you are using, you should cite it in the text of your essay as follows:

> (Cressey 1972, cited in Wright, 2006)

No page numbers are required for this citation.
   Do not cite the original text if you have not consulted it, as doing so is a form of plagiarism – you are claiming to have consulted material that you have not actually read.

Quotations

Direct quotations should be presented in the text of your essay in one of two ways.
   If the quote is a relatively short one (below 20 words), it should be included within the paragraph and placed in quotation marks. You may use

single or double quotation marks. For example, if you are writing about popular concerns regarding crime and disorder and are using Michael Tonry's text as a source, you might argue in your essay that:

> It has been argued that when politicians direct constant attention at a problem such as anti-social behaviour they run the risk of increasing the public's fear of crime and make them 'more mistrustful and more receptive to populist anti-crime appeals' (Tonry, 2004: 56).

If the quotation goes beyond 20 words, it should be separated from the paragraph and indented (but not placed within quotation marks). If you wished to expand on Tonry's ideas regarding the consequences of this approach you would do it thus:

> It has been argued that when politicians direct constant attention at a problem such as anti-social behaviour they run the risk of increasing the public's fear of crime. It has been argued
>
> > By making anti-social behaviour into a major social policy problem, and giving it sustained high visibility attention, Labour has made a small problem larger, thereby making people more aware of it and less satisfied with their lives and their government. (Tonry, 2004: 57)

The bibliography

A bibliography is placed at the end of a piece of written work. It commonly contains a list of all material that has been consulted in writing the work, whether cited or not. However, it is acceptable to produce a list of works that have been cited (titled 'References') followed by a bibliography that contains all works used whether cited or not.

For the purposes of this chapter, the term 'bibliography' includes material that has been cited *and* material consulted but not cited.

The bibliography relevant to a piece of written work should be placed at the end. It is prepared in the same manner whether you have used the Harvard or the Chicago system of referencing in the text of the work.

The authors whose works appear in the bibliography should be presented in alphabetical order. If you have cited several works written by the same author, present these in order of date of publication, commencing with the work written earliest. If you have cited several works by an author, some of which were single authored and some of which were joint authored, the single authored works should be cited first, in order of date of publication, followed by the joint authored material. If you have cited authors with the same surname, take the initial of their first name for the purposes of alphabetical ordering (i.e. Smith, J would precede Smith, S.).

Different referencing criteria are used depending on the nature of the source that has been used. At postgraduate level, when written work is likely to be lengthy, it is common to present the bibliography under several headings, such as books, chapters and articles, primary sources, etc. But at undergraduate level, especially in the early years of undergraduate study, this division is not necessary and all sources can be arranged in one list.

The material below gives suggestions as to how sources should be cited in the bibliography. The order in which information is provided should be adhered to, although variations regarding punctuation are acceptable and these suggestions should be regarded as advisory rather than mandatory.

Books

Books that have been referred to should provide information in the following order and format:

- Author's surname (followed by a comma) then initial(s) (followed by a full stop)
- Year of publication (placed in brackets)
- *Title of book* (in italics, followed by a full stop)
- Place of publication (followed by a colon)
- Publisher

For example:

Rowe, M. (2008) *Introduction to Policing.* London: Sage.

Electronic copies of books require no changes to referencing practice since they contain the same content as the hard copy of the work.

If a book has been written by more than one author, you should cite the authors as in the following example:

Grieve, J., Harfield, C. and MacVean, A. (2007) *Policing.* London: Sage.

Variations

* If the book consists of a collection of material edited by one person, the reference should be:

- Author's surname (followed by a comma) then initial(s) (followed by a full stop)
- The abbreviation (ed) (placed in brackets)
- Year of publication (placed in brackets)
- *Title of book* (in italics and followed by a full stop)
- Place of publication (followed by a colon)
- Publisher

For example:

> Rowe, M. (ed.) (2007) *Policing Beyond Macpherson. Issues in Policing, Race and Society.* Cullompton, Devon: Willan Publishing.

* If there is more than one editor, you should cite the authors' names followed by (eds) and then proceed as above. For example:

> Fine, B. and Millar, R. (eds) (1985) *Policing the Miners' Dispute.* London: Lawrence & Wishart.

* If the author is an organisation as opposed to an individual, the organisation should appear in place of the author:

- Organisation's name
- Year of publication (placed in brackets)
- *Title of book* (in italics and followed by a full stop)
- Place of publication (followed by a colon)
- Publisher

For example:

> National Council for Civil Liberties (1980) *Southall 23 April 1979. The Report of the Unofficial Committee of Enquiry.* London: National Council for Civil Liberties.

* Normally, it is sufficient to refer to the town or city as the place of publication. However, if this is relatively obscure, it is acceptable practice to accompany this with the county (UK) or state (USA), as is the case above in connection with Willan Publishing: the place of publication (Cullompton) is accompanied with the county (Devon) in which Cullompton is located.

Chapters in books

In the case of books to which a number of authors have contributed – usually edited collections – it is necessary to reference only those chapters that have been consulted. This may mean that the title of the book appears several times in the bibliography if several chapters have been used.

Chapters should be cited as follows:

- Chapter author's name: surname first (followed by a comma), then initial (followed by a full stop)
- Year of publication (placed in brackets)
- 'Title of chapter' (in inverted commas followed by a comma and the word 'in')
- Book author's name (or names)
- *Title of book* (in italics and followed by a full stop)

- Place of publication (followed by a colon)

- Publisher

Some guides to bibliography suggest you should cite the page numbers for the chapter when this is written by a person other than the authors of the book. It is not strictly necessary to do this, but there is no harm in adopting such a procedure should you wish to do so. You should use the abbreviation 'pp.' rather than the word 'pages'.
For example:

> Whitfield, J. (2007) 'The historical context: policing and black people in post-war Britain', in Rowe, M. (ed.) *Policing Beyond Macpherson: Issues in Policing, Race and Society.* Cullompton, Devon: Willan Publishing, pp. 1–17.

Variations

* It is permissible to cite this type of reference in a slightly different way: the initials of the editor(s) could come first rather than follow the surname. An acceptable version of the above example would thus be:

> Whitfield, J. (2007) 'The historical context: policing and black people in post-war Britain', in M. Rowe (ed) *Policing Beyond Macpherson: Issues in Policing, Race and Society.* Cullompton, Devon: Willan Publishing, pp. 1–17.

* If the author of the chapter is also the author of the book, it is not necessary to cite the author's (or authors') name twice. Instead cite is as follows:

- Chapter author's name: surname first (followed by a comma), then initial (followed by a full stop).

- Year of publication (placed in brackets).

- 'Title of chapter' (in inverted commas followed by a comma and the word 'in').

- *Title of book* (in italics followed by a full stop).

- Place of publication (followed by a colon).

- Publisher.

For example:

> Becker, S. and Stephens, M. (1994) 'Introduction: Force is Part of the Service', in *Police Force, Police Service, Care and Control in Britain.* Basingstoke: Macmillan, pp. 1–9.

Articles

Journal articles should be cited as follows:

- Author's name: surname first (followed by a comma), then initials (followed by a full stop)

- Year of publication (placed in brackets)
- 'Title of article' (in inverted commas followed by a full stop)
- *Title of journal* (italics, and followed by a comma)
- Volume of the journal (abbreviated to Vol. followed by a comma)
- Issue number of the journal (abbreviated to No followed by a colon)
- Page numbers for the entire article (abbreviated to pp.)

For example:

Gilinskiy, Y. and Zazulin, G. (2001) 'Drugs in Russia: Situation, Policy and the Police'. *Police Practice and Research,* Vol. 2, No. 4: pp. 345–364.

Alternatively, it is acceptable to omit 'Vol.' and 'No.' and abbreviate the volume and issue citation to a numerical format: in the above example use 2(4), instead of 'Vol. 2, No. 4'. Follow your choice of format consistently.

It is also permissible to miss out the abbreviation 'pp.', placing a colon after the issue number and then citing the pages. In the case of the Gilinskiy and Zazulin article above, the citation would thus be '2(4): 345–364'.

If the journal uses dates as opposed to numbers to differentiate issues, you should follow that format: for example, 'Vol 2, April 2001'.

Newspaper articles should be cited as follows:

- Author's name (surname and initials, followed by a fullstop)
- Year of publication (placed in brackets)
- 'Title of article' (in inverted comas followed by a full stop)
- *Title of newspaper* (placed in italics followed by a comma)
- Date (but not year) of publication (followed by a colon)
- Page number(s)

For example:

Davies, N. (2008) 'The IPCC: a catalogue of delays, rejections and basic failures'. *The Guardian,* 25 February: pp. 6–7.

There are differing opinions as to whether it is necessary to cite the page number of a newspaper article, but there is no harm in doing so, since it enables a reader to more easily cross-check references of this nature.

Electronic copies of journal articles require no changes to referencing practice since they contain the same content as the hard copy of the article. These do not constitute Internet or online sources.

However, newspaper sources obtained online do require an acknowledgement to be made of this fact and the URL also needs to be included. They should be cited as for Internet sources (see below):

- Author's name (surname and initials, followed by a full stop)
- Year of publication (placed in brackets)

- 'Title of article' (in inverted commas followed by a full stop)

- *Name of newspaper* (in italics and followed by a full stop)

- The word 'Online' [placed in square brackets]

- Date (but not year) of publication (followed by a full stop)

- Date when material was accessed [placed in square brackets, using the words 'Accessed on' followed by date month year]

- URL

Internet sources

Internet sources should be referenced in a similar manner to articles. If material derived from a website is being referenced, it is necessary to cite the name of the website or the organisation responsible for it and the website address (which is known as the URL – the Universal Resource Locator). Additionally, it is necessary to refer to the date when the material was accessed from the website, since sources of this nature are subject to change – they may be revised, updated or even removed.

Internet sources should be cited as follows:

- Author's name (surname followed by initials and a full stop or, alternatively, the name of organisation responsible for the material)

- Year of publication (placed in brackets)

- *Title of material* (in italics followed by a full stop)

- Name of website/organisation responsible for the material (followed by a full stop)

- The word 'Online' [placed in square brackets]

- Date when material was accessed [placed in square brackets, using the words 'Accessed on' followed by date month year]

- URL

For example, if you were asked to evaluate current trends in sentencing policy you might utilise the following reference:

Worrall, J. (2008) *Government Fails to understand Sentencing Policy Mess.* NACRO. [Online] [Accessed on 18 December 2008] http://www.nacro.org.uk/templates/news/newItem.cfm/20081022 00.htm

Variations

Journal articles obtained from the Internet are cited in a similar manner to that referred to above, save that the title of the journal replaces the title of the website. Material of this nature is cited as follows:

- Author's name (surname followed by initials and a full stop)

- Year of publication (placed in brackets)

- 'Title of article' (placed in inverted commas followed by a full stop)

- *Title of journal* (in italics and followed by a comma)

- Volume and issue number (followed by a colon)

- Pages (abbreviated as pp.)

- The word 'Online' [placed in square brackets]

- Date when material was accessed [placed in square brackets, using the words 'Accessed on' followed by date month year]

- URL

Electronic databases

For references of this type, it is necessary to identify the database source (such as Electronic Library, DIALOG, SIRS), which precedes information relating to the specific database that has been consulted and date of retrieval (although the latter is not required for CD-ROM databases.

Electronic databases (such as CD-ROMs) should be cited as follows:

- Author's name (surname and initials followed by a full stop or, alternatively, name of organisation responsible for the material)

- 'Title of the material' (in inverted commas)

- A retrieval statement that lists the database source, followed by the name of the specific database that has been consulted, followed by the CD-ROM release date and, if applicable, item number.

Parliamentary sources

Parliamentary proceedings constitute a range of important sources, in particular for criminal justice studies. Key sources are listed below.

Parliamentary debates, statements and questions

Matters raised within both Houses of Parliament (in the form of debates, ministerial statements, oral statements and written answers) provide good source material, in particular for criminal justice policy. A Second Reading debate, for example, will enable you to ascertain the government's motives for proposing a piece of legislation and to gauge the attitude of the Opposition parties to this measure. All material of this nature is found in the Parliamentary publication *Hansard*, which is available in hard copy or online.

You should cite material discussed in either House of Parliament as follows:

- MP/Peer/Minister making the remark (surname and initial followed by a full stop and comma)

- An abbreviation for the House of Parliament in which the remark was made (HC for House of Commons and HL for House of Lords)

- The abbreviation Deb (short for debate)

- Date of the parliamentary session (in brackets)

- Full date when the remark was made (followed by a comma)

- The volume number of Hansard in which the remark is located (abbreviated as Vol. followed by a comma)

- The column number (Hansard uses columns rather than pages), abbreviated as Col.

- A letter indicating the format in which the remark was made when this was other than in a routine debate: WS (for a Westminster Hall debate – a debate that takes place away from the main chamber of the House of Commons); WS (for Written Statement); W (for Written Answer); O (for Oral Question); OS (for Oral Statement).

For example, if reference was being made to the defence mounted by the Home Secretary Jacqui Smith of the government's intention to extend the length of pre-trial detention from 28 to 42 days, her speech would be referenced as follows:

Smith, J., Speech to the House of Commons HC Deb (2007–08) 7 November 2007, Vol. 467, Col. 227–237.

For older versions of parliamentary debates, the series number should be cited after the abbreviation Deb.

Standing Committee reports

Both Houses of Parliament contain committees that consider legislative proposals (termed 'bills') in detail. Each committee is identified by a letter of the alphabet. Their proceedings are found in separate editions of *Hansard*. You should reference these as follows:

- MP/Peer/Minister making the remark (followed by a comma)

- SC Deb (short for Standing Committee Debate)

- Parliamentary session (in brackets)

- Full date of the debate (followed by a comma)

- The words 'Standing Committee' followed by the Committee's identifying letter (A, B, C, etc.) (followed by a comma)

- The title of the legislation under consideration (followed by a comma)

- Column number

Acts of Parliament

In the text of a piece of written work Acts of Parliament can be cited in one of two ways. If you have consulted an Act and are quoting or paraphrasing material from it you should refer to the date of the legislation and its full title. For example:

> The 1998 Crime and Disorder Act introduced Anti-social Behaviour Orders . . .

If you have not consulted the Act directly, but have found reference to it in a text, your citation should be as for citing material that you have not read first-hand (above). For example:

> The Police and Magistrates' Courts Act (1994, cited in Jones and Newburn, 1997 [no page number is required]) stated that the primary duty of a police authority was to secure an 'efficient and effective police force for its area'.

In the bibliography you should provide the details that are found on the front cover of the Act (or front page if you have accessed it electronically):

- Title of Act and year (year is not placed in brackets)
- Chapter number (chapter is abbreviated to a lower case 'c' and placed in brackets)
- Place of publication (followed by a colon)
- Publisher

For example:

> Youth Justice and Criminal Evidence Act 1999 (c 23) London: TSO

If the Act was accessed online, you should cite it in the bibliography as:

- Title of the Act and Year (year is not placed in brackets)
- *Title of website from where the Act was accessed* (placed in italics followed by a full stop)
- The word 'Online' [placed in square brackets]
- Date accessed [placed in square brackets, using the words 'Accessed on' followed by date month year]
- URL

Older Acts are cited in a slightly different manner:

- Title of Act and year (year is not placed in brackets)
- Year of reign of the monarch
- An abbreviation of the monarch's name

- The chapter number of the Act (chapter is abbreviated to a lower case 'c')

- Place of publication (followed by a colon)

- Publisher

For example:

Public Order Act 1936 (1 Edw.8 and 1 Geo.6 c6) London: HMSO

If the reference to the Act was found in a secondary source, you should fully cite the secondary source in the bibliography: using the above example relating to the 1994 Police and Magistrates' Courts Act, you would cite in the bibliography:

Jones, T. and Newburn, T. (1997) *Policing After the Act.* London: Policy Studies Institute.

Command papers

Command papers cover a wide range of documents that include Royal Commissions, White and Green Papers, *ad hoc* enquiries or reviews and, in relation to policing, inquiries conducted under the 1964 Police Act. These are primary sources (see Chapter 3) whose publication is ordered by the monarch. These are typically presented to Parliament by the Secretary of State of the government department that commissioned the work and are identified by a number that appears on the document.

In the reference in the text, the author can be either the government department that commissioned the command paper or (in the case of an inquiry) the person who chaired it. This is followed by the date of publication and page number.

Thus if you were citing from Sir William Macpherson's report into the Metropolitan Police Service's handling of the murder of Stephen Lawrence and referred to his belief that the investigation was 'marred by a combination of professional incompetence, institutional racism and a failure of leadership by senior officers' you could cite this in either of these two ways:

(Home Office, 1999: 317)
(Macpherson, 1999: 317)

In the bibliography, a command paper should be referenced as follows:

- Government department (or departments) responsible for the report *or* the name of the person who chaired the inquiry

- Year of publication (placed in brackets)

- *Title of command paper* (in italics followed by a comma)

- Command number (Command is usually now abbreviated as Cm with the number followed by a full stop)

- Place of publication (followed by a colon)

- Publisher

- Name of person who chaired the report (placed in brackets): this is omitted if s/he is the accredited author of the publication

Using the above example, the citation in the bibliography would be either:

> Home Office (1999) *The Stephen Lawrence Inquiry: Report of an Inquiry by Sir William Macpherson of Cluny*, Cm 4262. London: TSO (The Macpherson Report).

Or:

> Macpherson, Sir W. (1999) *The Stephen Lawrence Inquiry: Report of an Inquiry by Sir William Macpherson of Cluny*, Cm 4262. London: TSO.

Other publications that should be referenced in a similar way include reports from Parliamentary Select committees. Select Committees monitor the workings of all government departments and those that scrutinise the Ministry of Justice and Home Office are of particular importance to criminologists.

Select committee reports have an official number (HC for House of Commons and HL for House of Lords) that should be cited preceded by the number given by the committee to their report and the parliamentary session in which it was presented to Parliament. For example:

> Home Affairs Committee (2008) *A Surveillance Society?* Fifth Report, Session 2007–08, HC 58. London: TSO.

Online parliamentary proceedings

If the material is obtained online, this should be referred to by citing the online source after the initial reference to the person making the remark and the forum in which it was made.

- *Title of website from where the reference was obtained* (in italics followed by a full stop)

- The word 'Online' [placed in square brackets]

- Date accessed [placed in square brackets, using the words 'Accessed on' followed by date month year]

- URL

Other official sources

Criminologists may draw upon a range of other official sources. Some of these are included below.

Government department circulars

Circulars issued by government departments were initially designed to give guidance on how legislation should be enforced. Their scope has subsequently been extended to impose requirements on official agencies. Although these do not have the standing of legislation, they frequently compel obedience by the threat of some form of sanction that will be imposed for non-compliance.

These are referenced as follows:

- Government department issuing the circular

- Year of publication (placed in brackets)

- *Title of the circular* (in italics followed by a comma)

- The number of the circular (followed by a full stop)

- Place of publication (followed by a colon)

- Publisher

For example:

> Home Office (1983) *Manpower, Effectiveness and Efficiency in the Police Service*, Circular 114/83. London: Home Office.

Legal cases

The decisions made by judges (either in UK courts or the European Court of Justice) sometimes impose requirements on criminal justice agencies.

Reference should be made to:

- The two parties (plaintiff and defendant) involved in the case (placed in italics and separated by the letter 'v.')

- The date of the ruling (placed in square brackets)

- The number of the volume of the official Law Reports in which the ruling was reported

- The court where the judgment was made (abbreviated, e.g. AC for Court of Appeal, QB for Queen's Bench Division, or, before the accession of our current monarch, KB for King's Bench)

- The case number (formerly page number where the report started)

For example, an important statement regarding the doctrine of constabulary independence was delivered in the case of:

> *Fisher* v. *Oldham Corporation* [1930] 2 KB 364

If the decision relates to a judgment by the European Court of Human Rights, the government of the United Kingdom will be one of the two parties to the case.

Here you will cite:

- The two parties to the case

- The date of the ruling (placed in square brackets)

- The report series in which the judgment appears followed by the abbreviation EHRR (which stands for for European Human Rights Reports)

- The case number

For example, an important ruling relating to the state's duty to protect its citizens, which had implications for the actions undertaken by the police service towards those who perceived danger arising from the threat of criminal actions of another, was contained in:

Osman v. *United Kingdom* [1998] 29 EHRR 245

European Union proceedings

The Council of Ministers is the EU's supreme law-making body. References to the decisions of this body should be referenced as follows:

- *Title of report* (in italics)

- The last two digits of the year of publication

- The serial number of the publication

- The word 'final' (when the publication is the final draft of the proposal).

If the material is obtained online, the above citation should be followed by:

- *Title of website from where the reference was obtained* (in italics followed by a full stop)

- The word 'Online' [placed in square brackets]

- Date accessed [placed in square brackets, using the words 'Accessed on' followed by date month year]

- URL

Other sources of information

Information on which you base a piece of written work may also be obtained from other sources such as interviews, letters, e-mails and television programmes or radio broadcasts.
    Letters should be referenced as follows:

- Letter writer's name (surname followed by a comma and initials)

- Year of writing the letter (placed in brackets)

- 'Personal communication by letter' (followed by a full stop)

- Place from which the letter was sent (followed by a comma)

- Day and month (but not year) in which it was sent

E-mails: should be cited as for letters, substituting the statement 'Personal communication by e-mail' for 'Personal communication by letter'.

Interviews: should be cited as for letters, above, with 'Interview with author' replacing 'personal communication by letter' and the place where the interview took place should be included instead of 'Place from which the letter was sent'.

Television programme or radio broadcasts: should be referenced as follows:

- *Title of the programme/broadcast* (in italics)

- Date of screening/broadcasting (placed in brackets)

- Channel/radio station responsible for the programme (followed by a colon)

- Producer's name, if this information is available (initial followed by surname)

A variation of this relates to the format you utilised to view/hear the recording. If you used a DVD or a video recording of a television programme this should be stated:

- Title of DVD/video (which is likely to be the same as the title of the programme)

- Year the DVD/video was released (placed in brackets)

- Director (Initial followed by surname and followed by a full stop)

- Format: DVD or video [placed in square brackets]

- Place of distribution (if known, folowed by a colon)

- Company responsible for distributing the DVD/video.

Speeches should be referenced as follows, if you attended the event where the speech was presented:

- Speaker (surname followed by a comma and initial)

- Year when speech was given (placed in brackets)

- Title of speech (followed by a full stop)

- Venue where the speech was given (followed by a comma)

- Day and month (but not year) when the speech was made

If the speech was delivered at a conference, the title of the conference should be inserted following the title of the speech.

If you refer to a speech given when you were *not* a member of the audience, you should provide the same information, but add the words 'cited in' and then provide details of your source (book, journal article, newspaper article or the Internet), referencing this as given above depending on the type of source (such as newspaper or online).

Dissertations or postgraduate theses should be cited as follows:

- Author's surname (followed by a comma) and initial
- Year when the dissertation/thesis was submitted (placed in brackets)
- *Title of dissertation/thesis* (in italics and followed by a full stop)
- The degree for which the dissertation/thesis was presented
- The name of the university

Other referencing issues

Joint authorship

If there are a large number of authors (take three as your upper limit) in the text of your assignment the name of the first author is cited followed by the Latin abbreviation *et al.* (which means 'and others'). But in the bibliography include full details of *all* authors.

For example, if you were using the work written by Eamonn Carrabine and others in 2004, in the text of your assignment you would cite:

(Carrabine *et al.*, 2004)

And provide the full details in the bibliography:

Carrabine, E., Iganski, P., Lee, M., Plummer, K. and South, N. (2004) *Criminology: A Sociological Introduction.* London: Routledge.

Additionally, do not reorganise the authors' names alphabetically – use the order they have adopted.

Multiple citations by same author

It sometimes happens that you will cite an author who has written several pieces of work in the same year, especially so if the author is an organisation that publishes material on a regular basis (such as the Home Office).

Where this is the case, the different pieces of material should be distinguished both in the text of the essay and in the bibliography by a letter (a, b, c, etc., in lower case) that follows the year of publication (2008a, 2008b, etc.). These letters are attached to the author's work in the order it appears in *your* work and not in the chronological order in which it was published.

Citing material that you have not directly consulted

You may decide to use, either indirectly or as a direct quotation, a source that is cited in a work written by another author. This situation is likely to arise when the original source is old, not readily accessible, out of print or written in a language other than English.

If the original source is obtainable, it is preferable to use it. It could be that the author in whose work you found the information has misinterpreted what the original source stated, or has made some form of error that you will replicate if you do not consult the original source.

There is nothing inherently wrong (especially at undergraduate level) in citing ideas or opinions that have not been taken from an original source, but have been obtained from a work written by another author. However, it is important that this fact is acknowledged in the citation in the text of the written work.

The text of the written work should adopt this format:

- Surname of original author

- Year of publication of original source (followed by a comma)

- The words 'cited in' followed by reference to the work from which the information was obtained, cited in the manner described earlier (surname followed by a comma and the year of publication). However, you do not include the page number.

In the bibliography you should provide details *only* of the secondary source: the source you have actually consulted.

Anonymity

Occasionally a source being cited has no author. This is highly unlikely with regard to books and journals but does sometimes arise in connection with newspaper articles or Internet sources.

If this is the case, you may either cite 'Anonymous' in place of the author in the text of your work and at the beginning of the reference in the bibliography, and then continue with the reference as outlined above depending on the type of source, or you may use the organisation's name on whose website the article appeared in place of the author.

It is particularly important to be critical of sources of this nature. There may be very good reasons for a source wishing to remain anonymous (e.g. he or she may be a civil servant who is revealing to the public information gained in the course of government employment and does not wish to run the risk of imprisonment under the terms of the 1986 Official Secrets Act). However, there is also the possibility that the material lacks accuracy or authenticity: the author is putting forward statements or ideas that cannot be substantiated and may also be doing so for mischievous reasons such as to discredit a person or an organisation against whom they have a grudge.

Absence of a date of publication

This problem may arise in particular in connection with Internet sources.

Adopt the procedures given above but cite 'no date' in place of the year of publication, both in the text of your written work and in the bibliography.

Where a book has several editions

Key criminology texts are frequently updated and republished. These changes are incorporated into what becomes a new edition of the book.

If the text you are using contains no reference to editions, you may assume that it is the first edition, which requires no mention in your bibliography.

However, if the book refers to an edition number, you should include this in the bibliography:

- Author (surname followed by a comma and initial followed by a full stop)

- Year of publication (placed in brackets)

- *Title* (in italics followed by a comma)

- Edition (abbreviated as 1st ed, 2nd ed, etc. followed by a full stop)

- Place of publication (followed by a colon)

- Publisher

For example:
Reiner, R. (2000) *Politics of the Police*, 3rd ed. Oxford: Oxford University Press.

May I cite notes provided in a lecture?

Lecturers will give varying advice on this issue and it is important to consult with your lecturer to obtain his or her views.

If you do cite from a handout provided by a lecturer, you should reference this as follows:

- Lecturer's name (surname then, initial followed by a full stop)

- Year when you were given the material (placed in brackets)

- *Title of the lecture handout* (in italics followed by a full stop)

- For place of publication and publisher, cite the location of your university and its full name (as in Manchester: Manchester Metropolitan University) followed by a full stop

- The word 'handout' (followed by a comma)

- The date (omitting year) when the handout was distributed, the lecture number and the title of the unit (the latter placed in inverted commas) (for example, distributed on 22 October in lecture 9 for the unit 'Development of Policing')

If you cite an author whose work was referred to in the lecture handout, cite this as you would for any other source you have not consulted first-hand, using the format referred to above in the text of your work and in the bibliography.

Other issues relating to written work

Footnotes

Footnotes are used to amplify an issue that has been raised in the text of a piece of written work. The use of a footnote may be preferred to an insertion in the body of the text, for reasons such as the technical nature of the additional material, or a desire not to complicate the text with information that may interrupt its flow. Where used they should be brief and to the point.

Appendices

An appendix (or appendices) can provide detailed information that is not appropriate to include in the text of a piece of written work because of its excessive length or complexity.

It is highly unlikely that appendices will be required in essays at under-graduate level, but they may be relevant to more detailed undergraduate work such as projects or dissertations. If a series of interviews have been conducted in relation to a piece of written work, for example, an appendix may usefully contain the transcripts of these interviews.

There are two important considerations relating to appendices:

- You should make sparing use of them and only employ them if the information they contain is integral to the work that is being presented. For example, an essay on contemporary crime prevention policy will make reference to the 1998 Crime and Disorder Act but it is not necessary to place a photocopied version of this legislation in an appendix.

- You must ensure that the contents or findings given in an appendix are fully incorporated into the text of the written work and are not used as a substitute for a discussion and evaluation of the ideas that it contains. For example, if a transcript of a series of interviews is provided in an appendix, it is essential that the text of the written work makes reference to these interviews and the opinions or ideas that they express.

Preparing a piece of written work

Regardless of the format in which your assignment is required (essay, case study, etc.) there are some common practices which should be applied to written work.

- Ensure that you understand the question or problem that has been set: at the outset make a brief list of points that will guide your answer and give it structure as well as content.

- Compile a list of sources you wish to consult (at undergraduate level these are usually contained in the course's unit outline).

- Make notes from your chosen sources. These notes should be relatively brief and focus on analysis rather than on factual content.

- Construct a more detailed plan for your answer, based upon the reading you have carried out.

Common questions related to written work

A number of questions or problems related to written work frequently occur.

How many sources should I consult?

There is no definitive answer to this question. The number of sources available will relate to a series of considerations that include the popularity of the topic for researchers and the extent of the debate that it engenders.

However, at undergraduate level, as a rough guide, year one work should rely on around six to eight sources and this number should progressively rise as you progress through your course of study.

There are no books in the library

Although university libraries frequently purchase multiple copies of key texts (and also utilise procedures such as limited or short-term loan) it is frequently the case that supply does not match demand, especially when a number of students are writing a piece of work to the same deadline.

There are ways round this problem. You can purchase copies of key texts or use journal articles, either in hard copy or electronic format, which will be more readily available than books. You should also be prepared to 'shop around' with your sources – if sources you wish to consult are not available, others that *are* accessible may be equally useful for your purpose. Lecturers who prepare course outlines typically include a wide range of sources for particular topics to cover an eventuality such as this.

Can I base my essay on material from the internet?

This depends very much on the nature of material that is taken from the internet. If the internet is being used to obtain material that constitutes secondary sources (see Chapter 3), it is unwise to be overly reliant on this. As an approximate guide, no more than 20–25 per cent of secondary source material should derive from the internet and preference should be given to standard academic material from books and journals.

However, this balance may legitimately change if the internet is being used to access primary material (for example, reports written by or for the Home Office or Ministry of Justice).

6 Studying criminology in higher education

The aims of this chapter are:

- To discuss the main methods used in higher education to deliver courses in criminology.

- To consider the main methods of assessment that are employed in higher education to assess a student's progress in criminology courses.

- To provide an understanding of the main ways through which methods of assessment are delivered in higher education.

- To discuss the construction of undergraduate research (typically a project or a dissertation).

- To give a brief summary of some of the careers available for criminology graduates.

Teaching methods

Higher education utilises a wide range of teaching methods to deliver units in criminology, although students will not necessarily encounter all of them in one institution.

Lectures

Lectures are a time-honoured way to impart knowledge and understanding and remain very widely used in higher education. They consist of one person (or several if team-teaching is employed) talking about a topic of which they have specialist knowledge, with students taking notes. Lectures commonly last for one hour and a range of supplementary devices (especially visual aids) are likely to be used to help the learning process.

The main aim of a lecture is to make learners aware of the key issues that relate to the topic that is under discussion. They are designed to inspire students to delve into the subject matter for themselves, thereby broadening their knowledge and understanding of it.

The do's and don'ts of lectures

As a student you should:

- Come adequately prepared (pen and paper, or laptop if there are facilities for using it) to take notes. Some lecturers are willing to have their lectures recorded – but their permission must be sought before doing this.

- Focus on the analytical or interpretative aspects of the lecture – descriptive material, facts, figures and details should be read from texts.

As a student you should not:

- Be a passive observer. Do not sit back in the belief that turning up to listen is sufficient. It isn't – you will forget most of what has been said before you leave the lecture room.

- Substitute note-taking with the use of a highlighter pen. Often lecturers make available outlines of their lectures in advance. Those who do this may regard it as a means of imparting some basic factual information, or as a way to outline the key analytical issues of a topic, and will then use the lecture to amplify and add to the material that has been provided. It is good practice for students to read material related to a lecture where this has been provided in advance. This enables you to appreciate the key issues and to pinpoint areas of the discussion that are adding to the material provided. Sitting in a lecture with a highlighter is a waste of time – this can be done anywhere without need to attend the lecture.

- Waste time writing up or typing out lecture notes. Lectures provide the key to unlocking the main issues and complexities of a particular topic. You should further your knowledge by additional research of your own rather than going over ground that has already been covered.

Tutorials/seminars/classes

These terms are often used synonymously. Technically a tutorial is a one-to-one session between a student and a lecturer whereas seminars or classes involve a group of students in discussion with a lecturer.

The aim of sessions of this nature is to enable students to test their knowledge and understanding of a particular topic. Typically the topic will have been the subject of a lecture and the lecturer's unit outline will provide a question or set of questions (accompanied by relevant reading) that will form the basis of the seminar discussion.

Do's and don'ts of classes

As a student you should:

- Attend a class adequately prepared. It is essential that you have studied at least some of the reading that has been suggested.

- Be prepared to speak. The ability to talk in public is a key transferable skill that is important in the workplace. Getting used to doing this in the context of a class discussion is a useful vocational practice.

As a student you should not:

- Regard the class as a second lecture and expect the lecturer to do all the talking. Classes are designed as opportunities for students to air their views and opinions and not for the lecturer to repeat what has been discussed in a lecture.

- Rely on other students to do the talking. The essence of classes is that they are interactive and that everyone in the room can learn from each other.

Methods of assessment

The performance of students in higher education is assessed on a regular basis in order to chart their progress on their course of study. Ultimately the class of degree obtained by a student is based upon tutors' assessments for a wide range of units that have been studied. Assessment may take various forms, including formative, summative and peer methods of assessment.

Formative assessment

Formative assessment consists of work that is formally submitted to a tutor but does not contribute towards the mark for the unit with which it is associated. Typically formative assessment will consist of a brief essay, an essay plan or a dissertation outline whereby a student's knowledge, understanding and the direction the work will take can be ascertained, strengths and weaknesses identified and bad practice eliminated. In other words, formative assessment is a mechanism for a tutor to provide feedback on a wide range of aspects affecting a student's academic progress.

Summative assessment

Summative assessment consists of material that is formally submitted and the mark that is awarded contributes to the overall grade the student gains for the unit with which it is associated. Summative assessment may take a number of formats including various forms of written work, examinations or oral presentations.

As with formative assessment, feedback by tutors is an essential aspect of the exercise (whatever form it takes) in order to explain why a particular mark has been given and to make recommendations for further improvement. Feedback on written work is typically provided on the work itself (often on a pre-formatted coursework feedback form), supplemented by discussions between a student and member of staff giving more detailed feedback or elucidating the written comments that have been initially made.

Some universities also make use of generic feedback in which the markers make a number of generalised comments based upon their reading of a batch of essays; this supplements the individual feedback given to students. Many universities also have mechanisms to provide for feedback on a student's examination performance.

Peer assessment

Peer assessment entails students having an input into assessing work presented by their fellow students. This process is frequently associated with oral presentations and group-based projects, and also with formative assessment. There are obvious difficulties with peer assessment: it may reflect a student's popularity (although anonymous review may help to circumvent this problem) and the quality of feedback may be less detailed or weaker than that provided by a professional tutor. For such reasons it is unlikely to contribute significantly to the student's overall assessment grade for a specific unit of study.

However, peer assessment does enable students to judge their own performance in relation to others working at a similar academic level. It also provides the tutor with feedback from students that is helpful in assessing their progress – for example, student feedback on a group-based project enables all of those responsible for a piece of work to comment on the contributions made by their colleagues and may help the tutor to identify those whose commitment and work rate needs to be addressed.

Mechanisms of assessment

Work that is presented for the forms of assessment referred to above can be delivered in a number of formats.

Oral presentations

Oral presentations entail a student or a group of students leading a discussion of a topic. This topic may be pre-selected by the unit tutor or the students may have chosen it themselves. Typically the students will present their findings to a tutor and other students in their class. An oral presentation is likely to last between 15 and 20 minutes and in many ways is like a mini-lecture. Ten or so minutes are allocated for questions at the end of the presentation. Although the discussion is presented orally, use should be made of visual aids – PowerPoint or flipcharts – in order to put the material across to the audience.

The quality of oral presentations is judged according to the extent to which the students display mastery of the subject matter and are able to put this across to the audience. The extent to which questions put to the presenters are successfully answered forms an important aspect of assessment.

Group-based work

Although much work undertaken by students for assessment in higher educa-tion will consist of individually prepared material, group-based assignments are relatively common. Working with others to complete a designated task is an important skill that has considerable relevance to the workplace.

Good organisation is the key to effective delivery of group-based material, whether presented orally or in the form of a written project. The task needs to be broken down to a number of manageable aspects, giving each member of the group responsibility for the completion of a task that contributes to the overall assignment. Allocating work may also enable a member (or mem-bers) of the group to demonstrate leadership skills.

A common difficulty with group-based work is that members may not find it easy to work effectively as a unit. This problem is more likely to occur when the composition of a group is determined by an 'outsider' such as a university tutor rather than through a process of student self-selection. Difficulties of this nature are not uncommon in a work-based setting, and meeting and addressing such issues is a useful vocational experience. Commonly agreed goals and the setting of deadlines for the completion of tasks will help the group to gel and achieve its objectives.

It is also usually the case that group-based projects contain an element of individual assessment, which may help to address concerns that some mem-bers of the group have worked harder than others.

Written work

All university courses require the presentation of written coursework. This may be handed in at specific times during the university year in order for a student's progress to be monitored and to provide feedback that identifies good and bad aspects of a student's work and enables him or her to improve their subsequent performance. Written work assumes various forms: essays, reports, case studies and book reviews. Guidance on the preparation of vari-ous types of written work is found in Chapter 5.

Examinations

Examinations are widely used in higher education, typically alongside other means of assessment. The purpose of an examination is to test the student's ability to apply knowledge that has been acquired in the study of a particular unit to specific problems or issues. These problems may be made known in advance (a *seen* examination) or be presented on the day of the examination (*unseen* examination).

How to prepare for an exam

Exams are often regarded as daunting exercises in which a student sets out to cram in as many facts as possible relating to a particular topic. Factual information has its place in an answer, but exams primarily seek to test a student's knowledge and understanding of a topic. This has ideally been gained during the study of a particular unit rather than being something that can be learned at the last minute.

How to answer exam questions

Bear in mind a number of issues when answering exam questions:

- Ensure that your answer is academically balanced, presenting all sides of the argument. Key words in exam questions guide this approach, such as *analyse, evaluate, discuss, to what extent do you agree with the statement that . . .* ? These indicate that the examiner is expecting an answer that considers all aspects of the issue that is under discussion, as opposed to a one-sided account.

- Referencing is an important feature of a good answer. References should be provided for key ideas and quotations. These may not be quite as precise as those included in assessed work when you have a copy of the text available (especially regarding page numbers and the volume and issue number of journals) but reference should be made to key authors and year of publication of the main texts.

Do's and don'ts of examinations

As a student you should:

- Read the examination instructions (rubric) carefully. There may be a compulsory question that you have to answer, which may count for more marks than other questions. The exam paper may contain sections and you are required to answer a question (or questions) from each section.

- Spend some time on preparation, jotting down a few key points that you wish to discuss in your answer to the question.

- Manage your time effectively, ensuring that you devote about the same amount of time to each of the questions that you answer (assuming that each question carries the same amount of marks).

- Answer the question that has been set for discussion.

As a student you should not:

- Devote an unreasonable amount of time to preparing an answer plan. If there are 45 minutes in which to answer a question it is not wise to spend 25 of them writing out a complicated essay plan, since it is not likely that the final answer will convey much additional information to that contained in the plan.

- Spend a disproportionate length of time on a question that appeals to you, to the detriment of other questions. For example, in a two-hour exam a student who devotes 1 hour 50 minutes to one question and only 10 minutes to the others) runs a high risk of failing (or perhaps scraping a pass), even if the answer that has occupied his or her attention for most of the exam scores a very high mark.

- Adopt a 'kitchen sink' approach to a question, throwing in every piece of information that relates to the topic under discussion, whether of relevance to the question or not. Focus precisely on the issues that the examiner wishes to see discussed.

- Write in note form. If you are running out of time towards the end of an exam, it is acceptable to finish off in this way, but avoid the excessive use of this style of presentation, since note format is unlikely to be sufficiently analytical.

Preparing a piece of research

Most undergraduate courses in criminology will expect students to embark on some form of research of their own, and projects and dissertations are common features of years two and three of undergraduate programmes. Commonly in research of this nature you are able to select the topic that you wish to explore.

Do's and don'ts of undertaking an undergraduate research project

As a student you should:

- Select an area of criminology that interests you, and is derived from material you have studied in your course.

- Carry out some exploratory reading related to this topic that will acquaint you with the key themes and ideas that you may wish to investigate.

- Narrow your subject down to a specific criminological issue or question that will form the focus of your research.

- Break your research topic or question down into a number of areas – these will form the draft chapters of your work.

- Compile a list of key sources that you wish to consult.

- Commence your reading and note-taking.

- Write the project up as you go – do not seek to complete the research before starting the writing as you may end up with a mountain of notes and the task will then appear insurmountable.

As a student you should not:

- Choose a very broad topic that is unmanageable. If you do this it is likely that your work, at best, will be overly superficial, adopting a descriptive rather than analytical approach.

- Define a topic that lacks a precise focus, typically one that asks a series of questions. This will complicate your research as it is not clear to anyone (yourself included) what exactly you wish to write about. The best way of avoiding this is to crystallise your research at the very outset into a theme or research question and then to break this down into a number of sub-themes that will constitute your chapter headings.

- Select a very narrow topic, especially one on which there is very little readily available information. Although at final year undergraduate level it is useful to conduct field research, it is necessary to put this into context by consulting established literature that you will be expected to analyse.

Methodological issues and literature review

Projects or dissertations require a statement relating to methodology (the methods you are using to construct your research) and a review of key literature. Depending on the length of the work, these sections may be included in the introduction or constitute separate chapters or sections.

Methodology

At undergraduate level it is acceptable that projects or dissertations are constructed from documentary research, although it is common that students writing material of this nature (especially at final year undergraduate level) will conduct some field research of their own.

The methodology section should contain a statement of the methods you have selected to compile your research and a rationale for choosing to conduct it through these methods. You should display an awareness of the strengths and weaknesses of the methods you have chosen and a rationale for not using other methods that would conceivably have been of relevance to the chosen topic.

More detailed guidance regarding methodology is provided in Chapter 4.

Literature review

A literature review is most appropriate to projects and dissertations and to work carried out in connection with postgraduate studies. It is thus most unlikely that you will need to undertake one in the early stages of your career in higher education. Nonetheless, some basic guidance regarding a literature review is useful even to those commencing their studies of criminology.

A literature review is an important tool through which the author of a proposed study gathers material that is relevant to a project or dissertation. It also demonstrates to those who will read and assess the assignment that key literature associated with the topic has been consulted and that the author has a good level of appreciation of the main themes and arguments relating to the chosen topic of research. At undergraduate level it is not expected that a student will have consulted all relevant literature – but it is important that key works are considered to give an overall impression that the author is the master of the chosen research topic.

Writing a literature review

When writing a literature review, the aim is to construct a balance between providing a fairly superficial list of relevant works (which may amount to little more than an annotated reading list) and a detailed chapter-by-chapter account of key works (which will be too lengthy and is likely to be insufficiently analytical).

A literature review should contain an abbreviated account of the main material related to the chosen field of study. This brief account should include items such as:

- The key arguments and main findings that appear in the literature: what the authors have to say about the topic.

- The methodology used by the authors on which their conclusions were reached.

- How your own proposed research relates to the reviewed literature. Perhaps you wish to test the validity of findings contained in existing material, or you may have identified gaps in existing knowledge that you wish to fill, or you intend to employ a different methodology from that used in existing research to see whether this produces a different slant on the topic.

It also needs to be organised in a coherent fashion. One way of doing this is to group the material thematically: that is, to identify the key themes of your chosen research topic and to discuss the main literature that relates to these themes. These themes may include considerations such as:

- The general context that is relevant to the chosen area of study.

- The specific topic or issue that you wish to investigate.

- The key findings contained in the literature you have consulted. It is often the case that key studies put forward divergent views, opinions and conclusions relating to a particular topic, which can form the basis of the way you organise your literature review.

For an extended piece of work, these themes may be contained under separate headings. Otherwise they can be presented in an essay-type discussion in which the paragraphs are organised around the key themes that you have identified in the literature.

Careers related to criminology qualifications

Although the transferable skills that are found in any degree course have obvious usefulness to the world of work, the subject matter of degree courses in criminology has vocational relevance. Those studying criminology frequently find work in the key criminal justice agencies (whose work is discussed in Chapter 2) and also in a wide range of public, private and voluntary sector organisations whose role in criminal justice affairs has expanded considerably in recent years, embracing activities such as crime prevention, community safety and work performed in connection with offenders in the community.

The police service

Recruitment into the police service is handled by individual forces. The basic criteria for appointment in England and Wales are that an applicant should be:

- Aged between 18½ years and 55 years (police forces may slightly vary the age limit).

- A British, Irish or a Commonwealth citizen, EC/EEA national, or foreign national whose stay in this country is not subject to any restriction.

- Of good character. Persons with minor convictions or cautions are not automatically excluded from entry to the police service. However, details of spent convictions, as defined by the Rehabilitation of Offenders Act, must be disclosed.

- Physically fit and healthy.

- Possess a full driving licence (or be in the process of learning to drive).

There are no formal educational qualifications required of a police officer, although all recruits have to pass a standard entry test: the Police Initial Recruitment Test (PIRT) in England and Wales or the Standard Entry Test in Scotland. Prior practical experience of police work is not essential, although a record of involvement with community groups or activities will be viewed positively.

Prospective entrants complete a detailed application form and medical questionnaire, and are assessed and scored against entrance criteria. The application form seeks to assess the applicant's capabilities in a number of key areas, including communication and problem-solving skills, literacy, the ability to work both independently and as part of a team, and respect for diversity.

Those who pass this aspect of the recruitment process proceed to an assessment centre where they undertake assessment tests and are formally interviewed. Successful recruits subsequently undergo fitness and medical tests, following which appointments are made subject to satisfactory references and security clearance. There is, however, often a delay between appointments being made and employment being secured.

All police officers commence their careers at the rank of constable. A probationary period lasts two years, during which time they learn the basics of policing, participating in activities such as residential training courses and attachment to an experienced tutor constable. Those who pass the probationary period are confirmed in the rank of constable. Following the successful completion of probation they are eligible to seek promotion. The rank structure in England and Wales is (in ascending order) sergeant, inspector, chief inspector, superintendent, chief superintendent, assistant chief constable, deputy chief constable and chief constable. The Metropolitan Police Service has a variation of this, whereby the most senior ranks are filled by (in descending order) Commissioner, Deputy Commissioner and Assistant Commissioner.

A number of national initiatives (such as the Accelerated Promotion Scheme for Graduates and the High Potential Development Scheme) have facilitated the rapid promotion of high calibre entrants to the police service in order that they can move speedily to senior management positions. A revised version of the HPDS is now administered by the National Police Improvement Agency for officers with the potential and commitment to reach senior levels in the service. All police officers, including probationers, are eligible to apply for this scheme, which is not limited to graduates.

The Crown Prosecution Service

The CPS operates a Legal Trainee Scheme which is available to those who are in their final year of study for a law degree or who have completed the Legal Practice Course or the Bar Vocational Course. The scheme includes 12-month pupillages (for barristers) and 24-month training contracts (for solicitors). Trainee solicitors will serve between six and eight months in private practice. Pupils may spend the entire one-year period with the CPS but will spend one month in Chambers to gain knowledge of the independent Bar.

The application process includes completion of an application form and verbal reasoning tests (both available online), the presentation of a written case study and an oral presentation and interview. Vacancies for the Legal Trainee Scheme are advertised one year in advance of the start date in October.

The probation service

Probation officers in England and Wales commence their careers in the service as a trainee probation officer (TPO). They must be at least 20 years of age. The academic background of TPOs is varied, and includes those with first degrees and (in the case of those over 25 years of age) those who possess no formal academic qualifications. Communication skills, the ability to relate to others, the capacity to work as part of a team and competence in problem-solving are key requirements for entrants to the probation service.

Trainee probation officers are required to undertake a two-year Diploma in Probation Studies. This qualification is a mixture of work-based practice and academic study. Successful completion of this course results in the trainee becoming a qualified probation officer for which a minimum age of 22 is required.

For the purposes of recruitment and selection, the 42 probation areas of England and Wales are divided into nine separate consortia. Vacancies are usually advertised in the Spring and those who are accepted as TPOs take up their posts in October or November.

The prison service

Most prisons in England and Wales are in the public sector, operated by Her Majesty's Prison Service. Those seeking employment in the prison service can do so either as prison officers or as instructors.

Prison officers are normally expected to possess five GCSE passes including maths and English, although they may as an alternative take the prison service entry test. Applicants must be aged between 18 and 57 and meet requirements relating to fitness and health. They must not have a criminal record and will be required to undergo a security check. Prison instructors are responsible for supervising and training prisoners and are required to possess a recognised apprenticeship in their trade and have work experience amounting to around five years.

Vacancies in the prison service in England and Wales are usually advertised in JobCentres.

The prison service has a hierarchal structure ranging from junior prison officers to prison governors. A fast-track option is available: a two-year programme that embraces the technical, policy and legal dimensions that are involved in running prisons. It is delivered through a mixture of coaching, mentoring and training and provides direct experience of the prison environment. Those who successfully complete it become senior operational managers, typically a deputy governor of a large prison, or a governor of a smaller one. The programme is available to those with managerial experience outside the prison service as well as to those employed within it.

Her Majesty's Courts Service

This agency was created by the 2003 Courts Act and commenced work in 2005. It is responsible for the administration and support for the Court of Appeal, the High Court, Crown Courts, magistrates' courts, county courts and the probation service.

A wide range of career opportunities exist in this agency, including administrative assistants, administrative officers, bailiffs, court ushers and court clerks. The qualifications for these posts vary.

Details of vacancies and the qualifications they require can be found on the HMCS website (www.hmcourts-service.gov.uk).

A career in law

A degree in criminology or criminal justice studies is not itself a qualification to secure entry to the legal profession, but graduates whose first degree is not in law may undertake a one-year conversion course, either the Common

Professional Examination or the Graduate Diploma in Law. These courses are virtually identical in content and equip those who successfully complete them to progress on to the Legal Practice Course (to train as a solicitor) or the Bar Vocational Course (to train as a barrister).

The Common Professional Examination and the Graduate Diploma in Law are one-year courses. There is an expectation that students will undertake 45 hours of lectures, classes and private study each week for a period of 36 weeks. A lower second class honours degree (2.2) is the minimum entry requirement for either of these courses. Applications for enrolment are made through the CPE/Diploma in Law Courses Application Board during the period November–February.

Volunteering in the criminal justice system

There are opportunities for those interested in or actively seeking careers in the criminal justice system to obtain useful experience by working in a voluntary capacity. These opportunities include the following.

The Special Constabulary

Special constables are volunteer police officers. Persons aged between 18½ and 55 years of age are eligible to join the Special Constabulary. Prospective volunteers are required to complete an application form, attend for a day or half-day at an assessment centre (where activities undertaken will include a written test – the Police Initial Recruitment Test) and pass a fitness test. Background checks will also be made, although those with minor criminal convictions may still be eligible for appointment.

Recruitment is undertaken by individual police forces, who should be contacted in respect of applications. The upper age limit is subject to slight variation between forces.

Youth Offending Teams (YOT)

Volunteers may undertake YOT work such as mentoring of young offenders. YOTs were created by the 1998 Crime and Disorder Act. Their personnel is drawn from a range of criminal justice agencies and they perform various functions in connection with young offenders.

Applications to work as a volunteer should be made to your local YOT or to your local authority. A Criminal Records Bureau check will be conducted.

Youth Offender Panels (YOP)

These panels include voluntary members of the local community who are given a key role in the requirements imposed on young offenders.

YOPs were introduced under the 1999 Youth Justice and Criminal Evidence Act. Persons aged 10–17 who are first-time offenders, who plead guilty and whose crime is of a minor nature, will receive a court order – the referral order. This triggers the summoning of a YOP whose role (in conjunction with offender and victim) is to draw up a contract that identifies actions that will enable the young person to make amends for his or her offence.

Each panel contains two community representatives who volunteer their services and are subsequently trained to perform this work.

YOPs are supervised by the Youth Offending Team for the area, and applications to serve on a YOP should be made to your local YOT.

7 Taking it further exercises

Chapter 1

Taking it further 1

Jeremy Bentham was an influential English thinker (a moral philosopher) whose views on crime and its prevention were inspired by classicist thought. Identify the key reforms with which he was associated and indicate how these relate to classicist criminology.

In this essay you would:

- Identify the key reforms with which Bentham was associated, namely, the reform of the penal code, the reform of the system of policing and the reform of prisons.

You would then develop your arguments by discussing:

- The key existing characteristics of the areas of the criminal justice system that the Benthamites wished to alter.

- The content of the reforms that were put forward.

- How and why these reforms were underpinned by classicist criminology – what specific principles associated with classicist criminology were these reforms designed to advance?

For example, the section on the reform of the penal code could be constructed around the key points that include:

- Classicists were opposed to the contemporary penal code in Britain which provided the death penalty for a very wide range of offences.

- They wished to adjust penalties to reflect the seriousness of the crime, the main thrust of their proposals being directed at removing the death penalty from a wide range of offences and substituting less severe penalties.

- They advocated this reform in the belief that the application of the criminal law was frequently disregarded because the penalties it prescribed were seen as unreasonable.

- This reflected the classicist concern that the punishment should fit the crime and their support for a criminal justice system that operated in a consistent manner and was not operated according to the whim of the judge or magistrate who was trying a case.

- This reform was underpinned by the principle of general deterrence: the belief that the certainty that those who had committed an offence would be convicted and sentenced would enable citizens to make informed decisions not to offend.

Finally, you should present a conclusion that summarises, on the basis of information you have presented, Bentham's contribution to the advancement of classicist criminology in the UK.

Taking it further 2

What do you regard as being the main differences between classicist and positivist explanations of criminal behaviour?

In this essay you would:

- Discuss the concept of free will (classicism) versus determinism (positivism).

- Compare the focus on the crime that had been committed (classicism) as opposed to a focus on the offender who had committed the crime (positivism).

- Contrast a belief that offenders should be punished (classicism) as opposed to a belief that offenders should be treated (positivism).

- Consider how the contrasting objectives of punishment versus treatment had implications regarding the notion of deterrence and the importance attached to the reform of the criminal justice system as the appropriate way to respond to crime (classicism).

- Contrast a reliance on philosophical speculation as the basis of their views (classicism) as opposed to a reliance on scientific investigation as the basis of their opinions (positivism).

- Present a conclusion that summarises, on the basis of information you have presented, the key differences, and also point to any similarities that you detect.

Taking it further 3

'Criminals commit crime because they are "born bad" – it is in their biological make-up to behave in this way.' Examine arguments for and against this view.

In this essay you would:

- Discuss the 'nature versus nurture' debate.

- Provide an account of the evidence that suggests that criminals are 'born bad': this would embrace biological explanations for crime spanning Lombroso to the arguments relating to the existence of a criminal gene.

- Consider alternative explanations as to why crime might 'run in families', which might include social and economic deprivation experienced by successive generations, bad parenting or deficient role modelling. You would not be expected to identify every possible alternative explanation but it is important that those that are put forward are linked to criminological schools of thought as opposed to being based on common sense-type generalisations.

- Present a conclusion that will, on the basis of evidence presented earlier in your essay, compare the strengths and weaknesses of both approaches, and might suggest that when a large number of circumstances exist that could affect an individual's behaviour, it is impossible to hold one of them to be solely responsible for that person's conduct.

Taking it further 4

Outline the key factors that Sigmund Freud and Hans Eysenck contributed towards an understanding of criminal behaviour.

In this essay you would:

- Argue that Sigmund Freud was especially concerned to explain how the early parent–child relationship shaped the formation of sexuality and gender in adulthood: however, his ideas could be adapted to explain criminal behaviour.

- Assert that Freud was concerned with the way in which the adult personality developed: here you would discuss the *id*, *superego* and *ego* – the three aspects of the human mind.

- Evaluate the views advanced by Freud and subsequent psychologists as to whether behaviour was fashioned by an overdeveloped or an underdeveloped superego.

- Conclude this section by arguing that Freud's views were deterministic and he viewed crime as the irrational consequence of conflicts occurring within the subconscious mind of the individual.

- Discuss the views of Hans Eysenck that personality is fashioned by biological and social factors rather than childhood experiences.

- Argue that Eysenck's ideas on the criminal personality were a synthesis of research conducted by Jung (who discussed extrovertism and introvertism) and Pavlov (who examined excitation and inhibition).

- Analyse Eysenck's belief that a criminal was thus viewed as being typically extrovert, with an enhanced desire for stimulation and a lower level of inhibitory controls. This made for a personality that was difficult to condition and hence to socialise, and was directed to the pursuit of excitement and pleasure regardless of the punishment that may arise in consequence.

- Consider Eysenck's later views that there were two components to extrovertism – impulsiveness and sociability – and that the former was of most importance in determining an individual's behaviour. This suggests that there is a link between offending and impulsiveness.

- Present a conclusion in which, on the basis of material presented in your essay, you would summarise the contribution made by Freud and Eysenck to an understanding of criminal behaviour, assess the strengths and weaknesses of their approaches, and evaluate their claims as important criminological figures.

> ### Taking it further 5
>
> For what reasons did the Chicago School suggest that crime and delinquency was a constant feature of certain urban locations?

In this essay you would:

- Present the general arguments put forward by the Chicago School locating crime as a constant feature of the 'zone of transition'.

- Explain the meaning given by the Chicago School to the term 'social disorganisation'.

- Put forward an account of the key features of a socially disorganised area. These would include rapid population changes, the existence of a wide range of social problems, and the inability of institutions such as the family or church to effectively uphold society's conventional values.

- Provide an explanation as to why socially disorganised areas were prone to crime, in particular pointing to the absence of an established set of values to guide the actions of those who lived there and the ineffectiveness of informal methods of control to shape communal behaviour, hence a reliance on outside agencies such as the police to maintain law and order.

- Present a conclusion in which, on the basis of material presented in your essay, you assess both the strengths and weaknesses of the views of the Chicago School concerning the location of crime and delinquency in the zone of transition.

Taking it further 6

Strain theory has been criticised for making assumptions that a high level of agreement existed within society about desirable objectives, and a tendency to ignore the deviancy of those who did not suffer from inequality.

A more significant objection, however, concerned whether social strain did, in fact, give rise to deviant subcultures that indicated a rejection of society's mainstream values.

Evaluate the concepts of:

- techniques of neutralisation (Sykes and Matza, 1957)

- subterranean values (Matza and Sykes, 1961)

- drift (Matza, 1964)

in connection with the assertion that social strain resulted in the emergence of deviant subcultures that indicated a rejection of the mainstream values of society.

In this essay you would:

- Examine arguments that linked social strain to the emergence of deviant subcultures.

- Outline what Sykes and Matza understood by the term 'techniques of neutralisation'. In brief, this alleged that delinquents *were* committed to society's mainstream values but justified their personal actions that were in breach of them by applying a concept of mitigating circumstances as an explanation for their behaviour. This was referred to as the 'techniques of neutralisation' that sought to explain or excuse delinquent juvenile behaviour and thus offset the negative views that society might otherwise adopt towards such action.

- Provide some examples of arguments based on these techniques: Sykes and Matza identified five of these techniques: a denial of responsibility for an action; a denial that injury had been caused to a victim; a denial that the victim was, in fact, a victim, an assertion that those who condemned the action were hypocritical; and seeking to explain a delinquent action by reference to higher loyalties (such as to friends or a gang). You could usefully amplify these techniques with some specific examples of your own: for example, the car thief who argues that as the victim was insured there was no harm done.

- Outline what Matza and Sykes understood by the term 'subterranean values'. This suggested that the values underpinning juvenile delinquency were not totally dissimilar from attitudes embraced by law-abiding, conforming members of society.

- Amplify the characteristics ascribed to delinquent behaviour (namely the search for excitement or thrills, a disdain for routinised work in favour of 'making easy money' and aggression) and explain how these were also embraced by law-abiding people. In brief, Matza and Sykes argued that these values were also espoused by respectable middle class persons, in particular in connection with their pursuit of leisure, and thus coexisted alongside society's dominant values. These 'alternative' values were labelled 'subterranean', meaning values 'which are in conflict or in competition with other deeply held values but which are still recognised and accepted by many' (Matza and Sykes, 1961: 716) and in this sense were 'akin to private as opposed to public morality' (Matza and Sykes, 1961: 716).

- Emphasise that the concept of subterranean values implied that there was thus no separate delinquent subculture: delinquents adopted one aspect of the dominant values of society but their behaviour was more regularly governed by them. This view also accounted for delinquency not committed by lower class juveniles, since 'some forms of juvenile delinquency . . . have a common sociological basis regardless of the class level at which they appear' (Matza and Sykes, 1961: 718).

- Provide an account of the relevance of 'drift' to the question: namely, many delinquents did not consistently behave in this manner (they might grow out of delinquency as they entered adulthood, for example). It was thus asserted that juvenile delinquents did not adhere to a body of subcultural values but, rather, drifted between delinquency and conformity. This 'drift' occurred when social controls were loosened enabling a person to pursue their own responses to whatever situations arose. The decision to adopt one or other of these two courses of action was primarily seen as a personal one, thus reintroducing the concept of individual choice into the discussion of the causes of crime.

- Present an overall evaluation based on the concepts you have discussed regarding the existence of delinquent subcultures and a rejection of society's mainstream values.

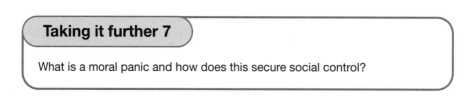

Taking it further 7

What is a moral panic and how does this secure social control?

In this essay you would:

- Define what you understand by the term 'moral panic'; namely, a situation whereby 'a condition, episode, person or group of persons emerges to become defined as a threat to societal values and interests' (Cohen, 1980: 9).

- Consider the timing of moral panics. When do they occur? In brief, they often occur in periods of rapid social change. Problems such as recession, unemployment or the growth of monopoly capitalism led many members of the general public to become disquieted concerning the direction society is taking, especially those whose interests or values seem directly threatened by these changes. Those affected by feelings of social anxiety are especially receptive to the simplistic solutions provided by scapegoating a segment of the population and depicting them as the physical embodiment of all that is wrong with society.

- Explain how a moral panic is produced. The media has been accorded a crucial role in the production of a moral panic. Initially it is responsible for making people feel uneasy concerning the direction that society is taking, often by reporting incidents that suggest a decay in traditional moral values. Having created an underlying cause of concern, the media then focuses attention on an action that epitomises the perversion of traditional social values. This incident is then amplified out of all proportion to its real importance through sensationalised treatment and the provision of selective information. The media associates the incident with a specific group of people (termed 'folk devils') who become scapegoated. The resulting moral panic is directed against this group and their anti-social activities, and causes public opinion to demand that the state acts to curb their activities, for example by new legislation giving the police additional powers or by the more vigorous use of existing ones.

- Discuss how the state's response aggravates the problem by creating what is termed a 'deviancy amplification spiral', in which actions directed against a particular stereotyped group result in an increased number of arrests and prosecutions of its members. This creates hostility from the targeted group, who view this intervention by the state as harassment. As a result, relationships between the targeted group and the police deteriorate, leading to confrontational situations which could then be cited as evidence of the existence of the original problem and also used as a justification for further tough action.

- Provide some examples of moral panics, drawing on key literature. The behaviour of young people (often but not exclusively of working class origin) is frequently the subject on which moral panics are based. Examples of moral panics include the clashes between mods and rockers at south coast holiday resorts in the 1960s (Cohen, 1980) and mugging in the 1970s where it was argued (by Hall *et al.*, 1978) that this term (which embraced a number of forms of street crime) was socially constructed by the media and utilised in a political way to divert attention from other problems of a structural nature that were then facing society. Subsequent examples of moral panics included activities associated with the 'underclass' (particularly urban disorder and juvenile crime) in the 1980s and 1990s. A particularly significant event was the abduction and murder of James Bulger by two ten-year-old boys in 1993. This resulted in a moral panic directed at the behaviour of young people and was also directed against single parents.

- Explain how moral panics facilitate social control. In brief, they do this in three ways. First, they enable the definition of criminal and deviant behaviour to be constantly adjusted: the ruling elite could respond to any threat posed to its interests by instigating a moral panic which would initiate coercive action to criminalise that threat. Second, they divert attention away from the fundamental causes of social problems: Marxists identified these to be associated with the workings of capitalism, particularly the unequal distribution of power and resources throughout society and the resulting levels of inequality and social injustice. According to this analysis, groups of citizens are placed in conflict with each other, thus impeding the development of class consciousness based upon common perceptions of injustice arising from the unjust nature of capitalism. Third, they manufacture consent for the introduction of coercive methods of state control: these were particularly important in times of recession when social harmony could not be achieved through the provision of socio-economic rewards.

- Present a conclusion in which, based on the material you have presented in your essay, you would analyse the arguments that relate to the authenticity of the concept of moral panics. For example, arguments alleging that moral panics are based upon manufactured sentiments are not universally accepted. There is no evidence to sustain allegations of conspiracies to create moral panics. Further, left realism asserts that the behaviour on which a moral panic is based often constitutes a genuine source of public concern and is not simply an artificial creation of the media.

Taking it further 8

Identify the key approaches to crime that were associated with new right criminology in the UK. What consequences did this approach exert on subsequent criminal justice policy?

In this essay you would:

- Define what you understand by the term 'new right criminology'. It was underpinned by an ideology of law and order that was summarised as consisting of a 'complex . . . set of attitudes, including the beliefs that human beings have free will, that they must be strictly disciplined by restrictive rules, and that they should be harshly punished if they break the laws or fail to respect authority', essentially it meant 'getting tough on criminals' (Cavadino and Dignan, 1992: 26 and 51) who would receive the 'just deserts' for their actions.

- Explain the political and social context within which it emerged in the UK. Although the two pillars of post-1979 Conservatism (neo-liberalism and the social authoritarianism of neo-conservatism) did not seem to be necessarily compatible, post-1979 Conservative politics made them closely connected. This view was excellently summarised by Stuart Hall who argued: 'if the state is to stop meddling in the fine-tuning of the economy, in order to let "social market values" rip, while containing the inevitable fall-out, in terms of social conflict and class polarization, then a strong, disciplinary regime is a necessary corollary. In "social market doctrine", the state should interfere less in some areas, but more in others. Its preferred slogan is "Free Economy: Strong State".' (Hall, 1980: 4).

- Identify the main features of new right criminology. In brief, these were a belief that those who broke the law should be properly punished for their actions, that social misbehaviour should be regulated by legislative sanction and that traditional moral values should be restored in order to reduce crime. This view was influenced by the American Charles Murray, who argued that liberal social welfare policy was chiefly responsible for creating a criminal underclass.

- A key consequence of new right criminology was the emergence of 'penal populism', aspects of which continue to underpin contemporary criminal justice policy. Populism advocates the pursuance of policies that are perceived to be supported by majority public opinion. Politicians 'talk tough' on crime in order to attract political support on the assumption that this is what the public want. This approach puts forward simplistic solutions to complex problems resting on 'common sense' assumptions. The terms 'penal populism' or 'populist punitiveness' were adopted during the 1990s and are characterised by the use of 'hard' policing methods, longer sentences and the increased size of the prison population. In answering this question you would provide a detailed examination of issues such as these.

- Present a conclusion in which, based upon material presented in your essay, you summarise the impact of new right criminology on contemporary criminal justice policy, putting forward the strengths and weaknesses of the policies that this concept has underpinned.

Taking it further 9

'The scale of white-collar, corporate and middle class crime is such that society should take it more seriously than is currently the case'. Discuss.

To answer this question you would:

- Provide some up-to-date estimates regarding the scale of crime of this nature. This may include issues such as death and injury in the workplace and work-related illnesses; harm caused to consumers by goods or products that the maker knew to be faulty or had concerns that this could be the case; dangers to workers and the general public caused by deliberately sacrificing health and safety considerations in the interests of saving money; and the scale of activities such as insurance fraud, tax evasion and thefts at work.

- Put forward some evidence to suggest that society does not take activities of this nature as seriously as they ought. For example, the reluctance of criminal justice agencies to investigate and prosecute deaths and injuries that occur in the workplace or that arise from the use of dangerous products or medicines.

- Identify reasons that might explain the reluctance of the state to intervene in these forms of activity. This might include considerations such as whether what is identified as a crime is actually a criminal offence (for example, a train crash might occur simply through bad luck rather than from any corporate shortcomings); many forms of white-collar and middle class crime (such as tax evasion) are not viewed as criminal by the general public; white-collar, middle class and corporate crimes are often difficult to discover and extremely complex to investigate and prosecute; some (but not all) middle class crime is 'victimless' in the sense that it lacks a tangible victim; also, unlike 'ordinary crime' (which threatens the work ethic), white-collar, corporate and middle class crime poses no fundamental threat to capitalist society or its underlying cultural values. You might also point to the difficulties associated with applying the criminal law to corporate shortcomings: in particular highlighting the problems facing a prosecution for the offence of corporate manslaughter.

- Suggest that activities of this nature, and in particular white-collar and corporate crime, are covered by regulatory rather than criminal law, which classes offences as technical violations rather than transgressions that are essentially criminal. You might identify the main forms of supervision, including self-regulation (in which commercial concerns regulate their own activities) and external regulation (whereby external agencies supervise the activities of a range of private and public bodies). Examples of the latter include the Health and Safety Executive, the Environment Agency, the Office of Fair Trading, and local authority trading standards departments and environmental health departments.

- Assess the effectiveness of regulatory supervision, citing difficulties such as the reluctance of regulatory bodies to prosecute, the extent to which their powers of supervision are adequate, and the adequacy of penalties that are imposed when companies have failed to meet their obligations.

- Present a conclusion in which you indicate, on the basis of material presented earlier in your essay, whether society takes this problem sufficiently seriously and what further steps you feel should be taken to address it.

> ### Taking it further 10
>
> Analyse the role performed by CCTV in contemporary crime prevention work.

In answering this question you would:

- Refer to the use made of CCTV by individuals, commercial organisations or public authorities in order to protect persons and property. You might discuss how CCTV works (for example, when used in public spaces, it involves banks of CCTV cameras being placed in fixed locations and remotely controlled with operators able to 'zoom in' on those acting in a criminal or disorderly manner) and the scale on which CCTV is currently used (estimating how many CCTV cameras are currently in use).

- Analyse arguments that suggest CCTV is a useful tool of crime prevention. You might discuss arguments that suggest that a potential offender may be deterred from committing crime (since there is an increased likelihood of detection if caught on film) and that, as with Bentham's *Panopticon*, the possibility that our actions are being observed by others may induce us to behave in a proper manner. The presence of CCTV also provides a constant reminder of the risk of crime and may alert potential victims to the danger, encouraging them to be on their guard.

- Evaluate arguments that are critical of CCTV as a method of crime prevention. You might refer to issues such as allegations of variable effectiveness (it tends to deter some forms of crime rather than all crime); the quality of the images that are produced; civil liberties objections arising from the activities of 'eyes in the sky' that observe on those going about their everyday lives in a perfectly law-abiding manner; the criteria used by operators when deciding to 'zoom in' on a particular subject (which may be based on stereotypical assumptions perhaps resulting in harassment of certain groups); and the extent to which CCTV leads to arrests.

- Present a conclusion, based on material presented in your essay, regarding the effectiveness and weaknesses of CCTV. One aspect of this evaluation that you may wish to emphasise is the extent to which concerns about the 'surveillance society' have been tempered by legislative developments including the 1998 Human Rights Act and the 1998 Data Protection Act.

> ### Taking it further 11
>
> Examine the strengths and weaknesses of situational methods of crime prevention.

To answer this question you would:

- Discuss what you understand by the term 'situational methods' of crime prevention (methods that seek to adjust the environment thus reducing opportunities that are favourable towards criminal acts being carried out). Refer to key initiatives associated with this approach and briefly explain the key theoretical underpinnings of situational methods of crime prevention.

- Evaluate the main strengths of situational methods of crime prevention, such as the reliance this approach places on practical methods as opposed to abstract theories; the wide range of activities with which this approach is associated; and the ability to evaluate the effectiveness of initiatives by comparing crime levels before and after they were introduced.

- Analyse the problems raised by this approach. A key issue concerns displacement, which alleges that situational crime prevention methods may not prevent crime but instead merely alter the pattern of offending behaviour. Displacement may take four forms: temporal (in which the same crime is committed but at a different time), spatial (in which the same crime is committed but in a different place), tactical (in which the methods used to commit a crime are adjusted to take account of initiatives such as target hardening) or target/functional (in which the criminal adjusts to crime prevention initiatives by carrying out a different crime) (Pease, 1997: 977).

- Other problems posed by this approach include victim-blaming (Walklate, 1996: 300) whereby individuals and communities that have failed to adequately protect themselves against crime might be held partly to blame for its occurrence – thus transferring the focus of blame away from the criminal and onto those who have suffered as the result of the criminal act. You might also consider the civil liberties implications posed by those situational crime prevention methods that utilise intrusive surveillance (such as CCTV cameras) and the extent to which these methods may enhance social exclusion by creating what are termed 'gated communities' whose purpose is to keep outsiders out of an area.

- Present a balanced conclusion based on your earlier discussion of strengths and weaknesses, perhaps highlighting evidence that suggests such methods of crime prevention are sometimes effective in reducing crime but also pointing out that they are more effective in countering crimes such as robbery, burglary and street crime rather than all forms of criminal activity.

Taking it further 12

Critically assess the work performed by Crime and Disorder Reduction Partnerships.

To answer this question you would:

- Explain what CDRPs are: namely, multi-agency bodies created by the 1998 Crime and Disorder Act which placed a statutory duty on police forces and local authorities (termed 'responsible authorities') to act in cooperation with police authorities, health authorities and probation committees in bodies that became known as Crime and Disorder Reduction Partnerships or, in Wales, Community Safety Partnerships. The 2002 Police Reform Act amended the 1998 legislation. Police and fire authorities became 'responsible authorities' as defined by the 1998 legislation in April 2003, and in the following year were joined by Primary Care Trusts in England (and health authorities in Wales). Crime and Disorder Reduction Partnerships were required to work closely with drug action teams in areas with a two-tier structure of local government and to integrate their work with drug action teams in areas that had a unitary structure of local government by April 2004.

- Discuss their role (namely to develop and implement a strategy for reducing crime and disorder in each district and unitary local authority in England and Wales) and how this is performed (referring to the local crime audit process on which the local crime reduction strategy is built). In addition they provide a mechanism for pooling information collected by the participants to the process, and conducting community safety projects. The funding for these is scarce, with most initiatives being fixed-term projects conducted at neighbourhood level funded from sources that include the Home Office.

- Examine their operations, particularly drawing attention to the role of community safety units (which link local authorities and CDRPs), to the superintendence of their work by the Government Offices for the Regions, and to the work carried out by Local Strategic Partnerships whose role is to bring together the public, private, voluntary and community sectors in order to tackle problems that require a response from a range of different bodies acting in partnership. Typically, the LSP develops themes to advance the local authority's community strategy which is delivered by CDRPs.

- Analyse some of the main benefits derived from their operations, in particular in connection with sentiments of empowerment derived from local people being able to help set the agenda for CDRP activities and the advantages of multi-agency work.

- Evaluate some of the key difficulties associated with their operations. These might include problems affecting the reliability of information gathered through the crime audit process (which initially tended to rely heavily on police data); the difficulties in getting a number of separate agencies (not all of whom had a traditional involvement in crime and disorder issues) to work together effectively; the tension between CDRPs seeking to respond to local concerns but also having to address issues imposed on them above by the Home Office (especially in connection with targets); and the extent to which the operations of CDRPs is subject to adequate mechanisms of local accountability and coherent leadership.

- If the word limit permitted it, you might usefully draw on some primary material (see Chapter 3) detailing the activity of your local CDRP based upon its crime and disorder reduction strategy.

- Formulate a conclusion in which you might refer to the importance of issues such as strong leadership as a key to the effectiveness of CDRPs and methods that may be advanced to enhance their responsiveness to local concerns.

Chapter 2

Taking it further 1

In England and Wales the police operate with the consent of the public. To what extent had the principle of policing by consent been achieved by the end of the nineteenth century?

To answer this question you would:

- Indicate what you understand by the term 'policing by consent', the essence of which concerns policing being carried out with the cooperation of the general public: the alternative to this is 'policing by coercion' in which the police serve the government rather than the people.

- Place the concept of policing by consent in its context by explaining why police reform was initially unpopular among all sections of society. One key reason was the fear that a reformed system of policing would be an agency of central government and act in a tyrannical fashion, riding roughshod over the rights and liberties of English people. Other reasons included cost and (especially in rural areas) a perception that the old system remained workable and should be shored up rather than be replaced.

- Analyse the main methods that were used in order to secure policing by consent. Here you might refer to issues such as control (outside of London, local people were given considerable power over their local policing arrangements, which were therefore not dominated by central government), police powers (which were initially the common law powers possessed by all citizens), recruitment (whereby most police officers were drawn from the working class who would behave deferentially towards their social superiors and act sympathetically with members of their own social background), and the concept of minimum force (which was designed to ensure that police officers would not act in tyrannical fashion, an objective that was underpinned by the limited weaponry – a truncheon – carried by officers only to be used for their self protection). You might also draw attention to the importance of the service role of policing in advancing the goal of policing by consent.

- Evaluate the success of these methods in achieving policing by consent by around 1900. Here you need to consider the diverse arguments presented by police historians: in particular, you should contrast the views of the 'orthodox' historians such as Charles Reith and Thomas Critchley (who argued that widespread consent had been achieved by this time) with the 'revisionist' police historians (such as Robert Storch and Michael Brogden) who alleged that police–working class relationships remained a problem for much of the nineteenth century.

- Present a conclusion based on your analysis of the arguments you have presented by police historians regarding the extent to which consent had been achieved by around 1900.

> ## Taking it further 2
>
> The 1994 Police and Magistrates' Courts Act was underpinned by the principles of new public management. Analyse the ways in which this legislation reflected the concerns of new public management. To what extent have these reforms resulted in a more centralised police service controlled by the Home Office?

To answer this question you would:

- Discuss what you understand by the term 'new public management', in particular drawing attention to the desire that public services should be driven by the concerns of efficiency, value for money and quality of service (which gave rise to performance measurement in which the public services were set targets by central government and their attainment was measured by a number of performance indicators); the view that citizens should be regarded as consumers; the setting of an organisation's goals by central government while giving considerable flexibility to agency heads as to how these goals were implemented; and the practice of 'hiving off' functions from public sector organisations to a range of bodies.

- Briefly refer to attempts dating from the 1983 Home Office circular, *Manpower: Effectiveness and Efficiency in the Police Service*, to introduce the principles of new public management into policing, which includes developments such as the 1993 Sheehy Report and the 1995 Posen Report.

- Analyse in detail the key provisions of the 1994 Police and Magistrates' Courts Act that are underpinned by new public management, including: the ability of the Home Secretary to set national objectives for the police service accompanied by performance indicators to measure their attainment, thus eroding the power of chief constables to set priorities for their force; the introduction of a cash-limited budget; the reform of the composition of police authorities and changes to their powers, especially in relation to the production of a local policing plan; and the granting of new powers to the Home Secretary in connection with issues that include finance and the amalgamation of forces. You must ensure that you discuss how these innovations are related to the key concerns of new public management.

- Evaluate the impact of this legislation in connection with the accusation of centralisation. To do this you should consider how the power of the Home Secretary increased by this legislation but also assess arguments that suggest chief constables and police authorities also obtained new powers: for example, the lessening of detailed controls governing how chief constables spent their budget and the enhanced ability of police authorities to hold their chief constable to account. However, in the context of central control you might argue that performance measurement has exerted considerable influence over police actions, ensuring that resources are directed into activities that can be measured, at the expense of activities that are less susceptible to easily quantifiable assessment.

- Put forward a conclusion based upon material presented earlier in your essay in which you summarise the key features of new public management as applied to the police service and evaluate the key question as to whether this has resulted in increased centralisation.

Taking it further 3

Analyse the developments that resulted in the creation of the Serious Organised Crime Agency in 2005. What dangers are posed by this body?

To answer this question you would:

- Discuss the changing patterns of crime in England and Wales after 1945 (the transition from craft-based to project-based crime, and contemporary crime that includes international terrorism and drug and people trafficking).

- Analyse the steps taken by the police service to deal with this changed criminal environment (such as the introduction of regional crime squads during the 1960s and the establishment of the National Criminal Intelligence Service and the National Crime Squad in the 1990s).

- Discuss the role, structure and organisation of SOCA and the powers that it possesses in relation to dealing with serious crime.

- Consider the advantages that a body of this nature brings to contemporary police work: for example, it placed personnel drawn from a number of separate agencies under one roof, and provides one point of contact with which police and criminal justice agencies abroad can liaise.

- Evaluate arguments related to dangers posed by this body. These principally concern the powers given to this agency to combat serious crime that might be viewed as eroding civil liberties. Although they may be defensible in connection with the issues SOCA deals with, there is a danger that innovations such as forcing witnesses to answer questions and produce documents may be extended to other less serious areas of criminal activity if SOCA finds them useful.

- Present a conclusion based on the material you have presented in your essay that establishes the rationale for the creation of this body, what issues of concern are raised by it and whether these problems outweigh the usefulness of SOCA in combating serious crime.

Taking it further 4

What criticisms have been made of the operations of the CPS and how successfully have these been resolved?

To answer this question you would:

- Briefly set out the rationale for the creation of the CPS and discuss the work it performs.

- Outline some of the difficulties that were encountered in the early years: these included suspicion by the police regarding the agency's work, remoteness and lack of accountability (especially in connection with its decisions concerning prosecution), and a concern that financial constraints were influencing its operations (for example, offences might be 'downgraded' in order that they could be heard in a magistrates' court rather than a Crown Court, thus saving money since magistrates' courts trials are cheaper).

- It would be useful to provide some examples of your own to illustrate the above arguments. For example, actual bodily harm might be downgraded to common assault. This might save the CPS money, but might also result in the victim feeling cheated by the system.

- Analyse some of the reforms that have been introduced to remedy perceived deficiencies. These include organisational reforms that have aligned the structure of the CPS with that of other criminal justice agencies (thus improving liaison between the CPS and other agencies); developments affecting victims that have had implications for the operations of the CPS (for example, initiatives arising from the 1990 Victims' Charter), and the more recent change whereby CPS lawyers (who may be based in police stations) have taken over responsibility from the police for decisions relating to charging offenders.

- Evaluate the effectiveness of these reforms. To do this you might consider statistics that relate to issues including discontinuance and conviction rates, and analyse whether these have improved in recent years in the wake of the reforms you have considered.

- Present a conclusion, based upon the material contained in your essay, in which you assess the key changes made to the operations of the CPS, analyse the extent to which these have answered criticisms made of this agency, and assess what further steps should be taken to improve its operations.

Taking it further 5

Evaluate the significance of changes made to the operations of the probation service since the late 1960s.

To answer this question you would:

- Briefly discuss the historic role performed by the probation service, referring to developments such as the work of the Church of England Temperance Society in the 1870s and the 1907 Probation of Offenders Act. What was this legislation seeking to achieve?

- Assess the functions performed by the probation service as it developed during the twentieth century, referring to areas of activity including supervising offenders in the community, providing reports to the courts regarding appropriate sentences for offenders and seeking to prevent recidivism by working with offenders while in prison and upon release.

- Evaluate the key changes made to the role of the probation service, including legislative developments affecting its work that include the 1972, 1991 and 2003 Criminal Justice Acts. Of particular importance is the move away from providing individualised treatment to assessing the risk posed by offenders and 'slotting' them into accredited offending behaviour programmes. This re-oriented the work of the probation service as an agency whose key concern was to protect the public.

- Analyse other key changes affecting the probation service, in particular its governance, its involvement in multi-agency operations (the 1998 Crime and Disorder Act is an important development in this respect in connection with CDRPs and YOTs) and the creation of NOMS.

- Present a conclusion, based on the material you have presented, regarding what you consider to have been the initial role of the probation service and what its current role is, in the light of developments that you have discussed.

Taking it further 6

Analyse and explain why prisons have traditionally found it hard to secure the rehabilitation of offenders.

To answer this question you would:

- Provide information that indicates that prisons have traditionally failed in this respect. Statistics relating to re-offending (or what we term 'recidivism') are an important source of evidence.

- Analyse changes to the role and purpose of prisons (in particular the move from the treatment model to the justice model and the impact of this on the prison environment).

- Evaluate issues relating to the day-to-day lifestyle of prisons that might make rehabilitation hard to achieve. You might draw upon the sociology of imprisonment literature and discuss issues that include the emphasis on security; issues that relate to psychological deterioration arising from being 'locked up'; the emphasis placed on purposeful activity (for example, is sufficient relevant education or work experience supplied to prisoners?); brutalisation and the view that prisons constitute 'universities of crime'. Additionally consider issues arising from more contemporary problems affecting the prison environment, especially overcrowding due to the large increase in prison numbers since the early 1990s.

- Analyse initiatives that have been introduced to tackle recidivism, in particular the creation of NOMS.

- Present a conclusion, based on your earlier comments, regarding the problems related to prisons securing the rehabilitation of offenders and the ways whereby this issue can be more effectively tackled.

Taking it further 7

Evaluate the effectiveness of the way in which complaints against police officers have been investigated since 1976.

This question is best answered by a chronological examination of the key developments that have been introduced to develop the police complaints machinery.

To answer this question you would:

- Place the police complaints machinery in context by explaining what it does (that is, handle complaints made by members of the general public against individual police officers) and explain the way in which the actions of police officers are regulated both by the law and by the service's professional code of conduct.

- Discuss the way in which police complaints were handled before and after the 1976 Police Act, which set up the Police Complaints Board.

- Evaluate the shortcomings of the Police Complaints Board, in particular its limited remit which was concerned only with behaviour that had breached what was then termed the Police Disciplinary Code, and the lack of confidence in a system in which complaints were investigated by police officers.

- Analyse the strengths and weaknesses of the Police Complaints Authority, which was introduced by the 1984 Police and Criminal Evidence Act and replaced the Police Complaints Board. The strengths of the new system were that the remit of the PCA was broader and able to consider complaints related to misconduct of both criminal and disciplinary nature. Additionally, the PCA had the ability to supervise a complaint (although the investigator remained a police officer). However, there were weaknesses, in particular the low level of complaints that were upheld, the ability of officers found guilty of disciplinary offences to avoid meaningful punishment and the concern that complaints remained investigated by the police.

- Evaluate the key provisions of the 2002 Police Reform Act, which replaced the PCA with the Independent Police Complaints Commission. The main strength of this reform was that the most serious complaints would be investigated by persons other than police officers. You should also identify potential weaknesses: in particular, the need for the system to be adequately funded and a concern that police officers may not fully cooperate with independent investigations conducted by the new body.

- Present a conclusion, based on the arguments you have presented above, pointing to the potential benefits to be derived from the IPCC provided it is able to overcome the problems you have identified. In this context you might refer to the resignation in 2008 of around 100 lawyers who specialised in handling police complaints from the IPCC's advisory body. Their concerns included allegations of inadequate oversight of investigations conducted by police officers, extreme delays in resolving complaints and favouritism being displayed towards the police.

Taking it further 8

Juries are an important feature of Crown Courts. Assess the strengths and weaknesses of trial by jury.

To answer this question you would:

- Briefly describe what a jury is: how it is constituted and what role it performs.

- Evaluate the main strengths of trial by jury: for example, it provides for the involvement of ordinary citizens in the judicial process and may enable them to introduce popular perceptions of right and wrong into sentencing decisions.

- Analyse the main problems historically associated with trial by jury: include issues such as the extent to which they are socially representative; and whether decisions are made solely on the basis of evidence presented or are influenced by factors such as the performance of lawyers, race or gender bias, inability to understand the law, the evidence presented and court proceedings or the nature of jury decision-making (for example, one or two jurors may dominate proceedings).

- It would be helpful to illustrate your arguments with some specific examples of jury trials.

- Evaluate the rationale for recent reforms proposed to the system of trial by jury: for example, the perception that this enables an accused person to 'play for time' perhaps in the hope that witnesses may fail to turn up or the prosecution would settle for a lesser charge when faced with the prospect of a costly jury trial. Consider the suggestions that have been put forward for reform: for example, to reduce the number of offences that are triable 'either way' (or to remove the defendant's right to decide where these cases should be heard), to eliminate jury trials in complex areas of law such as fraud (a reform that was proposed in the 2003 Criminal Justice Act but which has yet to be implemented).

- Present a conclusion giving your views based on the future of trial by jury, based on the arguments you have put forward.

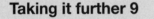

Taking it further 9

Evaluate the strengths and weaknesses of restorative justice.

To answer this question you would:

- Explain what you understand by the term 'restorative justice' and what it seeks to achieve, especially in connection with securing the reintegration of offenders into society. You might also provide a brief account of its historical development (especially in New Zealand and Australia).

- Discuss the 'mechanics' of restorative justice: how it works both in theory and in practice. Here you might consider key issues related to restorative justice, in particular the role played by shaming and also the practical aspects such as conferencing and its usage in England and Wales (in particular in connection with Youth Offender Panels provided for in the 1999 Youth Justice and Criminal Evidence Act).

- Examine the strengths of this process: for example, victim and offender involvement, empowerment of those most affected by a criminal act at the expense of the involvement of the impersonal state.

- Consider the problems associated with restorative justice, such as levels of victim involvement, public concerns regarding its alleged leniency towards offenders and difficulties associated with seeking to influence a wrongdoer's actions through the process of shaming.

- Present a conclusion, based on your analysis of the strengths and weaknesses you have identified above, which might additionally refer to issues such as effectiveness in preventing future wrongdoing and securing the reintegration of offenders into society and problems associated with the involvement of the public in sentencing decisions.

Taking it further 10

Evaluate the initiatives undertaken in the latter years of the twentieth century to provide an effective remedy against miscarriages of justice.

To answer this question you would:

- Define what you understand by the term 'miscarriages of justice'.

- Analyse explanations as to why these mistakes occurred: for example, abuses committed by the police, inadequate work by defence lawyers, failure by the prosecution to disclose evidence to the defence that is unearthed during the course of a police investigation, and erroneous evidence supplied by expert witnesses. It would be helpful to cite some specific examples of miscarriages when referring to these explanations (for example, the expert testimony given by Sir Roy Meadows in connection with the wrongful conviction of Sally Clark, which was overturned by the Court of Appeal in 2003).

- Refer to initiatives that were introduced in the late twentieth century to remedy these problems, such as the 1984 Police and Criminal Evidence Act, the 1996 Criminal Procedure and Investigation Act (and the subsequent 2003 Criminal Justice Act) and the creation of the Criminal Cases Review Commission by the 1995 Criminal Appeals Act. You should fully explain how these initiatives were designed to provide a remedy against miscarriages of justice.

- Evaluate the operations of the CCRC, explaining the role performed by this body, how it was an improvement on the former remedy provided by the Home Office (for example, greater openness, transparency and speed), and highlight any problems that might undermine its operations (for example, in areas such as volume of work and funding). You might also refer to examples of the CCRC where positive results have occurred as the result of this body's intervention.

- Present a conclusion, based on the material you have cited, analysing the effectiveness of remedies now available to respond to miscarriages of justice and suggesting whether there is further scope for improvement.

Taking it further 11

Analyse the effectiveness of reforms put forward by Sir William Macpherson's 1999 report to eliminate institutional racism from the police service.

To answer this question you would:

- Discuss what you understand by the concept of 'institutional racism' and the context within which this issue was raised in the 1999 Macpherson Report.

- Refer to some of the main reforms proposed by Sir William Macpherson to eradicate this problem: such as, the Ministerial Priority to rebuild the confidence of minority ethnic communities in policing; reform of the 1976 Race Relations legislation; the recruitment of greater numbers of black and Asian police officers; providing a new definition of a racist incident; improved monitoring of stop and search powers; a review of racial awareness training; and the introduction of a tougher police disciplinary regime. In discussing these areas, it is important to indicate how they were designed to eliminate institutional racism from the police service.

- Discuss the steps taken to implement these reforms by both the government and the police service: for example, the targets set by the Home Secretary regarding recruitment from minority ethnic communities; the 2000 Race Relations (Amendment Act); changes to police disciplinary procedures, including the introduction of an Independent Police Complaints Commission; the introduction of new training packages dealing with race and diversity issues; the new definition of what constituted a racist incident; and the Metropolitan Police Service's 1999 report, *A Police Service for All the People,* which contained this force's initiatives to tackle institutional racism.

- Evaluate the impact of these reforms on institutional racism in the police service: here you might comment on the progress of initiatives (such as targets for minority ethnic recruitment or an increased willingness to report racial violence) but also analyse evidence that suggests progress has been limited (for example, that contained in the 2003 television programme *The Secret Policeman,* and the 2008 television programme *The Secret Policeman Returns*).

- If your analysis suggests that progress has been limited, you should suggest reasons that explain this: for example, reservations by rank-and-file police officers regarding Sir William Macpherson's analysis of institutional racism: the government's law and order agenda became reoriented to deal with security issues; and problems with the way in which existing law prevented the introduction of relevant reforms such as positive discrimination.

- Present a conclusion, based on your findings, as to the extent to which institutional racism has been eliminated from the police service and what further steps might be necessary. In connection with this analysis it would be useful to draw on material contained in reports prepared by David Calvert-Smith in 2004 and 2005 and Sir William Morris in 2004.

Chapter 4

> ### Taking it further 1
>
> Consider the following questionnaire that has been designed to obtain findings related to victims of crime. How would you improve upon it?

This questionnaire sought to elicit data regarding the experience of those who had suffered from crime with a view to suggesting further improvements.

It shows several weaknesses, which you should avoid when designing your own questionnaires. Comments on these are inserted where they apply.

As a general issue, the format might be improved by numbering the questions, since some questions refer back to previous ones.

Questionnaire on Victims of Crime

I am a student at the local university writing my final year dissertation on the treatment given to victims of crime. I would like you to complete the following questions. Where appropriate, please place a circle around the answer that applies to you.

The questionnaire is anonymous and the information is solely sought for the purposes of my own research.

Age
What is your age?

This question may reveal important issues related to those who are victims of crime: you might consider offering age bands, perhaps 18–25, 25–35, 35–50, over 50

Gender
Are you male or female?

This is also an important question which should be included in the questionnaire

Race/ethnicity
What is your racial background?

Issues of race and ethnicity are of considerable importance in assessing victimisation and the response of the criminal justice agencies to those who have experienced crime. It would be normal practice to present categorisations in a tick box format, asking the respondent, 'Which of the following best describes you?' for example:

White
 British
 Irish
 European
 Other (please specify)

Black
 British
 African
 Caribbean
 Other (please specify)

Asian
 Indian
 Pakistani
 Bangladeshi
 Chinese
 Other (please specify)

Other
 Please specify

Victimisation
Have you been the victim of crime in the past year?
 Yes
 No

This question is an obvious one to ask. If the answer is 'No' there is no point in the respondent continuing, and you could make this explicit thanking them for their time.

Location
If the answer to the above was 'Yes', where did the incident take place and did it occur during the daytime or at night ?

....

....

The location of the crime is of importance to studies of victimisation. You are asking two questions here: you might usefully subdivide them into (a) and (b).
 For (a), it would be helpful to suggest a number of locations in a tick box format: for example, 'In my home', 'In the street', 'In a club', 'Other (please specify)'.
 For (b), 'Daytime' and 'Night time' could also be presented in a tick box format, but be aware that these terms are imprecise and you might consider offering time bands in a tick box format, if one of your purposes is to relate type of crime to the time of day when it occurs.
 You should also consider whether any of this information will overlap with the following question.

Nature of the crime
What type of crime were you the victim of? Was it serious?

This is a very poorly worded question. As in the above question, you are asking two distinct questions, so you should subdivide them, (a) and (b).

For purposes of analysis, it would be useful to guide the respondent by putting forward categories of crime in a tick box format: such as, 'Robbery', 'Theft', 'Burglary', 'Assault' 'Hate crime', 'Other (please specify)'.

You should also bear in mind that although the theft of a mobile telephone is objectively less serious than murder, all crime is serious to those who have experienced it. Thus (b) should be removed.

Reporting the crime to the police
Did you report the crime to the police?
  Yes
  No

This is an obvious question that needs to be asked.

Reasons for non-reporting
If the answer to the above question was 'No', what factor(s) persuaded you not to report it?

  The crime was trivial.
  I was too embarrassed to report it.
  I was too frightened to report it.
  I was concerned the police would not take my complaint seriously.
  I was worried that there would be bad repercussions for me if I reported it.

These suggestions are perfectly acceptable, although the last one might confuse the respondent: if you are making the point that the perpetrator might exact revenge if their actions were reported, this could be made more obvious in the wording.

These suggestions are fairly standardised explanations for the non-reporting of crime: in many ways this aspect of your questionnaire would only help to support what we already know. In order to seek information from your respondents that may not be so obvious it would be helpful to include an open-ended suggestion – 'Other (please specify' – that may elicit information that is less widely known and commented upon.

Response by the police
If you reported a crime to the police, were you satisfied with their response?
  Yes
  No
If the answer was 'No' what weaknesses did you encounter?

....

....

It would be useful for the second part of the question to present some alternatives in a tick box format (such as 'The crime was too trivial to report', 'The police were not likely to take it seriously') accompanied by the open-ended 'Other (please specify)'.

Prosecution

If you have been a victim of crime, was the person who carried it out prosecuted?

Yes
No

If the answer was 'Yes', were you satisfied with the way in which the prosecution was handled?

Yes
No

The second part of this question is unlikely to reveal much detailed information and it would be helpful to follow up 'No' with some suggestions that could be presented in a tick box format to identify the problems. (For example, 'I was provided with little information regarding the progress of the case', 'the prosecution failed to consult me concerning court proceedings', 'The court procedure was intimidating', accompanied by the open-ended 'Other (please specify)' alternative. The answers obtained from this aspect of the question may provide your research with some original insights that will feed into the next question.

Reform

What changes, if any, do you think should be introduced into the criminal justice system to benefit those who have been the victims of crime?

....

....

This is an open-ended question, but is one that can be validly asked as it may provide insights that established literature have ignored or downplayed.

Thank you for taking the time to complete this questionnaire.

Taking it further 2

'Crime statistics are socially constructed'. What are the consequences of this and does it mean that they contain no information that is valid for criminological study?

To answer this question you would:

- Define what you understand by the term 'social construction': that is, official crime statistics are not objective realities but, rather, reflect 'outcomes of social and institutional processes' (Coleman and Moynihan, 1996: 16).

- Provide examples to explain how official crime statistics are socially constructed: for example, you might refer to people's willingness or inclination to report offences (meaning that official crime statistics contain not an objective account of crime that has been committed, but a selective record of those crimes the public choose – or feel the need – to report). Further official crime statistics reflect the internal and external factors that influence the actions undertaken by the police service in connection with the recording of crime (you might in this respect refer to police organisational culture as an internal pressure and the role exerted by the media over police actions and the Home Office in connection with recording procedures as external pressures).

- Give specific examples of the way in which crime statistics are socially constructed: you might refer to moral panics and how these influence police operations, resulting in certain social groups becoming targeted by the police and over-represented crime statistics. What will inevitably be perceived as harassment and discrimination by those on the receiving end of these police activities may create further crime through processes that include self-fulfilling prophecies and deviancy amplification spirals (see Chapter 1 regarding labelling theory).

- Consider the consequences derived from this situation: for example, it is not possible to use crime statistics to compare levels of crime committed across historical periods since the processes that underpin their construction are subject to change over time).

- Provide a balanced conclusion, in which you summarise the issues relating to social construction that you have already identified, but also point to the usefulness of crime statistics: for example, omissions regarding reported crimes – especially if these occur for long periods of time – can be a useful indicator of the confidence that certain groups have in the operations of the criminal justice system and provide an agenda for reform (you might mention sexual or racial violence in this context). Additionally, official crime statistics provide some information at a specific point in time that can be used to compare the performances of police force and can underpin police operations directed at certain types of crime.

Taking it further 3

Much criminological research carries ethical implications that must be considered. What ethical issues arise in the following scenarios.

1. You wish to undertake a study of paedophilia and you intend that one aspect of your research is to study examples of child pornography available on the Internet. What ethical considerations should you consider before embarking on this research?

In this scenario, the key ethical considerations are that you are likely to break the law in conducting research of this nature and possibly end up with a criminal conviction and a penalty of being placed on the sex offenders' register for viewing and storing obscene images. You may also be subjected to accusations that your motives for gathering information of this nature go beyond academic ones: it is often the case that persons taken to court regarding accessing and storing obscene images will use 'research' as their defence.

The first consideration, therefore, is to assess whether information of this nature is essential to your research – do you need to actually view obscene images in order to proceed with your work? Is it possible that information relating to this kind of material can be obtained from other sources – perhaps by contacting criminal justice agencies and seeking to interview practitioners whose job is to monitor, arrest and prosecute paedophiles?

However, criminologists may sometimes wish to conduct research into issues relating to the dark side of the human personality. To do this they must adhere to ethical procedures and guidelines that exist in universities covering research that may have illegal connotations.

It is important that the researcher does not unilaterally embark on such research without keeping their supervisor fully informed. The supervisor will, in a scenario of this nature, refer the matter to relevant committees concerned with ethical issues that exist at departmental, faculty and university level. Conditions will almost certainly be applied if permission is given to conduct research of this nature, including an assessment whether the research is of sufficient academic worth to offset any criticisms that might be laid against the university or researcher for conducting research of this nature. Assurances will be needed that the research will be rigorously monitored to ensure that the material being gathered is used solely for the purposes of research; that arrangements have been put in place to securely store material gathered during the research; and that the researcher is adequately protected in connection with possible legal consequences (for example, agreement from one or more criminal justice agencies can be sought).

2. You intend to monitor the activities of an extreme right-wing political organisation. To carry out this research you intend to covertly monitor meetings of this organisation and secretly tape record conversations with leading activists. What ethical considerations arise from this proposed research?

The activity referred to here is covert research, and this frequently raises ethical considerations regarding those who are subject to the research not being aware that they are being studied.

Nonetheless, research of this nature has sometimes made an important contribution to criminological debate: the television programme *The Secret Policeman* entailed the reporter Mark Daley enrolling as a police officer and secretly recording conversations with other police probationers to assess the extent to which racism had been eradicated from the police service in the wake of the 1999 Macpherson Report. In this case it could be argued that the public interest consideration outweighed the obligation placed on researchers to make their subjects aware of the nature of the research project.

In this scenario, a similar consideration might apply, especially if it was discovered that members of this organisation were actively involved in breaking the law. There is, however, a further important ethical consideration to be assessed before embarking on it: how can the personal safety of the researcher be guaranteed both while conducting the research and subsequently when its findings are made public.

3. You have gathered research in connection with drug taking among school children. They are informed that this is in connection with your final year undergraduate dissertation. Although the self-report questionnaires were completed anonymously, you are able to identify the children involved and decide to pass onto the head teacher information about those who admit to using drugs. What ethical issues does this course of action raise?

It is sometimes the case that the true nature and purpose of research can be withheld from its participants. However, in this scenario participants have been informed about why the research is being conducted and may feel that they have been treated unethically if the information they provide is used for a different purpose, namely to report their habits to an authority that has the ability to take punitive action against them.

4. You are conducting research into domestic violence. A contact you have made in a criminal justice agency provides you with a list of victims who may be willing to participate in research of this nature. You decide to send each person on the list a detailed questionnaire, which includes questions seeking to ascertain the nature of the violence they have experienced. What ethical considerations arise from this proposed course of action?

The key ethical issue in this scenario relates to the manner in which potential participants are approached. There is a very strong possibility that the nature of the research may cause undue distress and discomfort to those who receive the questionnaire if this arrives as an unsolicited item of mail. Considerable harm may be caused to those coming to terms with their victimisation by an approach of this nature.

Criminologists frequently conduct research into sensitive topics such as domestic or sexual violence, but it is important to go about this in an ethical manner.

It is highly unlikely that a criminal justice agency will provide researchers with a list of names and addresses in the way suggested in the scenario. But there are other organisations that deal with the victims of violence of this nature that you may approach who may provide you with a contact for your research. You can then get in touch by personal contact. An initial interview may then be supplemented by snowball sampling to gather relevant material.

5. You are conducting research into the sex industry and wish to interview some persons who are involved in this form of activity. To do this, you intend to visit a local red light area in the early hours of the morning and question sex trade workers and their clients. What ethical issues arise from this research proposal?

The key ethical issue here is your personal safety: walking around red light districts in the early hours of the morning may result in your arrest (should the police not believe your explanation as to what you are doing in that vicinity) or you becoming the victim of a serious crime. Additionally, it is possible that those who talk to you may place themselves in danger by doing so.

Criminologists often conduct research into complex social issues of this nature, but must ensure that their personal safety, and that of their respondents, is guaranteed. Interviews must always take place on neutral ground where others are present (such as a University coffee bar).

Chapter 5

> ### Taking it further 1
>
> Below are two sample essays.
>
> Assume that these are at first year undergraduate level. Your task is to assess them in line with the criteria presented above.

Essay 1

What is good about this essay?

- It is the right word length.
- The content is quite good – it presents a number of relevant arguments related to the routine arming of the police.
- It presents a balanced account, outlining arguments for and against the proposition that the police should be armed.
- It has an introduction and a conclusion that draws the issues together and makes a recommendation based on a weighing of the arguments.

What is bad about this essay?

- There is no bibliography: a list of sources that have been consulted must always be provided at the end of an essay.

- It does not contain a single reference in the text of the essay.

- The absence of references means that statements are presented that are not substantiated: for example, in paragraph six we are told that many police officers oppose routine arming. In paragraph eight we are told that the public are concerned that officers who make mistakes with firearms may not be held sufficiently accountable for their actions. But how do we know these facts? Are they true? Sources must thus be provided to substantiate comments of this nature.

- It is always useful to provide facts and figures to substantiate arguments. For example, in paragraph four we are told that violent crime has increased in recent years: citing the evidence (perhaps derived from official crime statistics) would be helpful. Paragraph five refers to the deaths of police officers in recent years at the hands of violent criminals. Again, one or two examples would be a useful addition to the answer.

What mark would you give it?

- The content is quite good, but the style in which it is presented is poor.

- The mark would be in the range of 45–48 per cent.

Essay 2

What is good about this essay?

- It displays a good knowledge of the subject matter. The ideas of classicist criminologists and the reforms with which they are associated are adequately discussed.

- The essay provides a balanced account, referring to the ideas underpinning classicist reforms and also suggesting some of the problems associated with their ideas.

- The essay reads coherently and is logically structured and is around the right word length.

- The text of the essay evidences that a relevant range of sources have been used to research the topic and the text of the essay contains appropriate references to ideas and statements contained in these texts.

What is bad about this essay?

- It is written in the first person; this should be avoided in academic discussions. It is better to say 'In this essay the key ideas of classicist criminologists will be discussed' rather than 'In this essay I will discuss the key ideas of classicist criminologists'.

- Some of the quotations are a little lengthy – especially the second paragraph.

- It is a little brief, perhaps superficial, in places: for example, a little more detail might be provided about the reforms to the criminal justice system that were inspired by classicists and the problems associated with classicism.

- The sources used are secondary sources: this is not a problem at this introductory level but at a higher stage of study you would be expected to use primary texts (that is, the original publications written by the key theorists) if these were readily available – which is not always the case.

- The bibliography should list authors alphabetically.

What mark would you give it?

- Overall this is quite a good piece of work in terms of content, understanding and analysis.

- The mark would be in range of 60–65 per cent.

References

Brogden, M. (1982) *The Police: Autonomy and Consent.* London: Academic Press.

Calvert-Smith, D. (2004) *A Formal Investigation of the Police Service in England and Wales: An Interim Report.* London: Commission for Racial Equality.

Calvert-Smith, D. (2005) *A Formal Investigation of the Police Service in England and Wales: Final Report.* London: Commission for Racial Equality.

Cavadino, M. and Dignan, J. (1992) *The Penal System: An Introduction.* London: Sage.

Cohen, S. (1980) *Folk Devils and Moral Panics*, 2nd ed. Oxford: Martin Robertson.

Coleman, C. and Moynihan, J. (1996) *Understanding Crime Data: Haunted by the Dark Figure.* Buckingham: Open University Press.

Critchley, T. A. (1978) *A History of Police in England and Wales.* London: Constable.

Hall, S. (1980) *Drifting into a Law and Order Society.* London: The Cobden Trust.

Hall, S., Critcher, C., Jefferson, T., Clarke, J. and Roberts, B. (1978) *Policing the Crisis: Mugging, the State, and Law and Order.* Basingstoke: Macmillan.

Home Office (1983) *Manpower, Efficiency and Effectiveness in the Police Service*, Circular 114/83. London: Home Office.

Home Office (1993) *Inquiry into Police Responsibilities and Rewards*, Cm 2280. London: HMSO (The Sheehy Report).

Home Office (1995) *Review of the Police Core and Ancillary Tasks: Final Report.* London: HMSO (The Posen Report).

Matza, D. and Sykes, G. (1961) 'Juvenile Delinquency and Subterranean Values'. *American Sociological Review*, Vol. 26, pp. 713–19.

Morris, Sir W. (2004) *The Case for Change: People in the Metropolitan Police Service – The Report of the Morris Inquiry.* London: Morris Inquiry.

Pease, K. (1997) 'Crime Prevention', in M. Maguire, R. Morgan and R. Reiner (eds) *Oxford Handbook of Criminology*, 2nd ed. Oxford: Clarendon Press.

Reith, C. (1943) *British Police and the Democratic Ideal.* Oxford: Oxford University Press.

Storch, R. (1975) 'A Plague of Blue Locusts: Police Reform and Popular Resistance in Northern England'. *International Review of Social History,* 20: 61–90.

Walklate, S. (1996) 'Community and Crime Prevention', in E. McLaughlin and J. Muncie (eds) *Controlling Crime.* London: Sage.

Key terms in criminology and criminal justice policy

Accountability This is a mechanism whereby a person or agency is required to answer to other people or agencies in respect of the actions they have undertaken. Accountability is often of an *ex post facto* nature, whereby an action may be undertaken but is subsequently subject to scrutiny and the possible deployment of sanctions against those who have taken it if objections are made regarding what has been done.

Anomie Anomie refers to a state of social indiscipline in which the socially approved way of obtaining goals is subject to widespread challenge resulting in the law being unable to effectively maintain social cohesion. The concept was developed by Emile Durkheim and subsequently developed by Robert Merton.

Attrition Attrition in criminal justice refers to the gap between the number of crimes that are committed and the number that end with the perpetrator of the crime being convicted. This gap occurs because there are a number of stages involved in the prosecution of crime. Crimes are weeded out at each stage so that the number of convictions represents only a small proportion of crime that has been committed. This is a major issue for crimes such as domestic violence and seual assault, where women are commonly the victims. Currently only around 6 per cent of allegations of rape made to the police result in conviction.

Best value Best value is a process designed to assess efficiency and effectiveness in the delivery of services by public sector bodies and also to enhance the quality of service: best value replaced the Conservatives' compulsory competitive tendering procedures and was introduced into the public sector by the 1997–2001 Labour government.

Bifurcation This refers to sentencing policy that seeks to sharply differentiate between serious and non-serious crime. It is based upon a 'twin track' approach whereby serious offences receive severe penalties (such as long terms of imprisonment) and less serious crimes are responded to in a more lenient manner (by responses such as non-custodial sentences served in the community).

Broken windows This refers to a view, put forward by and Wilson and Kelling in 1982, that it is necessary to take firm action to enforce the law against low level crime (characterised by vandalism and graffiti) which creates a fear of crime and has a detrimental impact on neighbourhood cohesion. Nipping behaviour of this nature in the bud may prevent the development of more serious manifestations of criminality.

Case studies These constitute a method of criminological research involving intensive and focused investigation and analysis that seeks to provide an understanding of an issue that could not be researched in an alternative manner. The object of research might centre on the behaviour of a person or a group of persons (such as a gang) or an episode or event (such as a riot) and a key concern is to discover why people act in a particular manner. The individual or episode is studied as an end in itself, although the analysis may help to develop an understanding of a more general nature.

Classicist criminology This approach to the study of crime emphasised the importance of free will and viewed a criminal act as one that had been consciously carried out by its perpetrator having rationally weighed up the advantages and disadvantages of undertaking the action. The main focus of classicist criminology was on the operations of the criminal justice system. It was believed that if this operated in a consistent and predictable fashion (with punishments graded according to the severity of a criminal act) it would eliminate crime committed by those who felt that they would 'get away with it'.

Code for Crown Prosecutors The Code for Crown Prosecutors is prepared by the Director of Public Prosecutions and gives guidance to solicitors working for the Crown Prosecution Service concerning the general principles to be followed when making decisions about whether or not to prosecute. These emphasise the need for there to be a realistic prospect of securing a conviction (the evidential test) and whether the public interest is served by pursuing a prosecution (the public interest test). The Code for Crown Prosecutors further puts forward guidelines to aid decisions as to what precise charge should be brought against a person who is being proceeded against.

Code of Professional Standards for Police Officers This replaced the former Police Code of Conduct in 2006 and sets out the standards of professional behaviour expected of police officers, the breach of which constitutes a disciplinary offence whose penalties range from admonishment to dismissal from the police service.

Cold case review This entails reviewing unsolved serious crimes that were committed many years ago in the hope that new scientific methods now available to the police service (in particular in connection with DNA profiling) may lead to the arrest and conviction of the perpetrator. This term does not apply to attempts to prove the innocence of a person previously found guilty of a serious crime.

Community sentences These embrace non-custodial responses to crime that are served by offenders within their communities. The 2000 Criminal Justice and Court Services Act provided for a range of such disposals – community punishment orders, community rehabilitation orders and community punishment and rehabilitation orders – and the 2003 Criminal Justice Act provided for a new generic sentence – a community order – that enabled sentencers to prescribe a wide range of requirements to address an individual's offending behaviour. A similar generic sentence for young offenders – the Youth Rehabilitation Order – was created by the 2008 Criminal Justice and Immigration Act.

Crime and Disorder Reduction Partnerships (CDRPs) The 1998 Crime and Disorder Act placed a statutory duty on police forces and local authorities (termed 'responsible authorities') to act in cooperation with police authorities, health authorities and probation committees in multi-agency bodies which became known as Crime and Disorder Reduction Partnerships (CDRPs), although this term did not appear in the legislation. In Wales CDRPs are termed community safety partnerships. The role of these partnerships was to develop and implement a strategy for reducing Crime and Disorder in each district and unitary local authority in England and Wales. They act as the driving force for community safety initiatives.

'Cuffing' The practice of 'cuffing' entails a police officer either not recording a crime that has been reported, or downgrading a reported crime to an incident which can be excluded from official statistics. The decision to do this was initially motivated by a desire to avoid the time-consuming practice of filling out a crime report for minor incidents, but the introduction of performance indicators for the police service in 1992 intensified pressures on the police to avoid recording all offences notified to them. Crime statistics were a key source of evidence of police performance, so increased levels of reported crimes could imply inefficiency.

Cybercrime This term broadly refers to crime involving the use of computers. There are two main forms of computer-related crime – computer-assisted crime (involving the use of computers to perform crimes that predated their existence such as fraud or theft), and computer-focused crime (which refers to the emergence of new crimes such as hacking and viruses as the result of computer technology).

'Dark figure' of crime This term refers to the gap between the volume of crime that is actually committed in society and that which enters into official crime statistics. This discrepancy is explained by the nature of the process of crime reporting, which consists of a number of stages, each acting as a filtering process reducing the number of crimes that are officially reported.

Deviancy This refers to actions, committed by individuals, that society disapproves of but are not illegal. Those who carry them out may thus encounter hostility from their fellow citizens resulting in their ostracism from society.

Director of Public Prosecutions (DPP) This office was created by the 1879 Prosecution of Offences Act. The role of this official was to initiate and carry out criminal proceedings and to advise and provide assistance to other officials (such as police officers) concerning the prosecution of offences. The 1985 Prosecution of Offences Act made the DPP head of the newly created Crown Prosecution Service that henceforth became responsible for the conduct of criminal proceedings carried out in the name of the Crown.

Discretion Discretion refers to the ability of an official, organisation or individual to utilise their independent judgement to determine a course of action or inaction to be pursued. Discretion is frequently exercised in the context of an encounter between an individual and criminal justice practitioner.

Doli Incapax This term applies to those who have committed crime but due to their age are not held responsible for it, because they are considered insufficiently mature to be able to discern right from wrong. Currently, children below the age of 10 (the age of criminal responsibility) are deemed to be in this situation. Formerly children aged 10–13 were also in this position, but this presumption was ended by the 1998 Crime and Disorder Act.

Economic Crime This term refers to a range of activities that include bribery, corruption, cybercrime, money laundering, and various forms of fraud that are associated with white-collar crime, middle-class crime and organised crime and which particularly impose a burden on business enterprise.

Home detention curfew In January 1999 the government introduced this procedure that provided for the early release of short-term prisoners serving sentences between three months and less than four years, for up to the last two months of their sentence, provided they stayed at an approved address and agreed to a curfew (usually from 7 pm to 7 am), monitored by an electronic tag. The curfew would be for a minimum of 14 days and a maximum of 60 days. Those who breached the conditions of their curfew (including attempting to remove the tag) or who committed another offence while on curfew were returned to prison.

Home Office (or Home Department) This government department was reorganised in 2007 with the task of public protection at the heart of its new functions. It is responsible for the police, immigration and passports, drugs policy and counter-terrorism and is headed by the Home Secretary.

Human rights These consist of basic entitlements that should be available to all human beings in every country. Unlike civil rights (that are specific to individual countries), human rights are universal in application. A full statement of human rights is to be found in the European Convention for the Protection of Human Rights and Fundamental Freedoms (1950). It includes entitlements such as the right to a fair trial, and freedom of thought, conscience, expression and religion, and prohibits torture, inhuman and degrading treatment. The declaration is ultimately enforced by the European Court of Human Rights but its incorporation into UK law by the 1998 Human Rights Act means that accusations that public bodies (including the government) have breached an individual's human rights will be initially heard in domestic courts.

Institutional racism This refers to the use of discriminatory practices against members of minority ethnic groups by an organisation. The term is capable of a number of definitions that include a deliberate organisational policy to discriminate or discrimination that is derived unwittingly from an organisation's working practices.

Joined-up government This approach seeks to enhance the level of coordination between the various agencies whose work is of relevance to crime and disorder. It entails developments such as the use by all agencies of the same organisational boundaries and the construction of mechanisms to provide for multi-agency working. Joined-up government suggests that crime can be reduced not by structural reforms seeking to achieve a greater level of social equality but by managerial improvements affecting the way in which the criminal justice system operates.

Judicial review This is a legal procedure whereby the court is able to strike down an action undertaken by any public body, including the executive branch of government, on the grounds that it has failed to follow the correct procedures that are laid down in law.

Justice model This refers to an approach to the punishment of offenders that is underpinned by reductivist rather than rehabilitative ideals. In particular it seeks to ensure that punishments reflect the seriousness of the crime that has been committed, thereby ensuring that offenders get their 'just deserts' for their actions.

Other features of the justice model emphasise the desirability of consistent sentences (especially by curbing the discretion of officials working in criminal justice agencies) and the need for the criminal justice process to effectively protect the accused's rights.

Mandatory sentence This imposes an obligation on sentencers (magistrates or judges) to hand out a predetermined response to those convicted of crimes that are subject to this provision. Murder, for example, carries a mandatory sentence of life imprisonment. Judges are required to administer this penalty, regardless of the circumstances surrounding the crime. The raft of mandatory sentences was considerably added to by the 1997 Crime (Sentences) Act, which was subsequently amended by the 2003 Criminal Justice Act and the 2008 Criminal Justice and Immigration Act.

Ministry of Justice This was established in 2007, replacing the former Department for Constitutional Affairs. It is responsible for the courts, prisons, probation service, the criminal law and sentencing. It is headed by a minister with the title of Lord Chancellor and Secretary of State for Justice. When Jack Straw MP took up this post in 2007, he became the first Lord Chancellor not to sit in the House of Lords.

Moral panic This refers to a process in which a specific type of crime is focused upon by the media in order to whip up public hysteria against those who are identified as carrying it out. The aim of this is to secure widespread public approval for the introduction of sanctions directed against the targeted group and is often used to distract attention away from more serious problems facing society by implying that the targeted group epitomise all that is wrong with the current state of society.

New deviancy This approach to the study of crime and deviancy rejected the existence of consensual values within society, and asserted that it functioned in the interests of the powerful who were able to foist their attitudes throughout society because of the control they exerted over the state's ideological apparatus (such as religion, education and the mass media), its political system and its coercive machinery (especially the police and courts). Deviancy was viewed as behaviour that was defined as 'bad' or 'unacceptable' by this powerful group of people who were able to utilise their power to stigmatise actions of which they did not approve. New deviancy theory thus concentrated on social intervention and social reaction to activities that were labelled as 'deviant' rather than seeking to discover their initial causes. Labelling theory is an important aspect of new deviancy theory.

New managerialism This term refers to the approach adopted by post-1997 Labour governments towards the performance culture of the public sector. Performance targets and indicators were retained, and the agencies within the criminal justice process were subjected to central inspection and monitoring which was extended beyond service delivery to embrace managerial processes. Additionally, this approach is identified with long-term strategic planning and developments associated with joined-up government. However, compulsory competitive tendering gave way to a process of best value, whereby agencies were required to justify why they were required to deliver a specific service and to ascertain the best way to deliver it.

New public management This approach towards the delivery of services by the public sector was identified with the new right. It emphasised the importance of public sector organisations providing value for money and sought to reorganise the operations of public sector agencies through the use of management techniques associated with the private sector such as the use of performance indicators and business plans. This approach was associated with a shift towards organisations attaining centrally determined objectives while at the same time being free to determine how to achieve them at the expense of having to comply with centrally determined bureaucratic rules and procedures.

OASys This is the Offender Assessment System, designed to assess the level of risk posed by all offenders aged 18 and over. It is used by both the prison and probation services.

Panopticon In 1791 Jeremy Bentham wrote a three-volume work, *The Panopticon*, in which he devised a blueprint for the design of prisons in order for them to be able to bring about the transformation of the behaviour of offenders. Central to his idea was the principle of surveillance whereby an observer was able to monitor prisoners without them being aware when they were being watched. The aim of this was to produce conforming behaviour. The design of Millbank Penitentiary and Pentonville Prison adopted many features of Bentham's panopticon.

Penal populism The terms 'penal populism' or 'populist punitiveness' were coined during the 1990s and this approach was especially directed at the rise of persistent young offenders. It denies the relevance of any social explanation for crime and emphasises the need to adopt a harsh approach towards those who carry out such actions on the grounds that they (and not the operations of society) are responsible for their criminal behaviour. It is characterised by factors that include the use of 'hard' policing methods, longer sentences and the increased size of the prison population, and harsher prison conditions. Governments following this course of action do so because they believe that the approach of 'getting tough with criminals' is viewed favourably by the general public.

Penology This term refers to the study of the way in which society responds to crime. It covers the wide range of processes that are concerned with the prevention of crime, the punishment, management and treatment of offenders and the measures concerned with reintegrating them into their communities.

Plural policing This entails an enhanced role for organisations other than the police service in performing police-related work. Those performing these activities effectively constitute a second tier of police service providers and the organisations supplying work of this nature may be located in either the public or private sectors.

Police authority Police authorities were initially established by the 1964 Police Act. They were composed of local councillors and magistrates and their role was to maintain 'an adequate and efficient' police force for their area. The make-up of police authorities was subsequently altered by the 1994 Police and Magistrates' Courts Act. Typically they are composed of 17 members – nine local councillors, three magistrates and five persons appointed by the Home Secretary. Magistrates ceased to be a separate category of appointees by the 2006 Police and Justice Act, although they may serve as independent members.

Political spectrum This model places different political ideologies in relationship to each other, thereby enabling their differences and similarities to be identified. Ideologies are placed under the broad headings of 'left', 'right' and 'centre', indicating the stances they adopt towards political, economic and social change – the right opposed this, the left endorsed it and the centre wished to introduce changes of this nature gradually within the existing framework of society.

Positivist criminology This approach to the study of crime adopts a deterministic attitude whereby offenders are seen as being propelled into committing criminal acts by forces (that may be biological, psychological or sociological) over which they have no control. Common to all forms of positivist criminology is the belief that society rests on consensual values and offenders should be treated rather than punished for their actions. Positivist criminology also insists that theories related to why crime occurs should derive from scientific analysis.

Pre-sentence report This is a report that provides information to sentencers regarding the background of an offender and the circumstances related to his or her commission of a crime. It is designed to ensure that the sentence of the court is an appropriate response to the criminal action that has been committed. Pre-sentence reports for offenders aged 16 and over are prepared by the probation service. Social workers write pre-sentence reports for those below the age of 16.

Privatisation This policy was favoured by new right governments and was consistent with their belief in the free market. It entails services previously performed by the public sector being transferred (or 'hived off') to private sector organisations. These services are either totally divorced from government henceforth, or are contracted out and are thus periodically subject to a process of competitive tendering by bodies wishing to deliver them.

Problem-oriented policing This is a method of policing that seeks to direct police action to recurrent problems as opposed to an approach that reacts to them after events have taken place. It thus emphasises the importance of identifying and analysing recurrent problems and formulating action to stop them from occurring in the future. Problem-oriented policing emphasises the multi-agency approach to curbing crime, whereby activities directed at crime involve actions undertaken by a range of agencies and not by the police alone.

Reactive policing This is a style of policing (also dubbed 'fire brigade policing') in which the police respond to events rather than seeking to forestall them. This method of policing tends to isolate the police from the communities in which they work and (because of the loss of contact between police and communities) tends to promote the use of police powers in a random way based on stereotypical assumptions. This style of policing was widely regarded to have been a significant factor in the riots that occurred in a number of English cities in 1981.

Reassurance policing The key aim of this style of policing is to tackle the fear of crime by making people feel safer. It is associated with a constant uniformed presence in a locality to tackle low level crime and disorder which can then be developed into securing local involvement in identifying and tackling problems of this nature. The reassurance agenda was developed in the early years of the twenty-first century and neighbourhood policing (which was rolled out nationally in England and Wales by April 2008) was a key development associated with this approach. This entails a uniformed presence being delivered in neighbourhoods by police officers, police community support officers and the Special Constabulary.

Recidivism This refers to the reconviction of those who have previously been sentenced for committing a crime. It is an important measurement of the extent to which punishment succeeds in reforming the habits of those who have broken the law.

Reductivism This term refers to methods of punishment that seek to prevent offending behaviour in the future. Punishment is designed to bring about the reform and rehabilitation of criminals so that they do not subsequently indulge in criminal actions.

Responsibilisation This entails governments shifting the task of crime control from the central state to local level where it is carried out by a range of actors including local government, private and voluntary sector bodies and the general public. Crime and Disorder Reduction Partnerships are an important example of this process in operation.

Retributivism This term embraces responses to crime that seek to punish persons for the actions they have previously committed. Punishment is justified on the basis that it enables society to 'get its own back' on criminals, regardless of whether this has any impact on their future behaviour.

Restorative justice A key objective of restorative justice is to enable the person who has broken the law to repair the damage that has been caused to the direct victim and to society at large by his or her criminal behaviour. Crime is no longer viewed as an impersonal act that has breached an abstract legal code but as behaviour that has caused genuine harm to a real person. The main intention of this process is that the offender can be more readily reintegrated into society than would be the case if s/he merely received punishment for their actions which, in the case of a custodial sentence, may result in long-term or permanent exclusion from society.

Risk This term refers to the important role that criminal justice policy accords to public safety. Agencies operating within the criminal justice system have increasingly formulated their interventions on the basis of predictions regarding the extent to which the future behaviour of offenders was likely to jeopardise communal safety. This approach has given rise to actuarial penal techniques seeking to assess the future risk posed by offenders.

Rule of Law This constitutional principle asserts the supremacy of the law as an instrument governing the actions of individual citizens in their relationships with each other and also controls the conduct of the state towards them. In particular it suggests that citizens can only be punished by the state using formalised procedures when they have broken the law, and that all citizens will be treated in the same way when they commit wrongdoings.

Sentencers This term applies to officials who deliver society's response to crime through the courts over which they preside. In the criminal justice system these comprise judges and magistrates.

Sentencing tariff The tariff sets the level of penalty that should normally be applied by sentencers to particular crimes. In the case of murder, the tariff was the period that had to be served in prison in order to meet the requirements of retribution and deterrence. In 2002 the Sentencing Advisory Panel recommended that the phrase 'minimum' term should be substituted for 'the tariff' in these cases.

Separation of powers This concept suggests that each of the three branches of government (executive, legislature and judiciary) should perform a defined range of functions, possess autonomy in their relationship with the other two and be staffed by personnel different from that of the others. This principle was first advocated by Baron Montesquieu, in his work *De l'Esprit des Lois,* written in 1748, whose main concern was to avoid the tyranny that he believed arose when power was concentrated in the executive branch of government. Although total separation of the three branches of government is unworkable in practice, the judiciary in England and Wales has historically enjoyed a considerable degree of autonomy and may overrule governments through procedures that include judicial review and their implementation of the 1998 Human Rights Act.

Situational crime prevention This approach to crime prevention entails measures directed at highly specific forms of crime that involve manipulating the immediate environment to increase the effort and risks of crime and reduce the rewards to those who might be tempted to carry out such activities. The situational approach is heavily reliant on primary prevention methods and is contrasted with social methods of crime prevention that seek to tackle the root causes of criminal behaviour, typically through social policy.

Social disorganisation This approach to the study of crime was associated with the Chicago School of Human Ecology. It suggests that crime was an ever-present feature of a specific geographical area of a city termed by Ernest Burgess in 1925 as 'zone two' or the 'zone of transition'. This area was characterised by rapid population change, dilapidation and conflicting demands made upon land use. New immigrants would initially settle in this zone (or ghetto) as rented residential property was cheapest here, but would move outwards into the other residential zones when their material conditions improved, being replaced by further immigrants. The absence of effective informal mechanisms of social control was viewed as the main reason for this area of the city being a constant crime zone.

Social methods of crime prevention Social crime prevention is based upon the belief that social conditions such as unemployment, poor housing and low educational achievement have a key bearing on crime. It thus seeks to tackle what are regarded as the root causes of crime by methods that aim to alter social environments.

Social strain theory This explanation of crime was developed by Robert Merton whose ideas were originally put forward in 1938. He asserted that anomie arose from a mismatch between the culturally induced aspirations to strive for success (which he asserted in western societies was the pursuit of wealth) and the structurally determined opportunities to achieve it. Social inequality imposed a strain on an individual's commitment to society's success goals and the approved way of attaining them and resulted in anomie, which was characterised by rule-breaking behaviour by those who were socially disadvantaged.

Taken into consideration (TIC) This term (also referred to as 'write-offs' or 'secondary detections') entails an offender who has been apprehended for committing a crime confessing to other offences. He or she is not specifically charged with these additional offences and is unlikely to receive further penalty for these admissions. The system was criticised for being a means whereby police officers artificially boosted their force's detection rates (since TICs constituted a crime being 'cleared up') even though confessions from criminals were not always reliable. For these reasons, TICs are now less relied upon.

Triangulation This term is concerned with research methodology and entails utilising a range of research methods in an attempt to derive reliable data. It may involve analysing data drawn from different quantitative sources or it may enable findings to be based upon the product of quantitative and qualitative research methods. The main benefit of triangulation is that findings are derived from a diverse range of data as opposed the use of one source. Those involved in the evaluation of criminal justice initiatives frequently use this approach to assess the effectiveness of interventions.

Tripartite system of police control and accountability This term denotes a three-way division for the exercise of responsibility over police affairs shared between police authorities, the Home Secretary and chief constables. This system was initially provided for in the 1964 Police Act.

Victimology This aspect of criminology concerns the study of victims of crime. In particular it seeks to establish why certain people become victims of crime and how personal lifestyles influence the risk of victimisation.

White-collar crime As initially defined by Edwin Sutherland, this term referred to crimes committed by respectable persons within the environment of the workplace. Subsequent definitions have differentiated between illegal actions carried out in the workplace that are designed to benefit the individual performing them, illicit actions that are intended to further the interests of a commercial concern carried out by its employees, and criminal activities by persons of 'respectable' social status to further their own interests but which are not performed in the workplace (such as tax evasion and insurance fraud).

Zero tolerance This approach is most readily identified with a style of policing that emphasises the need to take an inflexible attitude towards law enforcement. It is especially directed against low level crime and seeks to ensure that the law is consistently and inflexibly applied against those who commit it. Unlike problem-oriented policing, it does not require the involvement of agencies other than the police to be implemented.

Index